Bombers Fly East: WWII RAF Operations in the Middle and Far East

Martin W. Bowman

Pen & Sword
AVIATION

First Published in Great Britain in 2016 by
Pen & Sword Aviation
an imprint of
Pen & Sword Books Ltd
47 Church Street, Barnsley, South Yorkshire S70 2AS

A CIP catalogue record for this book is
available from the British Library.

Typeset in 10/12pt Palatino
by GMS Enterprises PE3 8QQ

Printed and bound in Cornwall by TJ International.

Pen & Sword Books Ltd incorporates the Imprints of Pen & Sword
Aviation, Pen & Sword Family History, Pen & Sword Maritime, Pen & Sword
Military, Pen & Sword Discovery, Wharncliffe Local History, Wharncliffe
True Crime, Wharncliffe Transport, Pen & Sword Select, Pen & Sword
Military Classics, Leo Cooper, The Praetorian Press, Remember When,
Seaforth Publishing and Frontline Publishing.

For a complete list of Pen & Sword titles please contact
PEN & SWORD BOOKS LIMITED

47 Church Street, Barnsley, South Yorkshire, S70 2AS, England
E-mail: enquiries@pen-and-sword.co.uk
Website: www.pen-and-sword.co.uk

Contents

Dedication

Captain Paul F. Stevens USN 27 April 1921-27 August 2014

Preface

In presenting this collection of stories of the RAF in action the author's endeavour has been to make his selection as widely representative of the many departments of the Service as possible. For this reason not only are stories of the various operational Commands included, but also narratives of action varying in latitude from the tropic seas to the ice-bound wastes of the Arctic and in longitude from the grey wilderness of the Atlantic waters to the lush jungles of Malaya.

Men of all Allied nationalities have worn the air blue of the RAF, for one magnificent year the only adversary of the Axis in the world's skies and have flown and fought in aircraft blazoned with the proud roundels of red, white and blue. The battle stories of these men - British, Empire and Allied alike - have become an integral part of a great tradition. Their victories, won over a determined enemy, over great distances, impossible weather conditions, intense pain and sometimes even death itself, are gloriously embodied in that tradition.

Battle Stories of the RAF **by Leonard R. Gribble, 1945**

Chapter 1

Mediterranean Missions

Take off for the Western Desert,
Fuka, 60 or 09,
Same old Lib, same old target,
Same old aircrew, same old time.

In May 1938 the French Government had issued a specification to the Consolidated Aircraft Corporation of San Diego, California, for a heavy bomber. The company's early study, designated LB30, was a landplane version of their new Model 29 flying boat (PB2Y). Early in 1939 the US Army Air Corps also drew up a requirement for a heavy bomber of infinitely better performance than the Boeing B-17, then in production. They were looking for a bomber capable of a top speed in excess of 300 mph with a range of 3,000 miles and a ceiling of 35,000 feet. Consolidated engineers initiated a further design study designated XB-24, which incorporated David R. Davis's high aspect ratio wing and the twin-finned empennage used on the Model 31 Flying boat (P4Y-1). In September 1939 France followed up its tentative order with a production contract for 139 aircraft under the original LB30 designation. A month later, on 26 October 1939, the Davis wing was first married to the fuselage and on 29 December 1939 the Liberator flew for the first time. William Wheatley was at the controls as it took off from Lindbergh Field next to the Consolidated plant in San Diego. In 1940 seven YB-24s, which had been ordered by the Air Corps shortly before the contract for the prototype, were delivered for service trials. Six YB-24s and twenty B-24As were diverted to the RAF and after the fall of France in June 1940, Britain took over the French contract for 139 LB30s. In 1942 a second Liberator production line was opened at Fort Worth, Texas, by Convair and this company turned out 303 B-24Ds. A third production line was brought into operation, at Tulsa, where the Douglas Company produced ten B-24Ds before changing production to B-24Es. At the end of 1942 a fourth B-24 production line was opened, by the Ford Motor Company at Willow Run where construction work had begun in 1941. In early 1943 the fifth and final major manufactory of Liberators was operated by North American at Dallas, Texas. The first Liberators to be used in the bomber role by the RAF were Mark IIs flown by Nos. 159 and 160 Squadrons. All Liberators up to and including the Liberator Mark III (B-24D) were supplied under direct British contracts. The Liberator Mark IIIA and subsequent versions were supplied under Lend-Lease and handed over to the RAF by the USAAF.

In November 1943 deliveries of the B.VI and GR.VI Liberators began. These versions were Convair-built B-24H and J with American turrets except for the tail turret which was by Boulton & Paul. By the end of the war over 1,800 Mark VIs and VIIIs had been used by the RAF, RCAF and RAAF, the greatest number of all models. In the Middle East the Liberator Mark VI was used mainly against enemy shipping in the Mediterranean. Beginning in July 1944, thirty-six Mark VIIIs were delivered to the RAF in that theatre, each equipped with centimetric radar designed for PFF operations against ground targets. In the Far East the Liberator Mark VI was the principal bomber used in the final Burma campaign ending with the capture of Rangoon. Fresh deliveries of Mark VIIIs arrived in May 1945. By the end of the war almost 2,500 Liberators of one sort or another had been delivered to the RAF, RCAF and the RAAF of which 1,694 were supplied by Consolidated alone.

Of all the theatres of operations in which the B-24 served during the Second World War, only in the Mediterranean did it see such widespread and diversified service with both the RAF and the USAAF. As early as December 1941 108 Squadron, then based in Egypt and equipped with Wellington bombers, received four Liberator Mark IIs, which had been originally intended for France. These unarmed Liberators remained in Egypt until it was decided that 108 Squadron should use them to convert fully from Wellingtons to Liberators. However, after they had been fitted with Boulton & Paul gun turrets and cannon, the plan to convert the whole Squadron to Liberators was abandoned and only two were ever used for bombing operations. Some others which had been used for conversion training were modified for supply-dropping duties. The four Liberator Mark IIs operated as a separate flight from the rest of 108 Squadron, which continued using Wellingtons right up to November 1942. For a time the flight operated from Palestine. William Foulkes, a fitter on 108 Squadron, recalls: 'Keeping the Liberators flying was a problem. Just prior to the Battle of El Alamein we were operating from a base on the Cairo/Alexandria road about sixty miles from Alamein. Two of the Liberators had suspect engines so the one that was nearest its next major overhaul was cannibalized and its engines used on the other aircraft. The cowlings, however, did not fit properly on their new mountings and had to be fastened with nuts and bolts and even wire!'

As a result of Operation 'Torch' in November 1942, RAF Eastern Air Command had been formed under Air Marshal Sir William Welsh primarily to support the British First Army in its advance on Tunis. Seven weeks after the landings Welsh was able to deploy about 450 aircraft and Major General James Doolittle's newly created 12th Air Force about 1,250 for the North African campaign. By the end of 1942 the growing success of Eastern Air Command could not hide the fact that there was still no integrated direction of the Allied Air Forces in North Africa. While EAC and Doolittle's 12th Air Force continued to act independently, the position was further complicated by the presence of Brereton's 9th Air Force, which was also playing a vital part in the North-African campaign. Air Marshal Tedder, Commanding Officer of RAF Middle East Air Command, urged a single unified air command over the whole of the Mediterranean as early as November 1942. In December General Eisenhower appointed General Carl Spaatz to co-ordinate the operations of Eastern Air Command and the 12th Air Force but it was not until mid-January 1943, during the Casablanca Conference, that Tedder's original proposition was accepted. In the third week of February 1943 Mediterranean Air Command and North West African Air Forces, commanded by Spaatz and consisting of Eastern Air Command, 12th Air Force and other units, were officially created.

In October 1943 General Henry H. Arnold proposed a plan to split the American 12th Air Force in two to create a Strategic Air Force, leaving the remaining half of the 12th as a tactical organization. The possibility of a Strategic Air Force based in southern Italy would enable the Allies more easily to strike at targets like Ploesti and the aircraft factories at Wiener Neustadt. It would also complement the vast aerial armadas already operating from England. Arnold's plan was accepted and on 1 November 1943 the 15th Air Force was officially established. Between December 1943 and May thirteen new Liberator groups joined the 15th Air Force.

Less publicized are the achievements of the Liberators of 205 Group RAF in the Mediterranean. They not only flew daylight missions in their B-24s but night missions as well. The Group started as 257 Wing in the Egyptian Canal Zone, equipped with long-range bombers, mostly Wellingtons. In September 1941 it was re-designated 205 Group and attempts were made to reinforce the Wellington squadrons with other aircraft. There were no suitable heavy night-bombers to be spared for 205 Group so it was decided to equip them with the Liberator, despite the fact that the B-24 had many operational disadvantages for night work, the principal one being the bright flames and white-hot turbo-supercharger exhausts which made the aircraft a beacon in the sky for night fighters. Since night-fighter activity was not as intense over Italy and southern Europe as it was in the northwest it was considered that losses from night fighters would not be high. A further disadvantage was the 0.50 calibre machine-guns which had a much better range than the 0.303 guns but as the gunner could not see far enough in the dark to avail himself of this, the only advantage was their superior hitting power. However, it was found that as soon as the gunner fired, the flash from the guns ruined his night vision so he had little chance of aiming on a second attack. The front gun turret was also useless, as was the under gun turret as the light from the turbo-chargers made it impossible to see fighters at night.

So the RAF removed the under gun turret and the guns from the front turret, which was then faired over with fabric. The beam guns were also taken out because it was found that fighter attacks always came from behind. However, conversion to the Liberator was slow. On 15 January 1943 178 Squadron was formed at Shandur in the Suez Canal Zone from a detachment of 160 Squadron and began receiving Liberator Mark IIIs. The following night three Liberators took off and bombed targets in Tripoli. It was not a full-scale beginning and 178 remained the only Liberator Squadron in 205 Group until October 1944, although on 14 March 1943 a 'Special Liberator' Flight was formed at Gambut, Libya. It was later re-designated 148 Squadron and began special duties, dropping arms and supplies to Resistance groups in Albania, Greece and Yugoslavia.

In January 1944 148 Squadron moved to Italy and when not engaged in special operations its aircraft joined with other squadrons of 205 Group on heavy bombing raids on northern Italy and southern Europe. By April 1944, the powerful Mediterranean Allied Strategic Force was playing a vital role in the conduct of the war which was by no means confined to Italy or the Italian Front. The 15th Air Force continued to pound targets by day while the RAF Liberators and Wellingtons struck under the cover of darkness. By June the combined forces bombed railway networks in south-east Europe in support of Russian military operations in Rumania. Throughout the summer of 1944 Austrian aircraft manufacturing centres at Wiener Neustadt were bombed day and night and oil-producing centres, too, were bombed, often in conjunction with Bomber Command in England. By the autumn of 1944 these attacks had assumed top priority. Vast aerial fleets of 15th Air Force Liberators and B-17s escorted by Mustangs and Lightnings, attacked the refineries at Ploesti and bombed Budapest, Komárom, Győr and Pétfürdő in Hungary, Belgrade and other cities in Yugoslavia and Trieste in north-eastern Italy. Meanwhile, Liberators and Wellingtons of 205 Group flew unescorted at night from their bases in southern Italy and stoked up the fires left by the American bombers.

Of special importance to the Germans were the Hungarian and

Rumanian railway systems. These came under constant Allied aerial bombardment and in the summer of 1944 the Germans were deprived of the use of the Lwów - Cernăuţi Railway by the Russians. The only alternative route linking Germany with the grain-lands of Hungary and the oilfields of Rumania was the River Danube, capable of carrying 10,000 tons of war material daily. It was estimated that eight million tons of material had reached Germany in 1942 by this waterway alone. By mid-March 1944 the Danube was carrying more than double the amount carried by rail. Even a temporary halt in this river traffic would seriously hamper the German war effort and in April 1944 205 Group began 'Gardening' operations, 'sowing' the waterways with mines. On the night of 8 April three Liberators and nineteen Wellingtons from 178 Squadron dropped forty mines near Belgrade. Over the next nine days 137 more mines were dropped and in May the total number dropped had risen to over 500. No 'Gardening' sorties were flown during June but on the night of 1 July sixteen Liberators and fifty-three Wellingtons dropped 192 mines in the biggest operation of the mining campaign. The following night another sixty mines were dropped.

At first the 'Gardening' sorties were only flown on nights of the full moon as the aircraft had to fly no higher than 200 feet and even heights of forty and fifty feet were reported. 'Gardening' sorties continued throughout July, August and September. On the night of 4 October four Liberators and eighteen Wellingtons flew the final mission of the operation and dropped fifty-eight mines in the Danube in Hungary west of Budapest, north of Győr and east of Esztergom. In six months of operations, 1,382 mines were laid by Liberators and Wellingtons of 205 Group in eighteen attacks.

The effect on the supply route was catastrophic. Several ships were sunk and blocked the waterway in parts and by May coal traffic had virtually ceased. Canals and ports were choked with barges and by August 1944 the volume of material transported along the Danube had been reduced by about 70 per cent.

Meanwhile the Liberators of the 15th Air Force and 178 Squadron continued pounding enemy targets throughout the Mediterranean and its immediate area. 178 Squadron had been using Liberators since the beginning of 1943 and had built up an impressive record, listing among its targets those of Crete, the Aegean Islands and the Ploesti oil refinery. Apart from a few scattered units employing a handful of Liberators, up to October 1944, 178 was the only true RAF B-24 squadron in the Mediterranean. But that month 37 Squadron at Tortorella began exchanging its Wellingtons for the Liberator Mark VI. During the year this Squadron had flown many operations not only dropping Partisans and mining the Danube, but also normal bombing raids.

Frank Mortimer, a Liberator air-gunner who joined 34 Squadron SAAF (Motto: *Initasela Zasebusiuku (We Strike by Night)* at Tortorella near Foggia in October 1944 recalled: 'Our living accommodation was four to a tent. It was raining at the time and ours was on a slope. There were no beds. I was fortunate to have a sleeping-bag with me. All around the airfield, which had been a maintenance unit for the Germans, were wrecked Junkers 88s. None of the Ju 88s had tyres. They had been stolen by the Italians to mend their plimsolls. I took a rudder off a Ju 88 and slept on that for a few weeks. We also made radio sets from parts of their wreckage which we finished off with bent pins and razor blades, using our aircraft headsets for earphones.

'There was no place to dry out flying clothes so we slept in them. The dampness was intense and on raids we flew in wet clothes. The dampness also got into the parachutes and it is doubtful whether they would have worked when needed. We tried to make the tents more habitable by digging down about four feet to make more headroom. We also stole runway sheeting and used that to prop up the sides. Cleaning was another problem. There was a bowser which brought one jerry can of water every day. In 'Foggie' we used to try and take a bath but it was over-populated with Americans and the British Army. Gradually as crews were shot down it was the custom to raid their tents and take little luxuries, like a wooden bed. It was dog eat dog, with little sentiment at all.

'Our first two operations were supply drops to Tito's Partisans in Yugoslavia. These were completed under code names, flying about 100 feet over the DZs [dropping zones]. I recall very vividly flying in the region of 500 feet. We dropped sugar, boots, rifles and other supplies and we could quite clearly see horses and carts coming to pick them up. During briefing for a raid on Yugoslavia we were told that there were three main Partisan groups involved - Tito, Dragoljub 'Draža' Mihailović's men and the Chetniks. We were told to watch out for the Chetniks because they were known to help the Germans look for downed airmen.

'The rear turret was fitted out for electrical flying suits, although we didn't get these until the end of the war. Owing to dampness in the tents we got a lot of shorting out. On one raid my gloves caught fire and I had to throw them out of the turret. After that I used only silk gloves. My main clothing was two pairs of silk underpants, two vests, probably a short and RAF pullover, plus an inner suit. There was no way I could wear an Irvin jacket in the cramped confines of the turret.

'Most of the RAF crews were posted to 70 (ATF) Squadron in January 1945 and the South Africans gave us a farewell party. I for one was proud to have flown with them. They were good men and I'll always remember the CO; he was a fantastic man. 70 Squadron's base was no better. The Sergeants' Mess was another cowshed and the food was foul. I lived off tins of South African pears and peaches. The place was infested with snakes and I even saw a warrant officer cutting one up to make a tie out of it.'

'Having so many groups in such a confined area caused many problems. Foggia Plain comprised four airfields very close to each other. The flight paths overlapped and the risk of collision was very high. On one occasion two Liberators collided and we had to take the corpses to Bari cemetery. We collected them from the hospital in Foggia which was piled up with coffins. While going through the dock area an ammunition ship exploded and within minutes we were surrounded by hundreds of running Italians. As a result of the collision an order was made stating that the rear gunner had to remain in his turret to look out and warn of collision. Inside the tail turret was a notice which said OWING TO HIGH ACCELERATION GUNNERS MUST NOT LAND WHILE IN THE TURRET: The first time I actually landed in the turret it was a daylight raid. We had been warned to brace ourselves because the tail unit shook terrifically on a tricycle undercarriage but fortunately it was a very smooth landing. An aircraft rarely lands straight, it lands sideways and this causes a lot of acceleration. The second time I landed in the turret was after a night raid and I suppose I was a bit cocky and didn't brace myself. I remember that I banged my head on the gun-sights.

'The other dangerous practice was dropping the photoflash to enable us to make a photo-record of the bombing. It was a very dangerous 'pyro' in a long cylinder about three foot long and usually dropped at the same time the bomb-aimer called 'bombs away'. It was well known that many photo flashes had hung up in the bomb-bay and blown the aircraft in two. Our pilot was very wary of them and asked the rear gunner to throw it out of the rear turret during bombs away. The flash had two safety devices on it. Two wires like hooks on a fishing line connected the fuse to two lines clipped on to the side of the fuselage. It was my job to see that the two fuses came out as the 'pyro' descended. It was a very 'Heath Robinson' affair and extremely frightening. Prior to throwing out the photo-flash we had to jettison large bundles of leaflets out of the window.

'The rear turret was fitted out for electrical flying-suits although we didn't get these until the end of the war. Owing to dampness in the tents we got a lot of shorting out. On one raid my gloves caught fire and I had to throw them out of the turret. After that I used only silk gloves. My main clothing was two pairs of silk underpants, two vests, probably a shirt and RAF pullover, plus an inner suit. There was no way I could wear an Irvine jacket in the cramped confines of the turret.'

In January 1945 Denis Allen joined 40 Squadron at Foggia Main from 1675 HCU at Abu-Sueir in the Canal Zone: 'I was delayed by the smallpox epidemic in Cairo and arrived on the Squadron a few days after my first crew (Skipper Flight Sergeant Smout), only to find they had gone on their first op without me and failed to return. I became acquainted with many US aircrew; both at Foggia and at Prestwick, where I did the automatic pilot course. I remember with great affection these quiet, serious young men with their easy-going temperament and good nature. The Commanding Officer of 40 Squadron, Group Captain Smythe, placed me with Pilot Officer Colin Dunn's crew who had lost their flight engineer. Pilot Officer Dunn and crew had already completed ten 'ops' and despite the natural reluctance of all crews to take on a 'rookie' like myself, they made me welcome and I always considered myself lucky to join such a friendly and experienced crew. I flew eight 'ops' with my new crew, including one daylight mission. Our daylight 'op' was interesting - the target, a wharf named Arsa, was too small to bomb at night. We went in just above the altitude for accurate flak at about 24,000 feet. This was too high for such a small target so we were instructed to drop one bomb as a marker, make the necessary corrections on the bomb sight and go round again and drop the rest of the bomb load. On approaching the target we were immediately subjected to deadly-accurate flak and after a brief discussion with our bomb-aimer we decided to use the marker-bombs dropped by two 'Libs' who were ahead of us. The bomb-run was very 'dicey'. When the bomb-doors were closed, full power was applied and a steep climbing turn executed. My hands were shaking so violently that I couldn't make my log entry for several minutes.'

By early 1945 the war seemed to get more vicious rather than the reverse. During a briefing RAF Liberator crews learned that one airman who had bailed out had been hanged on the nearest lamp-post by Italian fascists. RAF Liberator crews were still coming through to replace those lost on operations although their training was not as complete as it could have been. Deryck Fereday, a pilot who joined 178 Squadron in March 1945 recalls: 'Pilots for 178 Squadron were taken from those who had undergone the OTU (Operational Training Unit) on Wellingtons - several in Palestine. Then instead of going straight to a squadron at Foggia they went to 1675 HCU (Heavy Conversion Unit) at Abu Sueir. The OTU course was five weeks and HCU only three. I still cannot believe that in so short a time I sufficiently mastered the intricacies of such an advanced aircraft to be entrusted with the lives of seven men and 8,000lb of high explosive, not to mention thirty tons of Liberator. I joined 178 Squadron at Amendola along the Manfredonia road from Foggia, which we shared with 614 Pathfinder Squadron - just converting from Wellingtons to Liberators. The airfield had only one runway, 2,000 yards long (essential for a fully loaded Liberator), constructed of perforated steel planking laid straight on the ground. The surface was far from level with plenty of friction to retard acceleration on take-off. With only one runway it meant that we could be as much as ninety degrees out of wind which presented severe flying problems.

'Operations were mainly to northern Italy, Austria and Yugoslavia and nearly all the raids, until towards the end of the war, were to railway junctions. I did just two daylight raids, both to coastal targets. It would have been suicide to have tried to go inland with our depleted fire-power but a hit-and-run raid could be pulled off.

A typical raid took about five hours, usually taking off at 2200 or 2300 hours and returning in the small hours of the morning. For a maximum effort the Group could muster about seventy aircraft. For a 'sustained effort' this was cut back to about forty or fifty aircraft to ensure enough carry-over of serviceable aircraft to the next night. The Liberators had a much better serviceability record than the Wimpys, which were truly clapped-out.

'So the bomber force was much fewer than in operations from the UK. But we all had to be over the target in a bombing cloud or 'stream' within three minutes instead of the ten or fifteen minutes usual in north-west Europe. This was essential to prevent flak singling out individual planes and meant that we had to navigate very precisely indeed. The Liberator's wonderful electrical and radio equipment, stability in flying and good auto-pilot, was a big help in this direction. Incidentally, because the Air Ministry supposed Italian-based Liberators met less opposition than the heavy bombers based in the UK, the tour of duty for crews was increased from thirty to forty operations. The chance of survival for crew members (and planes) was therefore theoretically the same.

'The small towns on the railways through the Alps were defended out of all proportion to their size because of the vital German need to keep their supply routes open. Towns like Bruch and Villach in Austria and Ljubljana in Yugoslavia were typical. Certainly there were plenty of legitimate targets down there in the dark. For example, I remember one such raid to Pragersko, a tiny junction in Yugoslavia, where we obviously hit a munitions supply train as the explosions on the ground were like a firework display and even at 15,000 feet we had the feeling of flying right through an inferno.

'Most raids were flown at around 12,000 to 15,000 feet. There was no point in going higher and losing accuracy in bombing. Over the target we had to stagger our bombing heights to lessen the chance of collisions and sometimes we had to descend to say 8,000 feet, if we had been allocated one of the lower levels. This meant that instead of being able to get the hell away from the target, flak and prowling night fighters, we had to climb at slower speed to get back to bomber-stream height. Also on raids to Austrian targets, we had to get back over the Alps.'

Arthur Bernstein was a South African Liberator pilot on 34 Squadron operating from an airfield near Foggia, in southern Italy. 'Our worst, or luckiest, experience occurred on the night of 27 February 1945. We had bombed the marshalling yards at Verona in the Po Valley and after leaving target I headed 'Q-Queenie' back toward the Adriatic on an easterly course. Time was about 2000 and we were flying into a rising full moon. We were above 10/10ths cloud so you can imagine just how bright the sky was ahead. And how dark behind, called the gunners to keep their eyes skinned for night-fighters which we knew were operating in the area. My second pilot and I were likewise on our toes. Suddenly I saw red lights speeding past us on the port side below us, something which I had never seen before. In a flash I realised they were cannon tracer and slamming off 'George' instinctively thrust everything into the bottom left-hand corner, throwing the aircraft into a steep diving turn to port, cutting across the line of fire and making it impossible for the fighter to turn inside me and keep us in his sights.

Then all hell broke loose. The gunners screamed 'Fighters, Fighters' and opened with all their point fives. At the same instant we were hit by four 37mm cannon shells (We found that out after landing). The noise was incredible. I thought that the armour plating of my seat had received a direct hit. The aircraft shuddered violently as the shells slammed into her and the gun turrets blasted their 5,000 rounds a minute. Then we were in the cloud. Very, very carefully I pulled her back to straight and level and resumed course. I called all the crew and no one was hurt. The only damage reported was from the beam gunner, whose kitbag at his feet was smouldering. I sent the second pilot back to do a visual check and the only damage he could find was a badly damaged ball turret which we carried retracted inside the belly at night. The instrument check showed a runaway prop on No. 1, which we feathered. No. 3 was losing revs, but I boosted her up as best I could and kept an eye on the gauges. I wouldn't check the hydraulics just in case there was damage and I would need all the pressure in the system for landing.

'We made it back all right, but the shock came when we climbed out and examined the fuselage from the outside. The first shell had entered the wing above the trailing edge, next to the No. 1 motor, smashing the CS unit. The second shell had gone through the wing and burst a two-foot hole next to my cockpit. The third had entered the fuselage two inches from the tail turret, gone between the beam-gunner's legs and exploded against the ball turret in the belly. The fourth shell had gone through the wing, like the first two and blown a gigantic hole out of the leading edge next to No. 3 motor. 'Q-Queenie' was written off. But the amazement of all was how we had escaped. Three cannon shells through the wings, all of them missing the fuel tanks! Our Squadron Commander put it nicely. 'It's incredible,' he said the next day. 'Someone up there must like you an awful lot!'

On 16 March 1945 the crew on 'V-Victor' a Liberator on 37 Squadron, 205 Group, the only RAF heavy bomber group in the Middle East, at Tortorella airfield had a lucky escape on the bombing run on the Monfalcone shipyards in northern Italy. Flight Sergeant Ken Westrope the 25 year-old rear gunner recalled: 'We had just dropped our six 1,000lb and six 500lb bombs - fairly general for all aircraft on these raids - and got the photo. I felt an almighty thump and the Liberator just fell out of the sky. The intercom and hydraulics had all gone. The only thing to do was to get out of the turret, unplug the intercom and oxygen, open the doors, get out and put your parachute on. This was my 20th or 21st operation. We flew 'Wells' up to Christmas 1944 on 37 Squadron and changed over to 'Libs' in January 1945.

'Our Liberator had plunged 5-6,000 feet. It just dropped down and I thought 'This is it'. I just didn't know what had happened. We had experienced nothing like this. We had had one or two things happen because of duff engines. During a training flight on Wellingtons we had been forced to land at Beirut airport on a single engine, but we didn't suffer any damage from enemy action. Flak had been the main threat, more than fighters. We had done all sorts of trips; including supply dropping to Tito's troops and dropping mines outside the northern Italian ports.

'I hadn't given such dangers as bombs hitting us a thought. There had been the odd problem on supply drops when parachutes came down through when some aircraft were flying higher, but you were able to see and avoid them. It wasn't in our minds. We didn't realise or think it could have happened. As far as I could gather, I had been watching this aircraft, 'R-Roger', a 70 Squadron Liberator, flying more or less parallel and coming up on our port side. I got in touch with our mid-upper gunner and told him to watch it.

'OK', he said and then I lost sight of him.

'Then he came alongside and suddenly must have turned left and come straight over the top of us. When bombs drop, they do not just drop straight down. They go forward.

'By the time I could get out of the turret, unplug and open the doors,

Squadron Leader Lionel Saxby, the skipper, had 'V-Victor' under control. Then eventually we got on a level course again. I went forward and I saw this big hole in the aircraft. It was a bit shaky. The hole was about 6 foot by 4 foot. The bomb, or maybe there were two bombs, had fallen on the mid-upper turret. Wally Lewis was jammed in his seat. I don't know if he was unconscious; he was a bit bruised, but miraculously not badly hurt. Cliff Hurst, the wireless operator, got the worst of it. He was sitting on the starboard side with his back to the hole. Oil and steam were pouring out of the port inner but there was no fire in the engine. However, the prop was completely knocked off.

'Pieces of the engine had entered the wireless operator's back. He was a tent-mate of mine. At first we laid him on the flight deck. He was unconscious for some time and then he came to. I suppose he must have felt the pain, but there was no question of being able to do anything about it. You could not give him morphia. That would have knocked him out and he never asked for it. His set, everything, was out of order and even though he was wounded, he managed to repair the wireless and get a message through to base to tell them what had happened. I held his parachute harness away from his back so it did not chafe on him.

'It was a bit of a struggle on the flight back and obviously we slowed down. Lionel Saxby was a very experienced skipper. We just sat hunched up on the flight deck so that if anything happened we could all get out together, or attempt to get out, as there was no intercom to warn us when to go. You could not hear anything. It had to be by signs.

'We all got into ditching positions for the landing. They cleared the runway and were waiting for us. We did not know if the wheels were locked. We had to be prepared for anything. As it was we left bits and pieces of wreckage strewn on the runway. Cliff Hurst made a full recovery and was awarded the DFM. The pilot was not decorated. He got a green endorsement in his logbook, which represented a 'good show'. We did not think about decorations. We just did what had to be done.'

On 23 March 1945, after bombing a rail junction and marshalling yard near Innsbruck, Deryck Fereday's crew had to climb immediately in order to clear the mountains. 'Had we been only slightly off course we could not have made it, due to the higher peaks on either side. This night we entered cloud as we turned from the target for home. The cloud was coloured red from the ground fires and there was no visual contact with the mountain peaks all around. As we climbed the Liberator seemed slower than usual and we seemed to be heading directly for a mountain. I turned the electronic boost control into 'Emergency position 10' and the Lib seemed just to jump upwards. At that moment we broke cloud into a magnificent scene of the Tyrolean Alps in bright moonlight. Fortunately we were safe at the necessary height so I was able to reduce boost and avoid further overstressing the engine. The panorama below was breathtakingly beautiful and a strong contrast to the scene of death and destruction we had just created only a few miles away.

'Towards the end of the war a new type of operation was introduced. Instead of strategic bombing we switched to close support for the 8th Army's final offensive of the war as the front moved into the plains of the Po valley. We were 'blanket bombing' the German troop positions just before the 8th Army launched a local attack, sometimes going for a small bridge area or a bottleneck as part of the total operation. There was no identifiable bombing point that we could find on our own so we had to bomb on Pathfinder markers which were dropped using dead reckoning or radar.

'There was no 'Gee', unlike in western Europe as we were out of range, which was a pity as it was the best navigational aid in existence and highly accurate. Instead we had 'Loran', which used stations 500 to 1,000 miles away and allowed no instant fixes, so as far as we could we used other methods. On these tactical raids we were in effect using the Liberators at night to reinforce what the American light bombers were doing in the daytime.'

Arthur Jeffries, a beam gunner on 40 Squadron, flew on the Po raid on the night of 18 April. He recalls: 'The briefing for the raid took a little longer than usual due to the complexities of this range of targets. Our own particular sector was at Malalburgo. We could hardly believe our ears when we were told that we were laying a barrage only a 1,000 yards ahead of the 5th Army - and at night! The time for take-off was at 19.25 hours.

'The Pathfinders (614 Squadron Liberators) were to drop markers and our navigator and bomb-aimer would be further assisted by members of the ground units firing tracer shells at the enemy positions. Timing was of prime importance. We arrived in 'E for Easy' a couple of minutes early and had to resort to a navigational trick or two to rectify this. Right on time the marker flares were dropped and the tracer shells indicated the target. From then on our bombing run began. Ted Hawes, our bomb-aimer, was in complete control, cool and confident. A quick look at our target area and we all knew that this 'first' night-support attack had been a success. Only light anti-aircraft fire was encountered and the night fighters were conspicuous in their absence. Letters of congratulation were received from General Alexander and General McCreery on the success of the mission.'

On 25 April 1945, 205 Group crews were briefed for an operation that was a return to rail junction and marshalling yard raids after their close support work. Sixty-one Liberators were dispatched to the marshalling yards at Freilassing a border town between Germany and Austria about four miles northwest of Salzburg. 614 (County of Glamorgan) Squadron dispatched seven Pathfinder Liberators to illuminate and mark the yards.

Deryck Fereday was among the bomber crews who took part: 'The operation took an hour longer than usual due to the greater distance (I logged six hours five minutes, carrying two 1,000lb and ten 500lb bombs). It went completely to the pattern of other raids: heavy flak over the target, lots of ground explosions and flames indicating munitions in the rail trucks destroyed. Coming back we climbed with plenty of time before we reached the Alps so I permitted myself the luxury of 'listening out' on the pilot's standard frequency radio, which was controlled from above the pilot's head in the roof of the flight deck and could be tuned to almost any broadcast frequency (normally we used only the push button VHF radio for ground/air control, plus the WOp's Morse set). Loud and clear was an Austrian station playing Strauss waltzes, without commentary or other introduction, just showing that someone down there was determined to end the war in three-four time. Even today hearing the Blue Danube brings on instant Liberator nostalgia. This was the last bombing raid of the war. We stood by for other operations but none were confirmed: indeed the fighting lines were so fluid that no one quite knew what point the invading armies had reached. Then VI - Victory in Italy Day - was announced on 6 May 1945. We won the war in Italy with the help of the Liberator, two days before VE-Day was announced in the West.'

During 1945 Liberators flew British troops from Italy to Athens to help suppress the ELAS rising. This caused unrest among South African crews because many were of Greek extraction. On the very last day of the war and for a few days after the German surrender in Italy, Liberators transported petrol and supplies to the British 8th Army advancing from northern Italy into Austria.

Denis Allen on 40 Squadron recalls: 'During the summer of 1945 we made several flights to northern Italy carrying petrol and army rations. These flights were regarded as an 'easy' number but in fact proved just as hazardous as a 'normal' mission! The trouble arose from the temporary landing strip. The Liberator soon broke-up the sun-baked turf and produced large areas of soft sandy soil which hindered take-off. On one occasion I remember even with 120 on the clock the Liberator simply refused to leave the runway.'

148 Squadron was also involved with 'trooping' duties as G. J. Hill recalls: 'We were given the job of transporting PoWs back to the UK as

part of Operation 'Exodus'. Benches were fitted and bomb-doors were sealed with doped fabric to keep the draughts out. However, a steady slipstream blew through the holes and the fuselage was below freezing for most of the trip. We carried twenty-seven passengers at a time in the bomb-bays and during the flight we let them up into the back of the Liberator for a smoke, one at a time - the poor Bs! The passengers could see nothing and there was no method of communicating with them other than by shouting to the first man and asking him to pass it on.'

One by one the Liberator squadrons left Italy. On 6 November 1945 148 Squadron left Foggia and flew to Gianacalis in Egypt. G. J. Hill remembers the trip: 'We carried everything we could get on these aircraft and we took possibly the only two pigs to fly on Liberators. The pigs had been with 148 a long time and were well fed with the swill from three messes. It was a sight to behold to see pigs' heads looking out of large beam windows as the Lib took off from Foggia. On 25 January 1946 148 Squadron was disbanded at Gianacalis. We had a wonderful farewell party - and we ate our two pigs!'

On 13 November 178 Squadron moved to Fayid, Egypt and towards the end of December was disbanded. Crews were posted to 70 Squadron of 205 Group at Shallufa, Egypt. Trooping continued until in February 1946 crews heard that they were to change to Lancs flown by new crews who would be coming out from the UK. The 'Libs' were to be given back to the Americans, as Britain saw no point in paying for them when ample British aircraft were now available for bomber squadrons.

Deryck Fereday recalls: 'We ferried the Libs one by one to Gebel Hamzi (formerly known as 'Kilo 40') on the desert road from Cairo to Alexandria and El Alamein. The last trip was made on 20 March 1946 and we had to suffer the indignity of being brought back by a Lancaster crew whose knees were still white and who had never seen a shot fired in anger. The 'Libs' at Gebel Hamzi were parked in two long lines stretching to the desert horizon. The Maintenance Unit closed down in September 1946 but not before German PoWs were brought in to chop through the aircraft, breaking the tail-plane off and hammering a spike sledge through each engine.

'By the time our last trip was made the first Libs had the sand washing over their tyres and had already been stripped by locals of anything saleable or of scrap value. It was a sorry sight, those beautiful and efficient flying machines in their graveyard, but they had done their job. It was the end of an era.'

Chapter 2

Warsaw Concerto

On 22 February 1944 a signal from Mediterranean Allied Air Force was received by HQ 249 Wing requesting that a Dakota on 267 Squadron be provided to carry out a very special operation. This followed permission from the Polish 6th Bureau and the Air Ministry granted as far back as May 1943 for Operation Wildhorn to take place. No further details were provided, until a conference held at Brindisi revealed the intention was to land in enemy occupied Poland in the middle of the night to fly in two important agents and fly out the GOC of the Polish Home Army (Armia Krajowa - AK) together with four members of his staff and numerous intelligence reports. The safe rescue of these officers from Poland would, to a certain extent, have a material effect on the conclusion of the war. Complete secrecy was obviously demanded. A total of six crews volunteered for this operation, without knowing the details and lots were drawn with the luck of the game falling to Flight Lieutenant Edward Joseph Harrod, his second pilot,

Flight Lieutenant Bolesław Korpowski on 1586 Polish Flight, the Australian navigator, Pilot Officer John Anthony Wells and Pilot Officer Noel Wilcock, the wireless operator. Dakota FD919 was set aside and fitted with eight long-range fuel tanks, giving it a flying time of about eighteen hours. The crew were taken off normal duties and spent the time studying plans and maps of the area and keeping their hand in by night flying on supply drop operations over Yugoslavia. They went on standby for the operation in mid-March 1944 and suffered intense bouts of anxiety and stress during this waiting period. On numerous occasions they were given the go-ahead, only to have the trip cancelled at the last minute. Many times they were actually airborne, waiting for the green light, when the radio would play the Warsaw Concerto, the signal to abort and they would return to base yet again, held back by adverse weather or ground conditions. Needless to say, this beautiful piece of music was not the crews' favourite after a few of these exercises! Finally, on 15 April, they were given the nod and set off from Brindisi at 17 hours 32Z, crossing the Dalmatian coast at 10,000 feet and setting course for a pinpoint landmark on the River Danube. They reached this mark without mishap and headed for the Vistula River. On crossing the Carpathian Mountains, the weather deteriorated and they flew in and out of cloud, relying entirely on Dead Reckoning navigation. Wells and Wilcock used radio fixes from enemy radio stations as the only means of navigation available! Passing Budapest they encountered searchlights and some flak, then the weather cleared after crossing the Carpathians, enabling Wells to get a decent fix on the stars, which showed a higher ground speed than expected, altering their ETA at the Vistula. They began a slow descent, crossing the pinpoint mark on the Vistula at 2,000 feet, as planned and heading for the target on a course almost parallel to the river.

With 40 seconds to go before ETA, they began a series of 'S' turns over the target area, flashing their downward identification light. This was answered almost immediately from the ground and the group of waiting partisans eagerly lit the hurricane lamps marking the edges of the landing strip in white and the green and red flares at each end of the zone. Without wasting any time with the niceties of studying the ground layout, Harrod undertook a normal approach, aiming to come in over the green lights at zero feet. As he did so, he switched on his landing lights and saw to his horror that he was coming in way too fast and heading rapidly for the red lights and farm building at the end of the strip, forcing him to pull up sharply for a second approach. Sensing that something was not right, he approached gingerly at stall speed and landed quite heavily just inside the green lights, but still saw the red lights approaching far too fast. He immediately applied the brakes with the tail still up and this, coupled with the boggy nature of the ground, enabled him to bring the aircraft to rest within just 25 yards of a large barn. As planned, the plane turned and headed back to the green lights to meet the ground party. The soft ground meant the craft had to be kept at full throttle the whole time to avoid sinking and on arrival at the green end of the strip the crew discovered that the ground party had changed the plans at the last minute, deciding to wait by the red lights in an effort to speed up the operation and putting the green at the wrong end of the field, resulting in a downwind landing which nearly had catastrophic consequences! No rational explanation was ever forthcoming as to why they had expected the Dakota to land downwind then simply turn around and take off up wind!

The frustrated crew swung the heavy machine round once more and headed back down the field, still at full throttle, where they at last met up with the ground group who emerged from the adjoining farm buildings. The passengers quickly disembarked, with time enough only for a quick farewell and the surreptitious handing over of a congratulatory bottle of Scotch to the pilot by one of the agents. The departing passengers were: Captain Narcyz Łopianowski (codename 'Sarna' after his favourite horse) and Lieutenant Tomasz Kostuch ('Bryla') plus dispatches and a cargo of US dollars and fake ID books for the AK. Without further ado, the waiting passengers boarded, consisting of: General Stanislaw Tatar (aka Tabor or Turski) Deputy Chief-of-Staff, AK; Lieutenant Colonel Ryszard Dorotycz-Malewicz - AK Head of Courier Operations; Lieutenant Andrzej Pomian - AK Dept of Information and Propaganda; Zygmunt Berezowski, Nationalist Party member and Stanislaw Oltarzewski, Government Delegation member.

The doors were closed. Harrod turned the craft once more with extreme difficulty and lined up with the hurricane lamps for a takeoff which he later confided he never expected to succeed. In front of him lay barely 800 yards of extremely soft, boggy, ploughed ground, ending in a row of trees, which cut at an angle across his path. Reaching this remote spot and landing successfully had been an exercise in its own right - getting out of here again was to be a further test of skill and courage!

After the excitement and stresses of the landing and takeoff, the return flight was relatively calm and uneventful. They experienced further flak over Budapest and took evasive action, then, with dawn approaching, as they crossed over the relative safety of the Adriatic, the pilot broke two cardinal rules of flying and allowed the crew to pass around a cigarette and the bottle of clandestine Scotch in celebration!

They landed at Brindisi at 03h45Z on 16 April where they were met by a large reception committee of both RAF and Polish officers. Three days later, after special dispensation had been granted to the crew, they accompanied their Polish passengers on the final leg of the journey to London. On the morning of 19 April they took off in another Dakota, assisted by another pilot and second navigator, flying non-stop to Gibraltar then on to England the next day, delivering their valuable human cargo to London, from where General Tatar was able to direct successfully the operations of the AK, together with the rest of the Polish government-in-exile operating from London.

On Wednesday 26 April at a specially convened investiture, Flight Lieutenant Harrod was decorated with the Silver Cross and created a member of the Military Order, Virtuti Militari, by the Polish Commander in Chief, General Kazimierz Sosnkowski. Later he also was awarded the DF C by King George VI.

The *Warsaw Concerto* is a short work for piano and orchestra by Richard Addinsell, written for the 1941 British film Dangerous Moonlight, which is about the Polish struggle against the 1939 invasion by the Nazis. The concerto is an example of programme music, representing both the struggle for Warsaw and the romance of the leading characters in the film. It became very popular in Britain during World War II. In his 1944 appearance on *Desert Island Discs*, Guy Gibson, leader of the Dam Busters raid, asked for it as his first choice.

By 0900 hours on Sunday 13 August 1944 it was clear to Lieutenant 'Bob' Klette, a South African Liberator pilot on 31 Squadron SAAF at Celone about ten kilometres north of Foggia in Puglia in Southern Italy, that his squadron would not be required to fly that night. Liberator VIs of 31 and 34 Squadrons SAAF in 205 Group RAF and B-17s of the 463rd Bombardment Group, 15th Air Force USAAF were based at the primitive airfield with its 6,000 feet PSP runway, extensive taxiways and hardstand parking areas and a steel control tower. Hardly the last word in comfort, this semi-permanent airfield, also known as Capelli or Foggia Satellite #1, was located 3.5 kilometres northeast of a farm called San Nicola d'Arpi on the banks of the Celone River, bordering the Adriatic Sea in the east, the Ionian Sea to the southeast and the Strait of Òtranto and Gulf of Taranto in the south. The lower half of Italy was now separated from the North by the German Army, fighting a stubborn rearguard action as it retreated slowly up the Italian mainland. The North was still under the control of the Mussolini government, with the support of the Germans under Hitler; the South had a provisional government with the support and control of the British and American forces. At any given opportunity Klette's crew were eager to swim in the cool, crystal clear waters of the Adriatic at Manfredonia Bay but it was not to be. 'My crew and I were stepping out to join the exodus of would-be swimmers from camp when our attention was caught by a cloud of dust preceded by a jeep approaching us in haste from the direction of the Ops tent. It was the CO's navigator, 'Lofty' Thorogood, with the terse instructions, 'No one to leave camp - briefing at 1100 hours.' This didn't satisfy our curiosity, for crews were only told that they were to fly to Brindisi after an early lunch for further briefing.'

In high summer and at mid-day it was so hot that it was possible to cook an egg in a hollow of one of the stones on the top parapet of the 'Castello Aragonese' off the coast at Brindisi. Klette parked 'G for George' [EW105/G] and ambled over towards 148 Squadron 'Ops room' where many other crews, both RAF and SAAF were assembled. 205 Group included 1586 Special Polish Duty Squadron, 178 and 148 Squadrons (334 Wing) and 31 and 34 Squadrons SAAF (2 Wing) and were based at the Foggia Airfield Complex, which formed part of a series of about thirty airfields on the Tavoliere delle Puglie plain in northern Apulia within a 25 mile radius of Foggia. The airfields were severely bombed by the USAAF and RAF in 1943 before the British 8th Army conquered the region during the Italian campaign. The US Army Corps of Engineers then repaired the captured airfields for use by heavy bombers and built new ones for operations against Nazi-occupied Europe and Germany. The airfields were used by 12th and 15th Air Force units, as well as the RAF. The complex did not just stretch out in the province of Foggia, but also well into Bari, Molise and Basilicata.

'Inside was a huge wall map of Europe and a route from Brindisi to Warsaw was marked with tape. We were totally ignorant of what was happening in that war zone and wondered what was in store for us. The mission was to drop supplies to the beleaguered Polish patriots in Warsaw and the background was rather sketchy. The briefing detailed the route, the position of the dropping area in Warsaw and the height and speed of approach (500 feet and 140 mph). The Met Officer forecast cloud with tops at 16,000 feet; handy for ducking into if night fighters showed up. A Polish pilot assured us that the trip there and back was 'a piece of cake'. He did it every week and advised that the high buildings to the south of the city should be avoided.'

However' recalled Bryan Jones, Klette's observer 'during a hurried coffee/sandwich break other locally based airmen told us that the Polish Flight had been almost decimated in their attempts to get through to Warsaw! The briefing ended with a very emotional Polish Squadron Leader saying 'Poland is in dire trouble and I plead with you South African and British gentlemen to save my country to-night.' With these words ringing in our ears these fine young men flew out into the setting sun to help our courageous allies in Warsaw. The rest is history. They were well trained and disciplined and many of them were also young men of faith and I believe that prayers of commitment and calls for Divine help went up as they wrestled with their crippled aircraft before plunging into the streets of Warsaw or nearby forests there to die alongside thousands of brave Polish men and women. At 25, my tent mate, Lieutenant Eric Impey [the observer on Captain Leonard Allen's crew] was older than most and after packing up his personal belongings, he sat down and wrote the well known *Airmans Prayer* before going out to Warsaw that night never to return. He was the reigning South African High Jump Champion and a young man of faith. I too was a young man of faith in God and His saving grace and in a definite way knew of the Lord's presence with me that night. Only years later I came to understand His last promise to his friends 'Lo I am with you always'.

In August 1944 the Russian armies had swept aside German resistance in Poland and were at the approaches of Warsaw. The Armia Krajowa - AK (Polish Home Army) under General Tadeusz Komorowski Bór ('The Forest') was persuaded to rise against the German occupation troops but the Russians made no attempt whatever to support the rising. On the evening of 1 August 1944 General Bór-Komorowski requested all possible air support for the rising but for some time the Russians refused to allow RAF and American aircraft, involved in supplying arms to Warsaw, to make emergency landings in Russian-held territory. Bór-Komorowski pleaded for the bombing of the environs of the capital, the dispatch of Polish fighter squadrons from France and even the dropping of the Polish parachute brigade into Warsaw itself. His pleas, however, were impractical. On 3 August British Prime Minister Winston Churchill decided to send assistance. The Special Duty squadrons in England were fully committed to 'Overlord' so the task of supplying the Polish Home Army was given to the Mediterranean Allied Air Forces. At first Air

Marshal Sir John Slessor the allied air commander in the Mediterranean opposed the plan on the grounds that the undertaking was suicidal. In any event only a small amount of ammunition and arms could be carried on each flight since the larger part of the carrying capacity of the aircraft was taken up by fuel. Usually, during ordinary flights, the calculated fuel reserve would be 25% to account for possible emergencies. For Warsaw, the estimated reserve was only nine percent. The supplies were packed in twelve canisters per aircraft, containing light machine guns, ammunition, hand grenades, radio equipment, food and medical supplies. Each canister had a small parachute to break the fall. Supplies had to be accurately dropped on identified street areas or into specified air-supply zones.

Despite opposition Churchill ordered 205 Group, commanded by a South African officer, Brigadier James ('Jimmy') Thom Durrant CB DFC to start with extensive flights from Italy to Warsaw, despite the extremely difficult circumstances that would seriously hamper these supply flights. Durrant went to see Air Vice Marshal Slessor and was surprised to be admitted to the presence of Churchill himself in an adjoining office. Slessor had become Commander-in-Chief RAF Mediterranean and Middle East in January 1944 and deputy to Lieutenant General Ira Eaker as Commander-in-Chief Mediterranean Allied Air Forces. In this role he conducted operations in the Italian Campaign and Yugoslavia, establishing the Balkan Air Force in the latter theatre. Durrant pointed out to Churchill that an airlift of 1,000 miles, most of it over enemy territory, could hold no hope of military success and that the loss of airmen and aircraft would be tremendous. Churchill's reply was brief and to the point: 'From a military point of view you are right, but from a political point of view you must carry on. Good Morning.'[1]

A small trial sortie was dispatched by 1586 Special Duty Flight on 8 and 9 August. When the crews arrived in the Operations room they were greeted with a large wall map of Europe, marked with a thick black route zigzagging over a sea, high mountains and from Foggia to Warsaw. For the aircrews involved, the trip to Warsaw was a most hazardous affair. It meant a round trip of nearly eleven hours, just short of 900 miles each way, starting in the last hours of daylight and ending back at base, if they managed to get back, somewhere around dawn the next day. Practically the whole distance was over enemy territory, which meant opposition from anti-aircraft fire and night fighters, while the high mountainous area of the Carpathians invariably provided dangerous electric storms. The route taken was in a straight line, north-east from the south of Italy, across the Adriatic, north over Yugoslavia and from there they crossed the Scutari Lake in Albania, then across the Danube to Hungary and Czechoslovakia and then southern Poland until picking up the Vistula to lead them into Warsaw. Pilots then had to follow the Vistula River for the last leg to Warsaw. On arrival over the city, the pilots were told to pass over four river bridges and then turn left toward the target area. They were to go in at 500 feet, with flaps down to reduce speed to 140 mph.

All aircraft returned safely but as the situation in Warsaw deteriorated, more aircraft were needed if the partisans were to survive and so on the night of 12 August, eleven aircraft from the Polish Flight and 148 Squadron flew to Warsaw. Three aircraft failed to drop their supplies, but the remaining eight were successful; again all returned safely. Then the position of the Polish Home Army deteriorated, as the Germans brought in more divisions and set about a systematic destruction of the city of Warsaw, razing it by gunfire and flame, block by block. A very much more concentrated supply effort was essential if the partisans were to survive. Their only hope lay in supplies from the outside world. As crews who took part in Warsaw Concerto', as the supply-dropping mission became known among the squadrons involved were told - the only alternative facing the partisans was annihilation.

When the first full-scale effort with twenty-eight Liberators on 31 and 34 Squadrons SAAF and 178 Squadron of the RAF took place on 13 August, ten crews on 31 Squadron (Motto: *Absque metu* (Without Fear) were ordered to Brindisi and briefed for a flight plan from Foggia to Warsaw to drop supplies for the encircled Polish resistance. One of the aircraft was 'G for George' skippered by Bob Klette: 'With canisters full of guns and ammunition packed in her bomb bays 'G for George' crossed the Adriatic in fading light. Bryan Jones our navigator called for a northerly course and the long flight across the Carpathians commenced. As night fell, all eyes were on the lookout for tell-tale glows in the sky which would indicate night fighters. Not much chatter from the crew - consisting, apart from Bryan, of second pilot, Lieutenant Alf Faul; 19-year old mid-upper gunner Warrant Officer2 Herbert James Brown from the Transvaal; wireless operator Warrant Officer Eric Winchester; waist gunner; Warrant Officer T. G 'Smiler' Davis and tail gunner, Warrant Officer Henry Upton.[2]

'All too soon the promised cloud loomed up ominously and although our height was above the forecasted ceiling of 16,000 feet, we plunged into the murk which turned out to be the brute of a cumulonimbus, vicious turbulence rocking, swinging and bumping the Liberator . It was like riding in a rodeo, the compasses spinning in all directions from north to south and east to west. Losing height didn't help; gaining height brought rapid icing on the leading edges of the wings as well as sluggish flying; so back to 20,000 feet. Eventually we were through the worst and

Bryan's calm voice came over the R/T suggesting that the mountains had been cleared and the descent could commence but I flew on for neatly half an hour before complying with his proposal. It was one hour fifty-five minutes after entering the cloud that we emerged with the altimeter reading exactly 1,000 feet and below stretching into the distance, was Poland.

Bryan pinpointed Kraków and we turned eastwards to observe the Vistula was a clear landmark beneath. While following the river northwards, a pin-point of light grew rapidly into the shape of a city in flames. This was Warsaw - an unforgettable sight. The river divided the main city to the west from its satellite Praga to the east and bridges linked the two clearly demarcated cities, flames illuminating the buildings and streets of Warsaw. We could visualise our heroic Polish allies waiting patiently for the supplies to be dropped while another mental picture was of trigger-happy ack-ack gunners preparing to welcome us.'

As they ran into the target at just 400 feet above the Vistula Bryan Jones was lying on his stomach in the nose of the aircraft, guiding Klette into their precise dropping area in the Old City. 'In the midst of the vivid fireworks display below, I heard a voice say 'Jones put on your tin hat'. We were obliged to take our steel helmets with us but never wore them as they were cumbersome in that confined space. When God's voice came for the second time, I reached for the tin hat on the floor behind me where I usually dropped it and put it on.'

While nearing the first bridge Bob Klette reduced height rapidly. 'As the bridge disappeared beneath, half a dozen searchlights beamed on the Lib and the heavens opened up with streaks of tracer and balls of flaming onions following from the east bank. Instinctively I pushed the stick forward and pulled it back again, roller coasting along through the muck. The noise was deafening as the flak thumped against the aircraft and our own guns fired flat out. There was little hope of accurate shooting by our chaps due to the rocking of the aircraft although there was an excited shout from Herbert Brown who was overjoyed when eliminating a searchlight. 'Smiler' Davis and Henry Upton were wounded during this battle but fortunately not too seriously. Eric Winchester was wounded in the head and arm. Number 2 engine spluttered to a stop and the aircraft slewed to starboard. Keeping straight was not easy and while Alf was feathering the engine and Bryan was guiding me over the dropping zone, number 3 engine also petered out. The problem now, with only the two outer engines functioning, was to maintain height, but I managed to stay at 500 feet while Brian talked me into position and after our load had been dropped he yelled, 'Canisters away; let's get the hell out of here' and he gave me a course to steer for home.

'We turned southwards away from the flames of Warsaw, the inky blackness ahead showing no sign of a horizon and inside the aircraft, the artificial horizon along with other gyro instruments, had gone for a total loop. A second or two later there was a severe jarring and scraping under the Lib's belly and then silence. The tall buildings to the south which the Polish pilot had warned us about, was my immediate conclusion as I tensed myself for inevitable death - but nothing happened. Various thoughts went through my mind: Had we crashed? Was I dead and in heaven? Then I stole a quick glance below to the left and couldn't believe my eyes. The Lib had made a perfect belly-landing on a grass surface. 'My God, we're on Mother Earth' I yelled, but the intercom was dead and only Alf heard me.

'We jumped out and ran to the aircraft's nose where Brian had been trapped and was hacking his way clear with an axe carried in that section of the 'Lib'. After freeing himself he joined us and we turned about intending to discover how the rest of the crew had fared, but while running around the port wing with its two engines spewing petrol on to the ground, the bean of a searchlight suddenly settled on us and at the same time a machine gun opened fire. Throwing ourselves flat on the ground, we crawled along towards the wing tip but my progress was suddenly halted by something which caught in my equipment. I gave a tug and with a *Shhhh* my Mae West began to inflate! Had the situation not been so traumatic, the scene could have been like something from a comic opera. I saw my shadow lengthening and felt my chest rising from the ground! Feeling a bit too vulnerable, I shed the Mae West and, still hugging the ground, scuttled along to catch up with Bryan and Alf. The searchlight went out and the machine gun stopped firing. 'Stay down,' I yelled, sensing a trap. I doubt whether anyone heard the warning, but sure enough the searchlights came on again along with the repetitive bursts of machine gun fire. (We were to learn later that the spirited young Brown had made a dash for it, possibly at this moment and was hit in the back of his thigh.)'

Bryan Jones walked away from the wreckage at Warsaw Airport. 'I knelt on the ground, stunned and said: 'Lord, for saving me, I will devote the rest of my life to you.'

'A moment or two later Very lights hovered over the Liberator' continues Bob Klette. 'There were voices in the dark and a gun seemed to be firing at the aircraft where, as far as I knew, our wounded gunners were trapped, so Bryan, Alf and I stood up and surrendered. Three Luftwaffe types, one a corporal, walked up. Ah Jannie Smuts se boys said the corporal eyeing our red tabs! A conversation proceeded in a mixture of German, Afrikaans and English when it was ascertained that we had landed on Warsaw Airport, unbelievably flying straight into the hornets' nest! I didn't mention that 'G for George' had landed herself with practically no help from me!'[3]

Bob Klette and five of his crew were escorted to a room in the airport building where a Luftwaffe officer volunteered to arrange for Bob to visit Herbert Brown who had been taken to hospital. This visit did not materialise and Herbert, who had been mortally wounded, was not seen again although the International Red Cross confirmed that he had been hospitalised in Warsaw. He was reported missing after the Russian advance but was not traced.'

Bob Klette and the rest of his crew were captured they were taken by train to Frankfurt and after three weeks' in solitary confinement prior to interrogation, were sent to PoW camps. Fortunately the war lasted only another ten months, when they returned home. After the war Bryan Jones held a number of senior managerial positions before becoming ordained as a pastor in the Rosebank Union Church in Jo'burg. 'It took a bit of time, but eventually I made good on that promise.'

For another crew on 31 Squadron, the outward flight on Liberator EW138 'K-King' skippered by Lieutenant William Norval was uneventful to within sixty miles of the drop zone, at which point the first of many difficulties was encountered. The hydraulics to the rear turret failed and constant manual operation had to be employed in the gunner's search tactics, because German night fighters were shadowing the Liberators. The previous flights to the Polish capital had alerted the Nachtjagd and crews could also expect increased flak and searchlight defences over Warsaw. At 0045 hours the Vistula was pinpointed just south of Warsaw: the river flowed to the capital and there was slight flak opposition on the starboard side. The activity of the ground defences increased on arriving over Warsaw at 0049 hours; 'K-King' was caught in the beams of a group of ten to twelve searchlights and came under very accurate and intense flak, knocking out the port outer engine. After a few terrifying moments, Norval succeeded in escaping the lights and he ordered the supplies to be jettisoned, although they were still one mile short of their briefed drop zone. Another battery of about a dozen searchlights picked up 'K-King' at a height of 4,000 feet and AA guns subjected the Liberator to intense fire. The aircraft started a power dive to starboard - and then without warning, Norval put on his parachute, opened the bomb-bay doors and bailed out!

The Liberator went out of control and began to lose height as it moved to and fro across the Vistula. Lieutenant Robert C. W. 'Bob' Burgess, the second pilot, took over and finally regained control at 1,000 feet. However, a glaring light in the cockpit indicated that the bomber was once again caught in searchlights. The gunner in the forward turret continued firing at them and succeeded in eliminating them, one after another, until Burgess managed to pilot the limping aircraft away from the burning city. The compass was out of order, the instruments were defective and one of the engines had died. The badly damaged aircraft was controlled only with difficulty and constantly threatened to nose-dive. Burgess and the navigator, Lieutenant Noel Sleed decided to fly on to Soviet territory. Aided by Sleed and Sergeant Alan Bates, Burgess managed to get the ailing B-24 up to 4,000 feet and then gave the crew the choice of either bailing out or remaining in the Liberator; they all chose the latter.

During the flight eastwards a fuel problem was overcome when Noel Sleed, with great difficulty, made his way to the fuel tanks in the rear of the fuselage via the narrow catwalk, which was then slippery because of leaking oil and coolly transferred fuel from the auxiliary to the main tanks. Then the propeller of the damaged engine suddenly began to turn uncontrollably, causing the bomber to dive towards the ground at high speed. With great effort, Burgess succeeded in regaining control at an altitude of only 2,700 feet. They flew on for three hours, finally reaching 8,000 feet, before tumbling to 5,000 feet at 270mph before Burgess regained control again. At daybreak, they flew over a village that had an old airfield and Burgess decided to attempt a landing. The aircraft circled the village eight times while the crew struggled to get its undercarriage and air brakes into operation. On the ninth approach, K-King' landed successfully at 0535 hours at Emilchino, about 100 miles west of Kiev. The crew were subsequently handed over to the British Mission. Burgess became the youngest and most junior SAAF officer to be awarded an immediate DSO and Sleed an immediate DFC. Fourteen Liberators dropped successfully that night, but eleven failed to find their drop zones, while three did not return. Those who did get back were badly battered.

The next night, 14/15 August, 26 Liberators set out for Poland once again. A Polish liaison officer attended the briefing and stated that a reserve Polish partisan division was situated in some undefended woods twelve miles to the west of Warsaw. 31 Squadron provided six Liberators for the supply drop. One of these was KG939 'A-Able' flown by Captain Jacobus Ludewicus van Eyssen, a Johannesburg mining executive. Jacobus or 'Jack' as he was known joined the SAAF in 1936 as a cadet in the Transvaal Air Training Squadron while an engineering student. He obtained his Engineering degree in 1940 and he then became permanently involved with flying instruction at various air schools in South Africa before joining 31 Squadron SAAF in mid 1944.

'As the aircraft climbed, course was set across the Adriatic' recalled Captain Jack van Eyssen. 'The enemy coast was soon reached in summer sunshine and although we felt too exposed for comfort we drew consolation from the fact that fighters could not surprise us as easily as they could in the darkness. The pilot and his gunners formed a very closely knit team, particularly when the aircraft was attacked by fighters. The pilots seldom accorded the fighters the courtesy of flying straight and level and turned violently up or down at the last second to spoil their aim and at the same time to give their gunners the advantage with their heavy machine guns.

'Darkness had set in and soon the Danube came into view as a thin blue ribbon. To the north lay the Carpathians and bad weather. We were tossed about in the clouds and frequently 'lit up' by lightning. At times our propeller discs created blue circles and blue flames trailed from wing tips and other projections. This frightening although harmless phenomenon is also seen on the masts of ships at night. Sailors call it St. Elmo's Fire. North of the Carpathians the weather cleared and we altered course away from Kraków which we knew to be a night fighter training centre for the Luftwaffe. A further course alteration led towards Warsaw. Before long we picked up jazz music from Radio Warsaw which was just what we wanted as it meant that we were out of the range of 'Gee'. Our radio compass needle led us directly to the city which first showed as a glow on the horizon. We started to lose height and as we drew closer to the city, were shocked by what we saw, in spite of having been told what to expect at the briefing. Rows upon rows of buildings were on fire sending clouds of smoke thousands of feet into the air. The smoke was, in turn, illuminated from below by the fires. It was obvious that a life or death struggle was taking place before us.

'According to our briefing we were to fly north along the Vistula dropping to 200 feet and then to turn left about a cathedral in the north of the city. We were then to turn south keeping the river on our left, to open bomb doors and to drop lower still to about 150 feet. By using optimum flap we could keep our large aircraft under control at only 130 mph. A greater speed could have snapped the shroud lines on the canister parachutes. We had to continue until we saw the letter of the night flashed in Morse from the ground. When we saw it we had to drop all of our canisters together and get away as fast as possible. An aircraft is most vulnerable to anti-aircraft fire at a height of 3,000 feet to 5,000 feet. Over Warsaw our aircraft attracted fire from hand-held machine guns, rifles and even pistols! Poor visibility due to smoke was also a serious hazard.'

At briefing the Polish liaison officer had said that supplies could be dropped to the Polish partisan division without great risk. He was only half right. Three Liberators on 31 Squadron received ground recognition lights and dropped successfully, while a fourth saw no signals but dropped in the target zone. Only twelve succeeded in dropping in the right areas and increased opposition was encountered as they flew over enemy territory on the way to the target. There was even stiffer anti-aircraft fire over the target and more night fighters on the return leg. Eight Liberators, including three on 31 Squadron, failed to return. One of these was 'A-Able' on 31 Squadron. After crossing the Vistula, 15 miles south of Warsaw at 6,000 feet, Captain Jack van Eyssen did one circuit to lose height before flying north along the east bank of the Vistula. At 0050 hours at a height of 1,500 feet and position two miles east of the river and three miles south of the city, 'A-Able' was caught by searchlights. As the Liberator turned it was engaged by six anti-aircraft guns and repeatedly hit. Numbers 2, 3 and 4 engines, petrol leads and the fuselage caught fire. Use of fire extinguishers and feathering of propellers failed to stop the fires. They were at 600 feet, so the supplies were jettisoned. Jack van Eyssen succeeded in restarting Number 3 engine and gaining height to 1,000 feet, on a south-easterly heading. He gave the order to the crew to abandon the aircraft as the Liberator's starboard wing was breaking up.

Lieutenant Basil Harvey 'Bunny' Austin the English wireless operator born at Slinfold in Sussex on 8 April 1913,[4] who had gained a reputation of being an expert wireless operator and a no mean handler of the machine gun, helped his fellow crewmembers and saw to it that they had their parachutes connected by both hooks before shoving them through the escape hatch of the doomed Liberator. When it was his turn to leave, Austin dived headfirst through the open bomb bay. He landed heavily amongst tall trees, thirty feet above the ground and swung suspended by his parachute. German patrols were active in the vicinity so Austin decided to walk away in the direction of the village of Aleksandrovo, fifteen miles south-east of Warsaw. He later took refuge in a girl's convent where he was tended by members of the Polish underground army. When movements were heard outside an alert was sounded at the approach of a German patrol and Austin was hidden in the bed of a twelve-year-old girl, Urszula Stupik. Next morning Austin was guided to a Russian field post where he gave himself up. Later other members of his crew joined him. Jack van Eyssen, Lieutenant D. R. F. 'Happy' Holliday SAAF, navigator; Sergeant George Peaston RAFVR, mid upper gunner and Flight Sergeant H. Stuart Lichfield RAFVR, bomb aimer, had all bailed out safely but Sergeants Leslie Mayes RAFVR, tail gunner and Herbert Hudson RAFVR, beam gunner were killed either by flak or so seriously wounded as to be unable to survive the jump and Lieutenant Robert George Hamilton SAAF, co-pilot was found 200 yards from the burning wreckage of the Liberator. His parachute had opened but failed to break his fall; the other two must have been too seriously wounded to survive the jump, or were hit by flak on the way down. 'A-Able' crashed and burned out after hitting the ground at Michalin 30 kilometres southeast of Warsaw. Polish sympathisers in the village of Alexandrov buried the three members of the crew in a common grave. Hundreds of villagers attended the funeral, covering the grave with flowers.

On the night of 15/16 August 31 Squadron sent out another seven aircraft. Another group of Liberators was ordered to be held in readiness for a repeat operation over Warsaw but 27-year old Colonel Dirk Uys Nel the fiery Commander of 31 Squadron, a descendant of the famous Voortrekker Uys family that was involved in many battles, stated that he could not agree to his aircraft going in unless at 7,000 feet. To do otherwise was suicide. Group Operations agreed that the squadron should stand down for the night. Four of the seven Liberators that were despatched reached Warsaw, approaching the target from the south up the river and turning in to the dropping zones at 300 feet after obtaining identification from the bridges. To the north-west of Alexandrov, the city of Warsaw was still burning, with a dense cloud of smoke blanketing large sections of its sprawling mass of ruins. The Germans put up a hail of anti-aircraft fire which holed all but one of the four South African Liberators, which managed to get back to Celone. As Captain F. C. Serfontein SAAF's Liberator on 31 Squadron approached the burning city, his navigator, Lieutenant John R. Coleman SAAF saw one Liberator explode in the air. They had barely completed their own agonizingly slow running of the gauntlet, when another Liberator became engulfed in flames and plunged earthwards. In all, three Liberators, captained by Captain van Eyssen, Captain Nicolaas van Rensburg and 25-year old Lieutenant Grattan Chesney Hooey, failed to return. All seven members of van Rensburg's crew died. Hooey's crew too were killed[6] when their Liberator (KG836) crashed after the wingtip hit a building in Warsaw Central Square while making an airdrop at Plac Krasiński.

Of the four remaining Liberators, three dropped their containers in target areas but Liberator KG872/V on 31 Squadron commanded by Captain William E. 'Bill' Senn was hit by the full blast of anti-aircraft fire as it turned into the target and its twelve containers fell on the east bank of the Vistula. Senn was seriously wounded in the thigh and the mid-upper gunner was hit in the hand. The rudder control cable of the Liberator was damaged; the elevator control was partially cut; and the hydraulic mechanism of the nose wheel was put out of action. Fuel began to leak and a fire broke out in the navigator's compartment, which was extinguished by the navigator, Lieutenant T. C. L. Symmes, who had been wounded in the face. Instruments, as well as the intercom system, were put out of action. Meanwhile, Warrant Officer Frank

Langford, the 23-year old tail gunner, continued firing bursts into a battery of German searchlights, of which he claimed to have destroyed four of them. Senn then gave the preliminary order to the crew to prepare to jump. They did not realise that he had been wounded and would therefore crash with the aircraft. The buckle of his parachute had been shattered. A fire broke out in the navigational compartment shortly afterwards, but was extinguished by the crew. One of the fuel tanks was shot to pieces, which forced the pilot to reduce speed in order to save fuel. This increased the danger of being shot down. The flight home was made without maps and using only the automatic rudder control. Senn reached the Danube at daybreak and went on to land safely at Foggia without flaps or wheels. The crew was at no stage aware that he had been wounded.[7] Senn was awarded the DFC for bringing back his badly damaged Liberator.

The operations of the two nights had been expensive. The 31 Squadron had despatched seventeen aircraft. Five had been lost; at most eight had successfully completed their mission. It was obviously uneconomical to send out aircraft with only a 50 per cent chance of success and equally impossible for the squadron, except with the certainty of annihilation, to continue to bear this high rate of loss among its best and most determined crews on a mission that was inspired by considerations of political rather than military necessity. The Poles sent enthusiastic telegrams of thanks, acknowledging receipt of the supplies and begging for more.

On 16/17 August three more Liberators on 31 Squadron failed to return. The crews captained by 31-year old Major Izak Johannes Meyer 'Nick' Odendaal, 27-year old Captain Gordon Lawrie[8] and 27-year old Captain Leonard Charles Allen (EV941/Q) which made a successful drop but was shot down was shot down near Kraków on return[9] were the ones lost. Odendaal was the skipper of Liberator EW248/P, which on 16 August was its second flight to Warsaw. Of all the narrow escapes during these sorties, his experience was certainly among the most surprising and dramatic. His Liberator reached Warsaw just after midnight. During the flight over the burning city, the aircraft was caught by searchlights and engaged by anti-aircraft fire. Hit several times, it soon became engulfed in flames. Odendaal ordered the crew to bail out. As Lieutenant J. J. C. Groenwald the second pilot, grabbed his parachute, the Liberator was hit once again and virtually blew up and he was hurled into the air by the violence of the explosion. He found himself falling with his parachute still clasped like a suitcase in his hand. Fortunately, he kept his presence of mind and managed to fasten the parachute to its harness and pull the ripcord. He landed uninjured, except for burns to his face and arms. Using the parachute as a blanket to keep warm, Groenewald spent the rest of the night in the German-controlled area at the spot where he had landed. At daybreak, he succeeded in stumbling to a farmstead where a sympathetic Pole took care of him and hid him under some hay. He was taken by horse-cart to a well-equipped little hospital run by an old professor who had earlier been a lecturer at Warsaw University. Nurses, disguised as farm labourers, manned the hospital. Groenewald was treated there for ten days, during which several skin grafts were performed on him by a Polish surgeon. When he had completely recovered he was provided with false identity documents and disguised as an old Polish farm labourer who was too old for military service he worked on a farm as a foreman. His new name was Jan Galles. Later, Groenewald joined the Polish partisans and fought with them against the Germans. In February 1945, six months after his Liberator had been shot down Russian divisions reached the area where Groenewald fought. He was taken to Moscow, where he was handed over to the British Military Legation. From there, he was able to send a cable to his wife, who had been receiving a pension from the widow's fund for several months.[10]

This loss of 50 per cent on an operation staggered the remaining crews of the squadron, though their concern was lightened by a brief message reporting that Captain Jacobus Ludewicus van Eyssen and four of his crew and were safe in Russia. When the aircraft was hit it sank to about 500 feet and before bailing out the pilot had to gain an additional three or four hundred feet in order to allow the chutes to open. With difficulty he achieved his object and the crew jumped. Captain van Eyssen landed in a clearing in a forest and spent about half an hour trying to round up his crew without success. He then started walking east and thinking that he was in German held country, avoided all buildings and roads. At dawn he hid in a thicket having covered about seven miles. The glow of burning Warsaw was still visible in the west and the sound of bombs was still clearly audible from that direction although occasionally he heard the sounds of firing from the east too. As he found out later this must have been Russian sappers exploding mines. Shortly after sunrise an old Polish woman came by his hiding place so he stepped out and tried to discover the position of the front lines by language and signs but she did not understand and appeared afraid of him. Then she departed. Considering his hiding place now no longer safe, he buried his Mae West and set off east again keeping to forests and plantations. On the way he passed bomb craters, wrecked transports, a burned out tank and several large fenced off areas that were probably minefields.

Captain van Eyssen and his navigator, 'Happy' Holliday soon found each other in the darkness but at first had some difficulty in contacting the Russian troops. Eventually they discovered that they had come down ten miles behind the line. Fortunately van Eyssen spoke German and was able to make himself understood fairly easily in their wanderings. The two officers always found someone who understood either English or German. Identification was fairly easy and it was here that the red tabs on their uniforms stood them in good stead and after a certain amount of questioning they were accepted as guests of the Red Air Force. The five survivors had to suffer days of intense interrogation at the hands of the Russians before being flown on to Moscow where they were handed over to No. 30 British Mission. In a magazine article of the time Holliday was quoted as saying that the Red airmen did everything possible to make them comfortable, heaping food and cigarettes upon them. The food was palpable and excellent in quality but not the type likely to suit the taste of a South African. Usually a type of soup called Borscht was followed by meat cooked in various ways - but nearly always a little too fatty for the South African palate. On the second day the airmen were taken back seventy miles and here many more comforts were available, including vodka. A cinema show was produced and shots of the fighting on the Eastern Front figured on the screen, while at the same time a glance out of the window across the sky showed rocket-firing guns in action against enemy aircraft. A day or so later saw the South Africans in Moscow. During the first two or three days of their stay in Moscow the two South Africans were accommodated in a small house. Afterwards they stayed with the British Mission. Here they enjoyed the comfort of familiar food and drink with a definite improvement in their digestive systems. On 4 September Captain Van Eyssen and his two South African crew members left Moscow on the first stage of their repatriation to South Africa. Three days later they reached Cairo. After recuperative leave in South African, Van Eyssen, Austin and Holliday returned to Italy to resume their interrupted tour of operations on 31 Squadron.[11]

The war diary of 31 Squadron during the days of the 'Warsaw Concerto' is a revealing document. On three nights the squadron sent out a total of 23 Liberators to Warsaw of which eight were lost. On the first night, ten aircraft took off, but four turned back early for a variety of reasons. The other six reached Warsaw after passing through a cold front and electric storms over the Carpathians. Three went in from the north-east and obtained definite identification of dropping area (four bridges, church spire, square) and dropped 36 containers. Another aircraft approached from the south-east, but obtained no positive identification because of thick smoke from the many fires in the city. It dropped twelve containers in an area close to the target zone. The first Liberators encountered few defences but later aircraft met very accurate fire from both banks of the Vistula as they were silhouetted in the flames of the fires. The Liberator of Captain Keith St. G. Hayward SAAF had its hydraulics shot up and was badly holed. As it turned out, crews had no difficulty in sighting the city. Warsaw was ablaze, its flames visible 100 miles away. As they went in to drop they were illuminated by these flames and also by the multiple searchlights, making them sitting ducks for the anti-aircraft batteries and other machine-gunners sited on roof tops. Often it was impossible to pick up the flares and recognition signals from the partisans to indicate the dropping areas, which meant that many loads of supplies were dropped off target or jettisoned.

The drops continued up to and including 27 August, though with fewer aircraft. Most of Warsaw was ablaze and pilots had no difficulty picking out the city from 100 miles away and as the partisans lost ground in the city the drops continued in woods outside the capital. As the Liberators dropped their supplies they were easy targets, illuminated by the flames and multiple searchlights. Flak guns and machine gunners on roofs picked off many of the four-engined bombers. Some dropped to as low as 100 feet, literally following the streets to the City Hall, which was one of the dropping zones, or in search of signals which indicated an area in urgent need of supplies., drops were made in the woods outside Warsaw, where a reserve Polish division was situated, with some success and with fewer casualties. Nevertheless, the casualty rate was high - something over 15 per cent, or three times higher than Bomber Command was normally prepared to accept. There were 196 11-hour night flights from Brindisi and Foggia in Italy (total between 31 and 34 Squadrons) to and from Warsaw from 4 August to early September 1944. Of the 80 aircraft involved, 31 were shot down, seventeen during the week of 13-16 August. Sixty-nine South Africans were killed and twenty-five SAAF Liberators were shot down. Fifty percent of the aircraft were from the RAF and 36% of the total force was South African. Air Marshal Sir John Slessor later put the losses at one bomber lost for every ton of supplies dropped. The 205 Group AOC Brigadier Durrant SAAF drew the attention of the Air Commander-in-Chief to these losses, but the operation continued unabated. Throughout the period of the supply operations 205 Group sent out 186 Liberators to Warsaw. Of these 92 succeeded in dropping supplies in the target areas, 63 were unable to find the targets and 31 did not return. The South African squadrons provided 41 of these aircraft of which eleven were lost. The Polish squadron suffered almost 100 per cent casualties.

The bravery of these men was almost beyond description as they sought to assist the gallant men and women of the Polish Home Army. Even after dropping the canisters of supplies the risk of being clawed out of the sky was still very real in the many hundreds of miles that lay ahead on the return journey. The figures of losses were frightening, yet it is remarkable that so many aircraft and crews went on that trip and returned. On the five nights between the 12 and 17 August, seventeen of the ninety-three aircraft despatched failed to return. With that operations ceased but operations were restarted after protests from the Polish authorities. Four of the nine aircraft on 1586 Flight failed to return on two nights and after further losses bad weather prevented any further flights to the beleaguered Poles. Of the 186 Liberators dispatched on 'Warsaw Concerto' operations, 92 succeeded in dropping supplies, 63 were unable to drop and 31 failed to return. In all, the South African squadrons sent 41aircraft, of which eleven were lost.

Altogether, the Polish, RAF and SAAF units lost thirty-one aircraft out of 186 Liberators dispatched to Warsaw in twenty-two nights of operations, 8 August-21 September. Of these, ninety-two succeeded in dropping their supplies in the target areas, sixty-three were unable to find their targets and thirty-one did not return. The South Africans of 31 Squadron lost eight Liberators in four nights. In six weeks 31 and 34 Squadrons lost twenty-four of their thirty-three aircraft. 1586 (Polish) Flight suffered almost 100 per cent casualties. Four of its nine Liberators failed to return on two nights and there were further losses; but then bad weather prevented any further missions. On 10/11 September Halifax BB422 FS-T on 148 Squadron captained by Pilot Officer David George Bryden was damaged by anti-aircraft fire over Yugoslavia while en-route to Warsaw. Bryden tried to return to base but crew forced to abandon the bomber over Yugoslavia. Three were taken prisoner and three survived with escape aided by the Chetniks. Captain Eric Arnold Endler SAAF and crew on 34 Squadron were shot down at Belgrade. Endler and Lieutenant Allan Graham McCabe the 22-year old air gunner were killed.[12]

On 16/17 October 34 Squadron lost two crews on a trip to drop supplies to partisans at Radomosko, southwest of Warsaw. Lieutenant James Arthur Lithgow DFC the 23-year old pilot flying KH152/F[13] and 27-year old Lieutenant Denis Osbourne Cullingworth who skippered EW250/L were shot down near Kraków en route to 'Cukinia 202' an Armia Krajówa area near Końskie. At 0830 when KH152 approached the Vistula in the sector between Kraków and Tarnów at a height of 11,000 feet about twenty miles north-east of Kraków, the aircraft was attacked by a night fighter (probably a Junkers Ju 88) piloted by Oberfeldwebel Karl Maisch of 2./NJG 100, which took off from Udefeld. Its controls were badly damaged and fuel tanks set on fire. The Liberator crashed 110 kilometres in the east from the Kraków in the Czarkówka village near Tarnów. Lithgow, who was broke his leg on landing was shot by a German policeman and was buried in the village of

Brzezówka. After the exhumation in 1947 he was re-buried in the Kraków-Rakowice Cemetery. Lithgow had received the DFC for sinking the Italian tanker *Prosperina* delivering food to Field Marshal Rommel's Afrika Korps in Africa on 26 October 1942. (It was his second and last flight to the Polish, the first taking place in the Piaseczna area on the night of 10/11 September when Lithgow piloted Liberator EW195/A). Four other crew members were killed on KH152.[14] Sergeant Ronald T. Pither RAFVR, air gunner was only survivor on EW250.[15]

Only a trickle of supplies actually reached General Bór-Komorowski's army and despite the capture by the Red Army of the suburb of Praga on 15 September, the rising was doomed to failure. On 18 September 107 USAAF B-17s dropped supplies from so great a height that less than twenty percent of the supplies reached Polish hands. The last attempt to supply the partisans from Italy was made on the night of 21/22 September, when twelve Liberators were dispatched. Only five B-24s succeeded in dropping their supplies, but all returned safely to Italy. Before any further sortie could be flown the Wehrmacht had crushed the uprising and by the time the Soviet Army relieved Warsaw, all partisan resistance had ended. When Bór-Komorowski surrendered to the Germans, the partisans had tried for 63 days, in vain, to liberate their capital. Of the approximately 40,000 men and women who were members of the underground army, roughly 18,000 lost their lives, about 25,000 were wounded (6,500 seriously) and the total number of civilian casualties was estimated at 180,000 people.[16] Nearly 10,000 Germans were killed, 7,000 went missing and 7,000 were wounded.

While the Polish Home Army was being destroyed, the Russians sat idly by a bare twenty miles away. Stalin realized that his western allies strongly disapproved of his handling of the Warsaw Rising and for the sake of 'window dressing', he was seen to relent, but only when he knew that it was too late. The Russians later, for 'window dressing' purposes, did drop supplies to the AK but made sure that these would be of little use. The Russian canisters were dropped without parachutes so that much of the contents were damaged. The firearms which the Russians supplied were so inferior as to have seemed to have been factory rejects while the cartridges which they provided were of a calibre which would not fit any of the Polish arms.

The Russians may prefer not to recall the days of the 'Warsaw Concerto', but each year the Polish communities in Johannesburg, Cape Town, Durban and other centres of South Africa, as well as in London, gather to pay homage to the memory of those gallant airmen who gave their lives in attempting to bring the means of survival to the valiant Polish men and women who were fighting stubbornly for their country.

On 12 October twenty Liberators on 31 Squadron were sent to North-west Italy on a supply drop mission to partisans at four different drop zones. Bad weather caused at least ten aircraft not to find the target areas. A further six aircraft failed to return and were subsequently reported as missing. Five crash sites were found in the Alps but the wreck of the sixth aircraft has never been found. It is generally assumed that the missing Liberator crashed into the sea. It is believed that the tragic loss of the six aircraft with crews was due to the bad/changing weather conditions and failure of the ground navigation electronic assistance system that night, forcing human navigation error. One of the missing Liberators was skippered by Charles Paul Nel. He had joined the SAAF in 1941 after he finished his matric in Oudshoorn. After qualifying as a pilot he was appointed as flying instructor at No.7 Air School, Kroonstad. In mid 1944 Charlie joined 31 Squadron and he participated in the Warsaw supply drops where half of the squadron was wiped out. On the night of 12 October Charlie's aircraft together with five other aircraft of the squadron, crashed in the Italian Alps with a total loss of life. The remains of Charlie's crew were found and buried by locals at a small town in the vicinity of the crash site. After the war they were reburied at the Commonwealth war cemetery in the outskirts of Milan.

Meanwhile yet another Air Command had come into existence in the Mediterranean theatre - the Balkan Air Force. Its formation in June 1944 was a logical step in the sequence of events which had begun in April 1941 when Yugoslavia had been invaded by the Germans. Various Partisan groups became a constant menace to the occupying troops and in February 1944 the British Prime Minister, Winston Churchill announced that no less than fourteen of the twenty German divisions as well as six other satellite divisions were being contained in the Balkan Peninsula, by a force of 250,000 Yugoslav Partisans supplied by elements of the RAF and American air forces in the Mediterranean.

Four Liberators on 148 Squadron had been supplying Resistance groups in Albania, Greece and Yugoslavia since May 1942. In March 1943 Halifaxes became available and this squadron provided the nucleus of a Special Operations Air Force, which by June 1944 consisted of eight squadrons, including one flight of Liberators and was manned by personnel from no less than five nations. Special Operations Executive (SOE) units also operated from the Mediterranean during the war. By May 1943 many flights had been made to Poland from England. Between August and October 1943 brief use was made of three Liberators (BZ859, 860 and 362, later transferred to 1586 Flight) but these long trips were subject to heavy fighter opposition and the risks were great. It was decided, therefore, to operate SOE aircraft from the Mediterranean theatre. 1575 Flight (which became 624 Squadron in

1943), 1586 Flight (which became 301 (Pomeranian-Polish) Squadron in November 1944) and 148 Squadron were based at Blida, Derna and Tocra in North Africa, although airfields in Italy were used on occasions in 1944, principally Brindisi but also Foggia. G.J. Hill, a fitter with 148 Squadron at Brindisi in August 1944, recalls the Polish Liberators:

'We used these Polish Liberators to convert some of the crews on to B-24s. Our Commanding Officer, Squadron Leader Dickie Knight and his flight engineer, had served on Liberators before so they were given the job of converting the rest of the crews. After a very short time we received a batch of B-24Js from a maintenance unit in Algiers. The old Polish Liberators were flown back by the crews who had ferried in the new B-24s.'

Liberators, Lysanders and Halifaxes based in southern Italy ranged throughout the Balkan countries, Czechoslovakia, southern France and, towards the end of the war, Austria and Germany, dropping 'Joes', Resistance leaders, arms and supplies. By the end of the war the Balkan Air Force had flown over 11,500 sorties into Yugoslavia and had delivered over 16,400 gross tons of supplies to the Partisans. On the personnel side, 2,500 persons had been flown in and 19,000 brought out of the country.

As more and more Liberators became available, three more Wellington squadrons converted to Liberators in the first three months of 1945. In January that year 70 Squadron at Tortorella began re-equipping with Liberator VIs, as did 104 Squadron at Foggia Main, a month later. In March 1945, 40 Squadron also began converting to Liberator VIs at Foggia Main. Crews were doubtless pleased with their new bomber, which was different in every way from the Wellington and most other aircraft. Although it did not have the standard British blind flying panel which contained all the vital flying instruments - the instruments were arranged somewhat haphazardly and checks for take-off and landing were only possible by having the flight engineer read out from a long check list - it did have a superb radio and auto-pilot. The auxiliary engine driven generator (for use on ground to ensure enough electricity for hydraulic brake pressures etc.) removed the constant anxiety of losing brake power when taxiing, which had been experienced with the Wellington, due to the slow running engines not being able to maintain pressure. Pilots found the flight deck a dream. There was more room than in the 'Wimpy' and there was even a carpet on the floor. (The ashtrays were removed on delivery as no smoking was permitted in any British service aircraft.) In its flying handling the Liberator was a lumbering aircraft - 'like flying a bus' but crews rapidly got used to its performance and even enjoyed its superior stability (and hence comfort). The tricycle undercarriage (which no British aircraft had at the time) was also vastly superior to tail-wheel designs both for visibility and ease of handling.

205 Group could now call upon six Liberator bomber squadrons including two SAAF Squadrons. The SAAF Squadrons had played a large part in the Mediterranean war, dropping supplies to guerrillas and taking part in the mining operations in the Danube.

My God, this night I have to fly,
And ere I leave the ground,
I come with reverence to Thy Throne
Where perfect peace is found.
I thank Thee for the life I've had,
For home and all its love,
I thank Thee for the faith I have
That cometh from above.
Come with me now into the air.
Be with me as I fly,
Guide Thou each move that I shall make
Way up there in the sky.
Be with me at the target, Lord,
When danger's at its height.
Be with me as I drop my load,
And on the homeward flight.
And should it be my time to die.
Be with me to the end.
Help me to die a Christian's death.
On Thee, God, I depend.
Then as I leave this mortal frame
From human ties set free,
Receive my soul, O God of Love,
I humbly come to Thee.
An Airman's Prayer

Endnotes Chapter 2

1   Durrant had joined the SAAF Reserve at the age of 19. In 1933-34, he successfully completed a Permanent Force Cadet Course whereafter he served in the SAAF and qualified as a pilot. He passed a special course at the RAF Photographic School at RAF Farnborough, the school which T. E. Lawrence had attended in 1922. He returned to the Union where he did aerial survey work. He was commissioned as a 2nd Lieutenant in November 1934. He held several posts between this period and the outbreak of war and proved himself to be a most capable Flying Instructor. In 1936 he was promoted Lieutenant and in 1937 Flight Commander. In 1938, he was promoted Captain and posted to Waterkloof Air Station. With the outbreak of World War II he was appointed Officer Commanding, Photo Flight with the rank of Major and later OC 40 Squadron SAAF which he commanded in East Africa from May 1940 to September 1941 when he was promoted Lieutenant Colonel and appointed OC 24 Squadron SAAF. He commanded this squadron throughout the bitter fighting in the Western Desert Campaign in 1941-42. He was then promoted Colonel and given command of 3 (Bomber) Wing SAAF in North Africa, Sicily and Italy. In 1944 he was seconded to RAF Bomber Command and placed in command of 205 Group RAF with the rank of Brigadier. In 1945 he was posted to the Far East as AOC 231 Group RAF with the rank of Major General. At the age of 32 he was the youngest Major General in the Allied forces. He died at his home in Parktown North, Johannesburg, after a short illness on 15 October 1990 aged 77.

2   Eric Winchester had joined the South African Army in 1940 at age 17 and was soon posted to East Africa. He was not seeing much action and tried to join the RAF but was turned down because of poor eyesight. Two years later he returned to South Africa where he eventually joined the RAF. He was posted to Cairo with 31 Squadron and was trained as an air gunner.

3   *Death Was Not Our Destiny* by Bob Klette.

4   Later, with his parents, he moved to Bexhill-On-Sea. From preparatory school Austin went on to Brighton College and after serving as a cadet in the Metropolitan Police Force, he transferred to the Palestine Police with whom he served from 1935 until 1942. While being repatriated to the UK in 1942, Austin's ship was torpedoed in the Mediterranean and after being rescued he reached Durban in May of that year. Austin later enlisted in the SAAF and after an initial disappointment at not being accepted as a pilot, he trained to become a wireless operator and aircraft machine gunner. He was subsequently posted to 28 Squadron, a Dakota transport unit that operated a shuttle service from Pretoria, carrying war goods and personal to and from North Africa.

5   Lieutenant Ray Arras Lavery SAAF, the 25-year old second pilot of Port Elisabeth; Lieutenant John Christopher Branch-Clark SAAF, the 18-year old observer of Plumstead, Cape Town; WO2 Joseph Arnold Meyer SAAF the 21-year old air gunner from the Transvaal; WO2 Reginald Walter Stafford SAAF, the 26-year old air gunner, husband of Dorothy F. Stafford of Cape Town; Sergeant Edward Turner Hall RAFVR and WO2 Ben Nevis Woods SAAF, the 36-year old air gunner who was born in Scotland but came to South Africa in 1939 where he looked after the polo ponies of a South African jeweller. He joined the SAAF in February 1942.

6   Lieutenant Peter Herbert Andrews SAAF the 20-year old second pilot; Lieutenant Cedric Arthur Cooke SAAF, the 30-year old navigator from the Transvaal; Sergeant Peter Henry George Lees RAFVR; Lieutenant Harry Allpress Ruston Male SAAF, air gunner who was born in England before leaving for Natal; Lieutenant Gordon Bruce Pitt SAAF, the 20-year old air gunner whose parents lived in Southern Rhodesia; and W/O Terence Desmond O'Keefe SAAF, the 20-year old air gunner of Cape Province.

7   See *The Warsaw Airlift, A Triumph Of South African Bravery* by Dr Pieter Moller, *Die Suid-Afrikaanse Krygshistoriese Vereniging* (The South African Military History Society Journal - Vol 13 No 1 - June 2004.

8   Lieutenant Allan John McInnes SAAF (22) (KIA); Lieutenant Oliver Coleman SAAF, observer (KIA); Lieutenant Herbert Henry Lewis SAAF (24) (KIA); Sergeant G. Swift RAF (20) (KIA) and Flight Sergeant R. Zambra RAF (22) (KIA).

9   Lieutenant Anthony James Munro SAAF the 20 year old second pilot from Natal (KIA); Lieutenant Walter Klokow SAAF, the 27 year old observer from Cape Province (KIA); WO1 Douwe B. Brandsma SAAF the 24 year old air gunner (KIA); WO1 Douglas John Palmer SAAF the 23 year old air gunner (KIA); WO1 E. Bradshaw RAF the 24 year old air gunner; Sergeant L. R. W. Nickerson RAAF the 22 year old air gunner (KIA); and Lieutenant Eric Ben Horton Impey SAAF (KIA)

10   The rest of the crew comprised the observer, Lieutenant Bernard Thomas Loxton SAAF; Sergeant G. T. Robinson RAF; Lieutenant Arthur James Hastings SAAF the 23-year old air gunner; WO1 J. B.

Erasmus SAAF, air gunner; WO2 John Atholl Campbell Steel SAAF the 18-year old air gunner and Lieutenant Thomas Tennant Watson SAAF, the 21-year old air gunner.

11   Jack returned to the squadron in early 1945 and finished his operational tour when the war ended. After the war he had a long and successful career in the mining industry as a mining engineer. Jack passed away on 5 November 1999. On 11 January 1958 Bunny Austin set out from Pretoria on his sentimental journey to Warsaw to trace Urszula Stupik, the twelve-year-old girl who had saved his life by hiding him in her bed. The project proved far more complex than even Austin had expected but reach Warsaw he did and he was re-united with former members of the Polish underground movement who had assisted him to escape the Germans. Five years later his book Urszula was published describing this adventure and how he had managed to snatch the now twenty-six-year-old Urszula Stupik from beyond the Iron Curtain and bring her to the safety of Paris. Unfortunately, his health deteriorated and in April 1977 he was moved to a nursing home suffering from Parkinson's Disease. 'Bunny' Austin passed away on 23 July 1977.

12   Other members on the crew consisted of Lieutenant J. W. P. Chapman, second pilot; Lieutenant T.A. Stewart SAAF (KIA); Sergeant C. Manley RAFVR (KIA); Flying Officer R.G. Devine RAF (KIA) and Pilot Officer G. Crook RAFVR.

13   His crew comprised Captain F. N. Murray SAAF, second pilot; Lieutenant E. Colbert SAAF; Lieutenant G. C. Dicks SAAF; Sergeant T. Myers RAFVR; Sergeant E. M. Stoves RAFVR; Lieutenant S. I. Fourie SAAF and WO2 G. J. Davies SAAF.

14   Lieutenant Keit Bernnand MacWilliam SAAF, co-pilot, whose parachute didn't open properly and as a result he crashed in the field of Szymon Dziekan in Brzezowka. After exhumation he was re-buried in Krakow. He left a widow, Elisabeth (Rissik); Lieutenant Evan Colbert SAAF, the 30-year old observer from Johannesburg survived thanks to help of Polish guerrillas, 'Stanislawa' in Szcucin, 'Malwina' in Medrzechow, Boleslaw - Mr. Kochanek and 'Drewniaki'; Lieutenant Graham C. Dicks SAAF, air gunner who managed to land safely. He was concealed by the AK in Kanna and Boleslaw villages and went to Moscow in February 1945 from where he left for South Africa via Cairo; Lieutenant Samuel I. Fourie SAAF, air gunner, who after the crash he was imprisoned by Germans; Sergeant Tom Myers RAF, bomb aimer; Sergeant G. F. Ellis RAF, air gunner; Sergeant William Francis 'Billy' Cowan RAF, the 31-year old air gunner from Belfast.

15   Those who died were: Lieutenant Denis Osbourne Cullingworth; Lieutenant Charles Stewart Searle Franklin SAAF, 2nd pilot, husband of Frances Franklin of Great Brak River; Lieutenant Kenneth James McLeod SAAF, the 27-year old observer; Lieutenant George Ray-Howett SAAF the 30-year old WOp/AG; Sergeant Jack Edwin Speed RAFVR, bomb aimer; Sergeant Ronald Cecil Bowden RAFVR, air gunner; and Sergeant Desmond Preston Richmond RAFVR, WOp/AG.

16   *The Citizen,* January 1978, K Swaift, *Death and destruction in the skies,* p.5).

Chapter 3

Three Men in the Mediterranean

Imagine a lovely sunny day in the Mediterranean, although on 9 January 1941 it was still a day to be enjoying the sun. Imagine also a fleet of ships consisting of battleships, cruisers, destroyers and an aircraft carrier, all in formation and carrying out there convoy duties escorting a number of merchant ships with vital supplies to the Island of Malta. The battleship was HMS Warspite with the Admiral aboard and the carrier was HMS Illustrious, a happy efficient ship still glowing from the recent success of her aircraft which had inflicted serious damage to the Italian fleet in Taranto harbour. Knowing the proximity to Sicily on that day, the Admiral had ordered that the fleet exercised their anti aircraft defences so that in the possibility of an air attack we would be fully prepared. This was for me my first experience of real gun fire being a young man! of 18 plus, in the Andrew for just over a year, having done my discipline and technical training and now in theory a fully fledged Air Fitter capable of goodness knows what. But I digress, to the uninitiated the awesome spectacle of a fleet of warships putting up an umbrella of fire through which no aircraft could penetrate, surely? was really something and I am sure that not only me but several hundred other so called sailors thought that we were pretty nigh invincible, should an air attack occur, but time would tell.

Another brilliant dawn, 10 January 1941, the ships routine went ahead as normal, the only worry was that one of or escort ships, HMS Gallant, had had her bows blown off after hitting a mine, what the injuries to her crew were we never knew, but in the meantime our aircraft were flying off and landing on and the ships company went about their normal duties. Come about noon, Up Spirits was over, although of course I was far too young to take part in that now forgotten ritual and I was on my way for'ard to the canteen for a goffa, soft drink, to us old salts, when action stations sounded. From that moment on life became rather hectic, guns were blazing, aircraft taking off, everybody trying to do their job while all hell was let loose around them. Near misses from dive bombers made the ship rise up out of the water like a phoenix but then the direct hits, the flight deck had a white line running down the centre, no doubt a wonderful marker for the enemy, one bomb went right through the centre of that line through the 4inch thick flight deck, through the hanger exploding in the wardroom, killing and maiming several officers. In all we received seven direct hits, one exploded down the fore lift well just as the lift was ascending, so you can imagine the carnage that caused, our steering gear was out of use and we were going round in circles, the remainder of the fleet seemed to have deserted us, no doubt with good reason, although we didn't think so at the time. During this hell I was doing my utmost to become invisible, as I am sure were a good many others, no aircraft could now fly so I and others had the unenviable job of trying to rescue the wounded and take them to the nearest sick bay, among them was a mate who only a short time before had shared a joke with me, his stomach was hanging out and he was crying out with pain, soon after I left him he died. This was going on all over the ship, stories of suffering and of heroism were too numerous to mention, but through it all the ship survived , a tribute to British workmanship, I doubt if a ship of similar design built in this era would survive such an ordeal. Eventually as sunset approached we limped into Valletta, as we entered the crowds lined the shore and cheered us in, I have often wondered since if those people would have been so eager to see us if they had known their future, as I am sure that when the Illustrious was tied up having temporary repairs, the attacks by the dive bombers on her was just the start of the terrific air onslaught that the island was to suffer during the next four years. So there it is, the calm before the storm and I can honestly say that before that day I was a simple youth, but that day will always remain as the day that a man was emerging and the subsequent situations that my service in the Andrew threw at me, more convoy work in the Med. including the Pedestal convoy and at least two convoys to Russia, I hope and believe gave me the strength and wisdom to become a fairly ordinary but quite a decent individual.

The Calm Before The Storm by Petty Officer Air Fitter Sydney William Millen.

The following story appeared in *Over To You,* one of several BBC broadcasts given by RAF officers and airmen between March 1942 and May 1943. On 12 September 1941 when eight Blenheim crews on 105 and 107 Squadrons found and attacked a large convoy of five heavily armed merchantmen 40 miles NNW of Tripoli. The attack cost two Blenheims on 107 Squadron and Sergeant Bill Brandwood's crew on Z7367 'L-Leather' 105 Squadron. His observer was Sergeant 'Jock' Miller and Sergeant Tony Mee, a Hounslow bank clerk in Civvy Street, was WOp/AG.

The pilot speaks: 'Except for Malta dog, a local germ which gives you a sharp pain behind the eyes and the Mediterranean sand-flies, the Island is a good place to work from. The Maltese themselves are cheerful, but every time an incendiary breaks on their hard and sun-baked sod they want us to go and bomb Rome. They have the utmost contempt for the Italians, whom we could occasionally see circling around the island at a safe distance, dropping their bombs in the sea and sheering off - no doubt to shoot a tremendous line when they got back to their bases. But when they came over and our fighters brought an 'Eyetie' down, you could hear the cheering from all over the Island. This was our twentieth operation. Once before, cannon shell had split open our petrol tank and fractured the main spar; and on another occasion, during an attack on a convoy of schooners and merchant vessels off Lampedusa, a ship carrying a gun looking like a howitzer opened up as we passed over and lifted us bodily into the air. Our score in the Mediterranean was already three ships sunk and a fourth shared with two other aircraft and once we had attacked a supply column on the Tripoli-Benghazi road and watched the drivers running in all directions into the desert while others took what they thought was shelter under the lorries. So that we weren't raw for this trip and that was just as well.

'We were briefed at 11 o'clock in the morning by Wing Commander Edwards [the 105 Squadron CO], who had recently won the VC for going through a balloon barrage in daylight over Bremen and he thought our target was pretty tough.[1] That morning a reconnaissance machine had reported eight merchant vessels and four destroyers, with Macchis escorting them above. We found, instead, six merchant vessels and seven destroyers. I was flying No. 4 in an elongated 'V' formation. My left window was open so that I could keep closer formation and get some air into the machine. Although we were flying in open shirt and shorts it was pretty warm. I think the observer and I saw the convoy at the same moment, didn't we 'Jock'?

The observer speaks. 'Yes. We were doing a square search and were on the last lag when we saw on the horizon a line of large ships and Bill called out, 'Here we go.' We batted in just above sea-level, flying in line abreast and at full five miles away I saw the lines of tracer coming at us from the destroyers. You could see the splash, splash, splash in the water around us and as we got really near, Tony in the tear turret had an awkward moment as the tracer lines seemed to scissor across him.

The air-gunner speaks: 'Awkward' is putting it mildly. Anyway it was a sheet, not a line, of tracer coming from the destroyers on either side of us. It started up a few yards from our tail, slowly caught up with us and then from my position in the turret I watched it entering the fuselage and creeping up towards me. I think another six inches and I should have had it; I could hear it ripping in like little stabs through tinfoil. As our bomb doors sprang to and we passed over the ship I had a look at the aircraft and saw smoke. I said to Bill, 'H'm, looks like your starboard engine's on fire.' I tried to make it sound as unconcerned as I could, as though it were his aircraft and not mine and I continued to

48

give him a running commentary on the situation in what was meant to be a detached manner. I took some photographs of the burning ship. I guess they were the best photos I ever took. I can safely say that, because they're 250 fathoms down and they won't be developed now. Then I smelt burning and this time I don't think I sounded quite so detached when I told Bill. The bomb well was alight and while I grabbed one extinguisher Jock grabbed the other.'

The Observer: 'Yes, Tony and I were on either side of the bomb well and were spraying the flames and smoke with fluid. I think my aim was better than his because Tony got more over me than I did over him. The aircraft was pretty well filled with asphyxiating smoke, because the wireless set was also alight. I pulled away the top hatch to get rid of some of it, while Tony went on giving Bill the latest news about the fire in the starboard engine.'

The Pilot: 'I must say it was pretty good, Tony. If it hadn't been our own aircraft that was burning, I should have been able to have taken a more objective interest in your power as a reporter. Anyway, your masterly restraint caused me to switch off the starboard engine, turn off the petrol and open the throttle to drain it. The aircraft flew on. I could now detect in the remaining engine a suspicious note and she began to surge. Probably what had happened was that a bullet had got embedded in the boost control. Slowly the port engine lost power and I asked Jock to find out our position.'

The observer: 'I was quite glad to have my mind taken off things, because it was a bit depressing watching the distance increase between us and the remainder of the squadron going ahead. I was taking Very cartridges out of the rack, because it was getting too hot from the fire, when I heard Bill call out that the other engine was going.'

'I wondered what it was going to be like. I never found out, for I suddenly went unconscious and the next thing I knew was that I was in the water with the plane three yards away, her nose pointing at an angle downwards and her wings lying flat on the sea. I jettisoned my parachute and looked around for Bill.'

The pilot: 'My escape wasn't as easy as that and for a moment I thought I wasn't going to escape at all. When I knew that 'L for Leather' was going in, I gave her as flat a landing as possible and felt her splash into the sea. I shut my eyes and felt a great sheet of water smacking hard into me. Somehow I was turned the wrong way and found myself facing the armour plating. I felt for the pin of the Sutton harness, which releases you from the straps which do you to the seat. Normally the pin lies across your middle and you could find it in your sleep. Automatically I groped for it, but found it was gone. Thinking I was free, I tried to rise but couldn't get away from the straps. They were doing their job. I started searching wildly around my body for the fastening and found the pin just below the shoulders at the back, pulled it out with my right hand and the straps fell away. I floated up. How did you get out, Tony?'

The air-gunner: 'Well, I felt a terrific pressure on my whole body, as though every part of me was being clamped in a separate vice. Everything inside the aircraft was smashing up. Almost immediately the water level had risen, going from Bill's sliding hatch to the tail, so that I knew we were nose down. I found myself sitting in about two and a half feet of water. I opened my hatch and saw Jock swimming six yards away, with Bill ahead of me struggling to unbuckle himself from the sinking plane. It was my job to get the dinghy out. It was floating inside the aircraft and I heaved it up. Jock and Bill used to chip me about a knife on a lanyard I always carried at my waist and Jock shouted to me now to use this famous weapon. I cut the cord and released the dinghy. It became automatically inflated by the compressed air cylinders. At the first crash of water I had been thrown on my back and banged my head on something hard. I didn't notice much wrong then, but now I felt that I had broken my arm and seemed to have injured my spine. Anyway, I got out and saw that Jock was in the dinghy.'

The observer: 'From my safe seat in the boat, Tony, you looked pretty comical. You probably don't remember it, but one of your flying boots had come off and was filled with water. You were hugging it like a mother with a baby. Do you remember, Bill, arguing with him in the water about it?'

The pilot: 'Do I remember! I could have crowned him with it, but nothing would make him give it up.'

The air-gunner: 'I know. I developed a passion for that boot and would have fought you to the last for it, in spite of my limp arm.'

The observer: 'Anyway, from where I was in the dinghy I could see the scene pretty clearly. Bill was helping Tony along towards the dinghy and a few yards away I could see the tail of 'L for Leather' slipping into the sea. Then Bill dived down and got his shoulder under Tony's seat, while I grabbed him by the shoulders and hauled him in, boot and all. Then Bill got in and we looked at each other. The last tip of the rudder went down. Well beyond the horizon we could see the haze of smoke from the burning convoy. We made a sling for Tony from the lace of his Mae West. Bill was only scratched, although some of the skin had been torn off has legs and they were bleeding a little. We told him the salt water would help to heal them.'

The pilot: 'Yes, but it was stinging like blazes and anyway you couldn't do much grinning because of the gash near your knee. You had on one shoe and one sock, torn shorts, a ripped shirt, no helmet and a Mae West.'

The observer: 'I know, but I kept my watch. Both yours and Tony's were ripped off. Mine stopped at 2.25, the moment when the sea came in and the glass was broken. I've got it here now. Anyway, we didn't do much arguing then. We said nothing for half an hour. Tony took off his remaining flying boot.'

The air-gunner: 'I thought what an ass I had been. I looked at both my boots sadly and thought they had done me pretty well. Then I threw them both out and wondered how long it would take them to go down 250 fathoms. We kept on looking at each other and at the dinghy and at the sea and at the blue sky. A breeze was coming up and there was a slight swell. I forget who broke the silence. It was you Bill, wasn't it?'

The pilot: 'I remember wondering what all our mothers would say if they could have seen us then - their devoted sons, looking a pretty odd sight, if you can think of it that way, with no water and no food and a few flying fish for company. But as a matter of fact, come to think of it, Jock broke the silence first. He was sick eight times. And he was so beautifully polite over it. Each time he said, 'Excuse me' and went ahead.'

The observer: 'Yes, but I would like to make it clear that I wasn't being seasick. It was all that damn salt water I had swallowed.'

The pilot: 'Well, that's your story 'Jock'. Anyway, we all had to make ourselves as comfortable as we could and unfortunately every spot on which we sat hi the dinghy got a sort of dent which filled with the water dripping off us. I took off my shoes and started to bail out - in the old-fashioned sense. We took off most of our clothes to let the sun dry our bodies and tried finding comfortable positions for our legs. We sat away from the sea anchor, which is a kind of drag apparatus of ropes and canvas, so that the waves break under the prow of the dinghy. 'Jock' tried to dry some cigarettes in the sun. They had got soaked from the dripping.'

The observer: 'It wasn't any use, because, when they dried, the paper burst. Anyway we had no matches and our one lighter wouldn't work. As the afternoon wore on, our hopes of being rescued that evening grew thin. We had been pretty certain that a Sunderland would arrive to take us off. When we first got in the dinghy the rest of the squadron came back and waggled their wings at us to show they had seen us, so we weren't in much doubt. But after a few hours we began to wonder. We tried to take our minds off the subject by talking, mostly about beer and food. We thought of what they d been having in Malta just then, grapes and melons and pears. And then we talked about whether we liked prickly pears. And cigarettes, of course, kept on cropping up. Tony said we were certain to be picked up that day. We repeated that again and again. We were certain to get picked up all right. But nothing came and then it got dark. As the night set in it became cold and for some reason they put me in the middle.'

The air-gunner: 'You know the reason darn well 'Jock'. It was because you're the smallest and anyway you'd lost most blood. I think you were the first to go to sleep. We all dozed, on and off for a bit and filled in time watching the fish just beneath the surface of the water. You could see the moonlight glinting on their scales. The stars were much clearer than they are here. Three of them, part of the Plough, I knew pretty intimately. I had watched them as a kid. I remember thinking how extraordinary it was that they were the same stars that I had watched when I was at school and then later on from my garden at home and when I went out walking in the country. And now we were floating on a bit of rubber in the middle of the Mediterranean and looking at the same three stars. Of course it all seems damn silly now.'

The pilot: 'Do you remember Tony, those flashes we saw in the night? We couldn't make out whether they were natural or from a beacon. We heard noises of aircraft and you wanted me to let off one of our two distress signals to draw their attention.'

The air-gunner: 'Yes, I know and you refused, because you said you weren't going to use them until you knew for certain they would be seen. The next day I was mighty glad. We got stiffer and stiffer throughout the night and kept on trying a different angle with our legs. We were all thankful when the sun came up.'

The observer: 'Yes, but don't forget about the false dawn. The sky grew faintly yellow and we thought the night had gone and then it was all dark again. The real dawn, when it came, was sudden - first faintly red, a yellow burst and the sun was up. We thought we heard voices. But they were seagulls calling each other and the flying fish started to rise again with tails like twin spines and a little bit of fin on the end. They were blue and some of them were green - shoals jumping out of the water and catching the sun on their bodies and disappearing.'

The pilot: 'And do you remember the turtle that morning? We eyed him hungrily at first, thinking what a good meal he'd make for breakfast. And then we were scared of him. I expect he felt the same about us - greedy at first and then afraid. He dived down and we could see him coming under the dinghy. He had pretty sharp teeth and he could have ripped through the rubber like a kid biting a wafer. At ten to eight in the morning we saw a black oblong in the distance rather like an old square sail. We couldn't make it out, but it grew bigger and Tony flashed it with mirror, while I got a marine flare ready. We paddled towards it at about half a knot and when I guessed it was the conning tower of a submarine I let the flare off and thirteen white stars climbed from it about a hundred feet into the sky.'

The observer: 'Yes, but don't forget we didn't know the nationality of the submarine [it was HMS *Utmost*[2]]. We could see a chap in a green shirt on the conning tower and one in a red shirt on the hull. You said, 'Blast! They're ' Eyeties'! And we thought what a villainous couple they looked. As they came up to us we waved and called out, 'Are you British?' A Yorkshire voice came back, 'Yes'; and then, as an afterthought, 'Good show, lads.'

The pilot: 'Next day the submarine put us ashore. Before we left, we were able to tell them what had happened to the convoy. After our attack a reconnaissance aircraft found there were only three merchant vessels left in the convoy. That night other bombers went out and got two more. Next day the sole survivor was found beached. We shook hands with the men of the submarine and blessed them all. They said they'd do the same again for us. Any time.'

Postscript: Flying Officers Bill Brandwood and 'Jock' Miller were killed in action on the night of 15 June 1944 when their Mosquito on 571 Squadron was shot down by flak during a raid on Gelsenkirchen.

Endnotes Chapter 3

1   On 4 July 1941 Wing Commander Hughie Edwards DFC RAAF led a daylight attack ('Operation Wreckage') against the port of Bremen, one of the most heavily defended towns in Germany. Edwards' force of twelve Blenheims attacked at a height of about 50 feet through telephone wires and high voltage power lines. The bombers successfully penetrated fierce anti-aircraft fire and a dense balloon barrage, but further fire over the port itself resulted in the loss of four of the attacking force. Edwards brought his remaining aircraft safely back, although all had been hit and his own Blenheim (V6028) had been hit over 20 times. His actions in the raid earned him the Victoria Cross. In the last week of July Edwards took ten tropicalised Blenheims of 105 Squadron to Malta (two more aborted en route) in order to conduct operations against Axis shipping carrying reinforcements from Italy to Tripoli and Benghazi. The unit remained in the area until October, when they returned to Britain.

2   *Utmost* left Malta for a patrol in the Mediterranean in November 1942. On the 23rd she sank an enemy ship, but on 25 November, during her return journey to Malta, she was located, attacked and sunk south west off Sicily by depth charges from the Italian torpedo boat *Groppo*.

Chapter 4

They Captured their Captors[1]

The air war came early to Malta and stayed late. By spring of 1942 the battle-scarred islands of Malta and Gozo were in a dire state of siege. No supply convoys had reached them since an ill-fated attempt in March of that year. Then, the three remaining merchantmen that had won through to Valletta's Grand Harbour were all sunk by enemy bombs before any substantial portion of their urgently needed cargoes had been unloaded. Before that, the last convoy to arrive reasonably intact had anchored in the harbour something like nine months earlier. By June, therefore, the plight of the island's inhabitants was indeed precarious, with the spectre of starvation and disease hovering over the 174 square miles that comprised Malta and Gozo.

The spirits of both soldiers and civilians, however, were buoyed up by Malta's increasing military activity. In spite of acute shortages, Malta not only increased the fierceness of its defence, but also launched a heavy air offensive against the enemy's airfields in Sicily and against other enemy concentrations. As one fighter pilot phrased it, 'The tempo of life here is just indescribable. The morale of everyone is magnificent, but things are certainly tough. Bombing continues at intervals all day long. One lives here only to destroy the enemy or to hold him at bay. Everything else - living conditions, sleep, food and all the ordinary standards of life - has gone by the board.' In particular, British air and submarine attacks struck crippling blows at the enemy's shipping lines supplying Axis forces then rolling towards El Alamein.

These round-the-clock sorties against enemy shipping were at their height when Lieutenant Edward Theodore 'Ted' Strever, a South African seconded to the RAF, arrived in Malta in the early summer of 1942 to join 39 Squadron. Strever lost no time in being introduced to the air war over the Mediterranean. He weathered his first strike successfully; and thus, by the rugged standards of those days, he was something in the nature of an old hand by the time his big day came.

July the twenty-eighth started out cloudless and hot. By nine o'clock the photographic reconnaissance Spitfire had finished its daily scan over enemy coastlines and water. Its successful sighting report had earlier been flashed back by radio and even before the Spitfire touched down on Luqa aerodrome, the Beauforts on 217 Squadron were rolling out of their dispersal pens, each with a torpedo tucked under its nacelle. Airborne, the nine Beauforts quickly formed up in fluid pairs' formation and began letting down on a south-east heading, low over the water. Their target was an Axis convoy off the Grecian island of Sapienza. Three hours later the convoy, consisting of one tanker and three escorting destroyers, was intercepted in the shadow of Sapienza. At a mile and a half the destroyers' small-calibre armament spewed out a fine spray of Breda, Oerlikon and Bofors that drifted lazily in coloured balls across the water, then suddenly whiplashed by. The Beauforts fanned out and then banked into the attack.

Evasively skimming the water in air that seemed filled with tracer and flak bursts, Strever steadied his machine ['I' L9820] at sixty feet; laid off deflection and dropped his tin fish. Off his port wing Dawson's plane reared suddenly then crashed into the water. Strever opened her up to full throttle and jinked in a wild caracole past the tanker - only to run into more flak from the escort vessel positioned off the other beam. He was well out when he skidded right into a string of Bofors that caught his port engine. Frantically he wound on right rudder trim as the aircraft was carried out of the fray under its own speed. Almost automatically he began a slow turn to starboard - a turn towards base. But he knew without looking at his smoking port Wasp that it was useless. At best, his good engine might last twenty minutes before overheating. There was no choice but to ditch while he still had control.

The sea was freshening as he set her down; and, with gusts whipping the crests of the waves, Strever ran head-on through a trough. His Beaufort broke up fast. But... no one was hurt. Scrambling out of the fast-sinking wreckage, the crew got the wing dinghy out intact, quickly inflated it and pushed the little rubber boat away from the aircraft. All four men were aboard the dinghy when the Beaufort slipped beneath the waves.

When they got over the initial shock the four men took stock. The English navigator, Pilot Officer William Dunsmore from Maghull, near Liverpool, was unhurt, apart from a few superficial scratches, as were the wireless operator, Sergeant John A. Wilkinson, Royal New Zealand Air Force from Auckland and the air gunner, Sergeant Alexander R. Brown, Royal New Zealand Air Force of Timaru. To the east lay Sapienza with the larger bulk of the Peloponnesus and Messenia in the background.

They were adrift only a short time when they saw it. A dim speck, appearing low on the horizon and then the sound of aircraft engines, faint at first, then growing louder and louder, reached their ears. Their spirits sank when they saw the fasces markings of the Italian seaplane.

The enemy aircraft flew overhead and past them. Then... it turned round. The pilot had seen them and flying back in their direction, the aircraft settled down on the water and taxied over towards them. The dinghy being virtually uncontrollable, Strever pulled off his jacket, tore his shoes off his feet and dived over the side. A crewman slipped down on to the aircraft's float, uncoiling a line. The Italian aircraft, a three-engined Cant [Z.506-B] came up alongside and soon the enemy aircrew hauled the dripping South African and his colleagues light-heartedly aboard. Ted Strever was given brandy and a cigarette. The rest of the crew were then picked up and treated likewise, after which the plane taxied to a harbour in the island of Corfu where the bedraggled Beaufort boys were introduced to the Italian garrison officers' mess. They were feted royally by their enemy hosts. There followed a mid afternoon meal of steak, tomatoes and wine; an excellent supper, with more wine and cigarettes; comfortable beds in rooms vacated by the Italian officers; and eggs for breakfast in the morning. Their captors then informed them that they would be taken to a prisoner of war camp in Italy by aircraft. At this their hearts sank, for unlike a journey by train or car the mode of transport seemed to offer no chance of making an escape. The only possibility, they decided, was to capture the plane; but of how to do this they had no idea.

Thus it was almost with regret that Strever and his crew were forced to leave their generous hosts the following day. They were taken back to the harbour where their aircraft turned out to be the float plane of the previous day. The Italian crew of four - pilot, second pilot, engineer, a combined wireless-operator-navigator - was also the same, with the addition of an armed corporal to stand guard over the prisoners. Before boarding the Cant, for a trip to Taranto and imprisonment, the four men posed for snapshot after snapshot taken by the garrison officers. Cant had a crew of five: and a corporal guard for the captives. Flying, they were soon to discover, was not one of the corporal's strong points. Vibrating terribly, the aircraft lumbered through the air, sensitive to every up-current and down-draught. Before long the land-lubber corporal was looking considerably less happy. His sallow complexion turned progressively greener as the plane headed north-westwards towards Italy. Obviously, flying was not the corporal's forte.

It was Sergeant Wilkinson who first sensed that the time was right to turn the tables on their captors. Staring out of a nearby port-hole, Wilkinson pretended to be fascinated, then half-turned and gesticulated towards the unhappy corporal who was now holding his stomach and looking very ill and unhappy. 'Look out there!' Wilkinson's whole expression said. His inviting appearance distracted the air-sick groundling just long enough to allow for a solid right uppercut to the corporal's jaw. With a shout, Wilkinson gained his feet and with the guard sprawled helplessly on the floor, the stockily-built New Zealander snatched his automatic pistol and tossed it to Strever. Not to be outdone Pilot Officer William Dunsmore and Sergeant Alexander Brown promptly tackled the engineer, while the Italian pilot tried to draw his revolver and the second pilot began fumbling with a Tommy gun. This danger Wilkinson countered by advancing up the fuselage holding the corporal in front of him as a shield, while Ted followed brandishing the captured revolver. Sergeant Brown scooped up and threw a convenient wrench almost the entire length of the fuselage, scoring a lucky hit that stifled the attack before it began. A few more swift moves and the Italians were disarmed and tied up with their own belts and Ted had taken over the controls. All this proved too much for the corporal, who was on his first flight and who now added to the confusion by being violently sick. Strever, covered warily by Sergeant Wilkinson, stepped into the co-pilot's seat, took a firm grip on the controls and turned the aircraft purposefully around on to a south-westerly heading.

Meanwhile, the mopping-up party of Pilot Officer Dunsmore and Sergeant Brown had subdued the other Italians in the cabin and secured them. Then the four of them rested briefly and triumphantly, breathing hard, complete masters of the plane in which, only a few minutes before, they were being taken captive to Italy. For the next few minutes, Strever tried to hold the unwieldy aircraft reasonably straight and level, while his eyes took in the unfamiliar array of gauges and gadgets on the instrument panel. 'Maps! Get the maps!' he shouted to Pilot Officer Dunsmore. The English navigator searched the aircraft from nose to tail, but could find no maps or charts of any kind. Evidently the Italians were confirmed coastline crawlers. Using sign language Dunsmore persuaded his Italian opposite number to co-operate with him in drawing a map of the coastline from memory and between them they produced a passable map of the relevant section of Italy and Sicily, from which Dunsmore was able to work out a rough course and estimated time of arrival for Malta.

The next problem was how to fly a strange aircraft with no maps, no charts and no knowledge of the petrol consumption. Ted soon found it easier to free the Italian second pilot and asking kindly (at gunpoint) to fly to Malta and taking a chance in the matter of petrol. Ted at once ordered the pilot to turn south. At this the Italians, who were fully aware how Malta's fighter aircraft and ground defences would greet an Italian seaplane registered great alarm. The Italian pilot insisted in broken English, fright written all over his face, that they lacked sufficient fuel for the trip, but Malta was the nearest friendly base and so they had no choice but to carry on. After some deliberation Strever and Dunsmore worked out an approximate course to Sicily, agreeing that a landing off the island's east coast and a trust-to-luck inland dash would be the only course of action.

Two hours later, to everyone's immense relief, land loomed up ahead; and after Dunsmore had identified the toe of Italy and Cape Spartivento, they pin-pointed their first reasonably good fix. The Cant was swung on to a more southerly heading and they flew on, all but clipping the wave tops. At one tense stage, a Junkers 88 formated on them briefly and a pale-faced Strever exchanged friendly waves with the German pilot. After another hour the last headland of Sicily no longer lay on their right and suddenly they realised that they might just possibly make Malta.

And now, with barely sixty miles to go, events were moving to a climax. The Italian pilot who had taken over the controls again, at Strever's order, in case of attack by RAF fighters, tapped the fuel gauges excitedly.

Non c'e benzina! Non c'e benzina! he screeched. He flapped with reason. The gauges registered zero. The panic-stricken Italian made a motion to land, but Strever gestured him on, while, for numberless times, a pale-faced Dunsmore strained his eyes to the horizon, looking for signs of land. The float-plane was still almost clipping the wave crests as they tried to slip in under the island's radar defences; and for a while it looked as if they might. It was a shout of joy from Sergeant Brown that registered the tip of Gozo far off the starboard quarter. But joy turned to wild alarm a second later as three Spitfires swooped out of the sun and boxed the Cant. The next few minutes were terrifying ones. The Spits dived in from every quarter, raking the plodding, cumbersome float-plane with cannon and machine-gun fire. Brown frantically spun the rear guns to and fro as a gesture of peaceful intentions, while Pilot Officer Dunsmore took off his vest (the only white object handy) and trailed it behind the aircraft as a sign of surrender, proved unavailing. the Spitfires continued to attack and racked the Italian plane with a stream of bullets that poured through the wing. Ted decided the time had come for a more decisive gesture and he ordered the Italian pilot to put down on the water. The floats met the surface safely and then the propellers spun idly in the air as the last drop of petrol spluttered in the jets. Providentially, the marksmanship of the Spitfire pilots was ropy that day; for barring a hit in the starboard wing tip, the Cant came through unscathed. The reason for the fighter pilots' showing doubtless lay in their utterly unnerved state at finding a sitting duck right in their own back yard. Plainly it was too much for them. A profusely perspiring Italian pilot settled the

Cant down on the water as the cannon crackled all around. Even before the landing run was completed, the three fuel-starved engines coughed out one by one and the Cant began to weather cock into wind. Overhead circled the three Spitfires, their guns now silent.

Within a few minutes Air Sea Rescue Launch HSL 107 came roaring out from Kalafrana Bay, to be greeted by the sight of Lieutenant Strever and crew sitting on the wing of an Italian seaplane, cordially drinking Greek wine with five late members of the Regia Aeronautica. (The Italian crew, it seems, were to have gone on leave after the end of their trip and their suitcases were packed with wine.) Astonished to see four RAF's in the Italian plane a member of the launch team towing them back to St Paul's Bay said, 'We thought it was old Mussolini coming to give himself up!

An old Brooke motorboat then took over from HSL 107 and took the Cant to St. Paul's Island, where the five Italian crew members and the four airmen were taken ashore. The Beaufort crew, who were feeling a little conscience stricken at the way they had repaid the Italians' hospitality, offered their apologies and promised do all they could for the comfort of their captives. One of the Italians, cheerfully recognizing that war is war, took everything in good part and produced from his suitcase a bottle of wine, which he insisted on sharing with Ted and his crew. Ted then looked in on the Spitfire squadron, 603 Squadron RAF, where he had the doubtful pleasure of hearing the pilots slated by their commanding officer for bad shooting.

Ted Strever and William Dunsmore were both awarded the DFC, while John Wilkinson and A. R. Brown both received the DFM. The Spitfire pilots, regrettably, had a Commanding Officer not lightly swayed by the unusual circumstances and the trio caught a sizzling rocket from him on the strength of their poor marksmanship.[2]

Endnotes Chapter 4

1   Adapted from an article by A. M. Feast. *See On Laughter-Silvered Wings The Story of Lt. Col. E. T (Ted) Strever* DFC by Gail Strever-Morkel (Pen & Sword Aviation 2013).
2   Ted Strever died in Haenertsburg, South Africa in 1997 at the age of 77.

Chapter 5

The Middle East

Flight Lieutenant James W. Moore DFC

James Wharton Moore was born on 11 May 1920 at Hawes in Wensleydale, North Yorkshire, having an elder sister, Kathleen and a younger brother, Stanley. (As an air gunner on his first operation on a Short Stirling on 218 Squadron, Sergeant Stanley Peter Moore lost his life on 28 May 1943). Jim was educated as a boarder, at Barnard Castle School, County Durham. On 29 August 1939, three days before the outbreak of war he enlisted in the Royal Air Force on a six year engagement for training as a wireless operator. On completion of his six month course he volunteered for training as an air gunner, qualifying as a WOp/AG in June 1940. He joined 18 Squadron, flying on Bristol Blenheims, from RAF West Raynham on 12 August 1940. He also acquired the nickname 'Dinty' which was to remain with him for the rest of his service days. By the end of the year he had flown 28 operations before being hospitalised with pneumonia. On return to his squadron he flew 24 daylight operations before being posted 'on rest' as an instructor to 13 OTU, RAF Bicester. Before the end of the war he had flown two further operational tours; the first on the Douglas Bostons on 88 and 107 Squadron and the second on the North American Mitchells on 226 Squadron. On his demobilisation on 5 December 1945, his log book shows that he had flown 923 hours 35 minutes and taken part in 92 operational sorties. In November 1948 he joined the West Riding Constabulary, serving in different branches of the Force, in a variety of locations in the county. On his retirement in November 1975 he held the rank of Inspector.

Churchill's Light Brigade; The Bristol Blenheim Bomber Crews in Action by **Flight Lieutenant James W. Moore DFC**[1]

At 1645 on Monday 10 June 1940 the British Ambassador in Rome was handed a note stating *His Majesty the King Emperor declares that from tomorrow June 11th, Italy considers herself at war with Britain.* Mussolini, sitting on the sideline, had watched the rapid and decisive onslaught by the Germans in Western Europe and concluding that Britain had been defeated, felt it was time to share in the spoils of victory. His vision of the easy fruits of victory encompassed the French area of Savoy, as well as African countries such as Egypt, Sudan and Tunisia. Whilst his decision to act delighted his Axis partner, Adolf Hitler, it was not welcomed by the members of the German High Command. The British Army in Egypt was pitifully small compared with the large Italian Armies in the west in Libya and to the east in Eritrea, Somaliland and Ethiopia. The RAF in Egypt and Palestine, like the British Army, were ill-prepared for the conflict, having only the following aircraft at their disposal: forty single-engined biplane Gloster Gladiator fighters, seventy Bristol Blenheim Mk.Is, 24 Bristol Bombay and Vickers Valentia bomber-transports, 24 Westland Lysander army co-operation spotter aircraft and ten Short Sunderland flying boats. In so far as the Blenheim squadrons were concerned, five of them - 30, 45, 55, 113 and 211 - were based in Egypt, three of them - 8, 11 and 39 - in Aden, whilst in Iraq was 84 Squadron. Replacements for the Allied Armed Forces in the Middle East travelling from Britain had to make the 12,000 mile journey, via the Cape of Good Hope, as the route through the Mediterranean was now closed. Arrangements were being made for the delivery of aircraft by sea to Takoradi in West Africa. These would then be flown over land to Egypt. Other aircraft would also be flown via Gibraltar and Malta, as the reader is well aware, but both of these routes had yet to get off the ground. One of the early priorities was to replace the Blenheim I with the improved Mk.IV.

No time was lost in striking the first blow against the new enemy. Air Chief Marshal Sir Arthur Longmore the AOC in Egypt gave orders to Air Commodore Raymond Collishaw (a First World War fighter ace) that we were at war with Italy. Collishaw felt that with the RAF's weakness in the Middle East an aggressive strike should be made. So in the early hours of 11 June, twenty-six Blenheims on 45, 55 and 113 Squadrons strafed and bombed the Italian airfield at El Adem in Cyrenaica, destroying several enemy aircraft and disrupting a ceremonial parade. They were met by surprisingly fierce resistance, two of the bombers being shot down, whilst a third, severely damaged, had to force land at Sidi Barrani. Operations continued to be flown against Italian troop concentrations, ports and airfields then, on 13 September 1940, the Italian Army, commanded by Marshal Rodolfo Graziani, began to advance towards Egypt. The odds in favour of the Italians, both on the ground and in the air, were five to one, so the Allies had no option but to withdraw, with the Blenheims and Gladiators keeping up a constant attack on enemy columns. Having crossed the Egyptian border, capturing nothing of importance, the Italians halted and dug in at Sidi Barrani. Here they erected a number of camps, each surrounded by barbed wire.

The next event, which was to have a disastrous influence on the war in North Africa, occurred on 2 October 1940, when the Italian Army invaded Greece from bases in Albania. The latter country had been invaded and occupied by the Italians in 1939. The Royal Hellenic Air Force had 6,000 personnel and 120 aircraft, including two fighter squadrons equipped with obsolete Polish aircraft; with Fairey Battle, Blenheim I and French Potez 63 medium bombers as the strike element. Like the Greek Army they were hopelessly outnumbered by the Italians, though they were to prove more than a match for their opponents.

Meanwhile, in Egypt, General Wavell's Army prepared to attack the Italians at Sidi Barrani. In preparation for the attack the Blenheim squadrons, which were being re-equipped with Mk IV aircraft flown in from Takoradi, were in the forefront of daylight attacks on enemy positions and airfields. On 9 December 1940 the attack on Sidi Barrani began; involving not only the Army, but both the Royal Navy and Royal Air Force. What had been intended as a reconnaissance in strength turned out to be a rout, the Italians retreating as fast as they could. The offensive rolled on, the British Army occupying Tobruk, Bardia and finally, on 7 February 1941, Benghazi, where Wavell had to call a halt as his lines of communication were over extended, the enemy re-grouping at El Agheila. The Western Desert Air Force of two squadrons of Hurricanes and Gladiators, five squadrons of Blenheims, Lysander army co-operation aircraft and the obsolete Bombay and Valentia (makeshift night-bombers) made a very important contribution to the success of the offensive. Despite odds of five to one in favour of the Italians, at least 1,100 enemy aircraft were destroyed both in the air and on the ground. During the campaign 133,295 prisoners, 400 tanks and 13,000 guns were captured at a cost to the Allies of 7,000 casualties, so it was not surprising that it was felt that the Italians were a defeated Army which posed little threat. In consequence, troops, equipment and aircraft were withdrawn either for training or to be transferred to Greece, which was to prove to be a costly mistake. The RAF contingent in Greece was reinforced by 33 Squadron (Hurricanes), 112 Squadron (Gladiators) and two Blenheim squadrons (11 and 113). All the squadrons were based on poor aerodromes without adequate transport and bad telephonic communication and those based near Athens at Eleusis and Tatoi were about 200 miles away from the front.

The Blenheim crews experienced diabolical weather and over their targets in Albania, especially heavy anti-aircraft fire, so they seldom returned unscathed. During February some of the Blenheim squadrons were moved to airstrips nearer the front, where they operated in close-support. A further two Blenheim units (Nos. 84 and 211) and 80 Squadron with Gladiators moved to Greece, with the Blenheim fighter element of 30 Squadron remaining at Eleusis to defend Athens and 80

Squadron Gladiators moved forward to Trikkala in the Larissa plain.

During a counter-attack by the Italians, prompted by the presence of Mussolini, from 9-27 March Blenheim crews carried out 43 sorties against enemy troops, gun positions and transport columns. Other Blenheims carried out raids from Greece against the enemy airfields at Martza, Cattavia and Calato on the island of Rhodes, from which the Luftwaffe were launching raids on Allied convoys. The Italian mainland also received attention from the Blenheims, who attacked aerodromes at Brindisi and Lecce. These daylight attacks were supplemented at night by the crews of the few Wellingtons based in Egypt.

On 7 March the first fighting troops of the British and Commonwealth landed in Greece, followed by many more, the convoys being escorted by the puny British Air Force in Greece. A week before these landings commenced, units of the German Armed Forces, intended for the attack on Russia, had entered Bulgaria. This represented a very considerable threat to the Allies, which was followed on 5 April by Germany declaring war on both Greece and Yugoslavia, opening their offensive on Yugoslavia at dawn the following day. The city of Belgrade was subjected to a merciless aerial bombardment, comparable with the attacks on Warsaw and Rotterdam, so that Yugoslavian military resistance was speedily overcome. Employing the same tactics as in Western Europe the German armoured columns sped across the frontiers of Bulgaria and Yugoslavia into Greece, closely supported by hordes of fighters, dive bombers and medium bombers. At that time the British Air Force in Greece had about 200 aircraft, of which only eighty were serviceable, whilst the Greeks hardly had any. By contrast, in Rumania and Bulgaria, the Luftwaffe had 800 aircraft, whilst the Italians had 310 in Italy and Albania. In support of the Allied troops on the Albanian Front were one Squadron of Gladiators and 211 Squadron with Blenheims. On the Yugoslav/Rumanian Front was one Hurricane squadron, one of Lysanders and 11 and 33 Squadrons with Blenheims. Based close to Athens was one fighter squadron, 30 and 84 Squadrons with Blenheims and a small number of Wellingtons. This pitifully small Allied Air Force was all that could be mustered to withstand the German Blitzkrieg.

On 7 April Wellingtons and Blenheims successfully bombed many enemy positions along the whole of the front. This was followed on the next day by a raid by Blenheims crews on German motor convoys held up on a road through the mountains. However the German advance continued despite strenuous and courageous opposition, Blenheims bombing and strafing enemy motor transports and armoured fighting vehicles (AFV) during the day, the Wellingtons adding their contribution at night.

On 13 April six Blenheims on 211 Squadron took-off to bomb enemy mobile columns, without fighter escort and in daylight, when they were attacked by a swarm of Me 109s over Monastir. Every Blenheim was shot out of the sky, crashing into the mountains, only two of the aircrew surviving when they bailed out. These two lucky survivors, Flight Lieutenant Godfrey and Sergeant Simpson, although behind enemy lines, made their way to Larissa, where they were offered a lift in two Army Lysander aircraft, an offer they gladly accepted. However, as they took-off their luck ran out, both Lysanders being shot down by Me 109s, Simpson being killed and Godfrey losing two fingers.

The Germans had wasted no time in constructing airstrips close to the front, from which their fighters could operate and on 15 April the Luftwaffe turned their attention to the Allied aerodromes. For example, the Blenheim base at Niamata was subjected to both bombing and strafing by Me 109s and Me 110s several times in one day, ten aircraft being destroyed on the ground, equipment destroyed, personnel killed and injured, the squadron rendered impotent.

In order to conserve his small force, which on 15 April was reported as 47 serviceable aircraft, Air Vice-Marshal Sir John Henry D'Albiac decided to employ the few remaining Blenheims on night operations, bombing the Luftwaffe bases at Sedes, Katerini, Kozani and Larissa between the 15th and 22nd April. They were also engaged in bombing road bridges intended to impede the enemy's remorseless advance. The dilemma was that the Allied fighters on the single airfield immediately behind the Thermopylae Line was in danger of being wiped-out if they stayed and too far from the front if they moved to Athens.

As an indication of the odds in favour of the enemy, in raids on the city of Athens on the 19th and 20th April, a Luftwaffe force of 100 dive-bombers and fighters were opposed by a mere fifteen Hurricanes. On the 20th in an attack on Piraeus thirty of the enemy aircraft were believed to have been shot down for the loss of five Hurricanes. Fifteen Hurricanes of 33 and 80 Squadrons had to challenge the enemy. This was the scene where Squadron Leader 'Pat' Pattle, considered at that time to be the highest scoring RAF pilot, fell to the guns of the enemy along with four other of his companions.

The situation had by now become desperate, one Greek Army having already surrendered on the 21st, so it was time for the British Forces to be evacuated. The fourteen Blenheims on 30 Squadron, employed as long-range fighters, had already flown to Crete to cover the evacuation. On the 22nd and 23rd the few remaining Blenheims on 11, 84, 113 and 211 Squadrons flew to Egypt, whilst nine Blenheim fighters on 203 Squadron were despatched from Egypt to Crete to assist in covering the Allied convoys. During the campaign the RAF lost 209 aircraft due to enemy action, 72 being lost on operations. Despite heavy and sustained attacks by the Luftwaffe, between 24-29 April 43,000 of the 57,660 troops sent to Greece were re-embarked, leaving behind all their heavy equipment including 8,000 trucks.

The next major event in this theatre of operations was to take place in the mountainous island of Crete, which lies at the base of the Aegean Sea and about 155 miles south of Athens. The Allied High Command had never considered the island to be at risk and little had been done to prepare for its defence. During the campaign in Greece a naval base on the island, Suda Bay, had proved to be of considerable importance. Of the British and Commonwealth troops evacuated from Greece, 25,000 of them, with no equipment other than their rifles, were landed in Crete, making a total garrison of 28,600. The island was subjected to constant raids by the Luftwaffe, the three airstrips receiving special attention, these raids increasing in intensity, with Fliegerkorps VIII supporting Fliegerkorps XI by concentrating on the sea approaches to Suda Bay. Attempts to deliver arms and equipment by sea were hampered by aerial attacks as, for example, when eight of 23 Allied ships were sunk. Due to the constant attacks on the three airstrips they became untenable and the few surviving aircraft had to be withdrawn to Egypt on 19 May. The following day the assault on the island began with saturation bombing of Máleme airfield, the dropping of paratroops and the landing of gliders filled with German troops. On this first day 7,000 airborne troops were landed on the island, the prelude to the greatest airborne invasion the world had ever seen. At Heraklion and Retimo the German paratroops were wiped out and the glider landings at Canea suffered heavy losses, but at Máleme the glider-borne troops caught the defenders out during heavy bombardment and established a considerable foothold. In less than a week the Germans landed by air between 30,000-35,000 troops, which were supported by continuous bombing and strafing by the Luftwaffe.

The soldiers from Australia, Britain and New Zealand fought bravely despite their lack of equipment, although the outcome could never have been in doubt. The first Allied troops to be evacuated were taken off the island during the night of 28/29 May 1941, though sadly, of the 4,000 who embarked, 800 were killed, wounded or taken prisoner, when the ships in which they were travelling were sunk by enemy aircraft. The last evacuation took place during the night of 30/31 May, bringing the total evacuated to 14,580 though sadly, 15,000 were left behind. The cost of this German victory achieved by aerial supremacy is estimated to have cost the Germans between 12,000-15,000 men, of which the majority were killed. Hitler was reported to have been appalled by these losses and it is interesting to note that this was the last large airborne operation mounted by the Germans during the war. The Royal Navy had suffered grievously. For example, over a period of three days two cruisers and four destroyers had been sunk, whilst one battleship, two cruisers and four destroyers had been severely damaged.

During this short and bloody campaign, operations against the enemy were flown by the Blenheims based 200 miles away in Egypt. In one such raid by 14 Squadron they destroyed at least twelve Junkers Ju 52 transport aircraft on Máleme airfield, though in a second raid on the same target they lost three aircraft and crews. Another unit involved was 55 Squadron, who flew similar low-level daylight operations against the enemy on Crete. The disastrous and ill-advised involvement of the Allies in Greece led indirectly to altering the course of the war in favour of the Allies. The German invasion of Russia had been delayed until 22 June, which meant they were unable to defeat the Russian Army before the onset of the winter. This delay, coupled with the appalling winter weather, gave the Russians the opportunity to hold and to ultimately defeat the enemy.

Meanwhile, in the Western Desert, during the absence of so many Allied units in Greece and Crete, early in February the Germans had landed a Light Armoured Division at Tripoli manned by specially trained troops. The Luftwaffe also began a build-up of operational fighters, dive-bombers and medium bombers, who soon began to make their presence felt. On 31 March, the German offensive began, under the command of the legendary Erwin Rommel, against the few Allied units left in Cyrenaica. The Allies had no option but to retreat from this well-armed and superior force, withdrawing over the ground they had occupied during their spectacular advance, which had only ended on 7 February, with the capture of Benghazi. The retreating Allied units were supported by daylight raids by the few remaining Blenheim squadrons (39, 45 and 55) in the desert, who attacked enemy airfields, troop concentrations and ports, their efforts being supplemented at night by the Wellington squadrons. At this time 39 Squadron were the first Blenheim squadron to have its aircraft replaced by Martin Maryland twin-engined bombers, a pattern which was to continue. By 27 April 1941 the Germans and their Italian allies had driven the weakened Allied Army back across the Egyptian frontier, although Tobruk was still occupied in strength, mainly by the Australians. During the three days from 1 April more than 400 fighter and bomber sorties were launched against enemy targets, of which eighty were flown by Blenheim crews. Considering there were only three Blenheim squadrons involved, this was a remarkable achievement.

Mussolini was not the only one who was under the impression that Britain and her Allies were defeated, other problems were to beset the Allies during their involvement in Greece and Crete coupled with the withdrawal in Cyrenaica. The first occurred early in April 1941, when four pro-German Iraqi Generals forced a coup d'état, which posed a real threat to Allied access to the precious oil in Persia (Iran) and Iraq. British and Indian forces were landed at Basra and deployed to protect Allied interests, whilst Iraqi forces moved in strength against the RAF aerodrome at Habbaniya. This was a Flying Training School having about sixty aircraft, none of which were operational. These training aircraft were hurriedly converted to carry bombs and guns, being flown by the instructors and some of their pupils, taking-off to attack the Iraqi gun positions, which were a mere thousand yards from the airfield. Their gallant efforts were quickly supplemented by Wellingtons on 70 Squadron and Blenheims on 203 Squadron, the Iraqis withdrawing during the night of 5/6 May. The coup d'état was quelled by the Allied Army and peace restored by 1 June.

The other threat in that area arose in the French colony of Syria, now governed by the pro-German Vichy French Government. The latter had given Germany permission for the Luftwaffe to use air bases in Syria for refuelling, which represented a real problem to the Allies, as it placed the Luftwaffe in a position to threaten Cyprus, Palestine and our oil-fields in Iraq and Iran. On 14 May a 203 Squadron Blenheim piloted by Flying Officer A. Watson carried out a reconnaissance of the area and found German aircraft re-fuelling at Palmyra. Later on in the day Watson was given permission to attack this target, by which time four other Blenheims had arrived and so an attack was carried out. During the following days more raids were carried out against airfields at Rayak and Damascus as well as a large fuel dump at Beirut.

On 8 June the Allied Army of Australians, British, Free French and Indian infantry invaded Syria, being opposed by their former Allies, the French, who fought fiercely. The Vichy Air Force in Syria flying LeO 45 and Martin 139 (Maryland) bombers carried out attacks on the Allied naval and land forces and were opposed by 80 Squadron Hurricanes and 3 Squadron RAAF P-40s, with 11, 45 and 84 Squadron Blenheims carrying out bombing raids on military targets. Eight Blenheims were lost in aerial combat and two more when they collided. These losses, sad though they were appear even more tragic when one considers they were inflicted by airmen we had so recently looked upon as colleagues.

The Vichy forces fought fiercely and 'Habforce' moving from Habbaniya to Baghdad and then towards Palmyra was bombed heavily by Vichy aircraft. However, on 28 June P-40 Tomahawks of 3 Squadron RAAF caught six Martin 139 aircraft attacking our troops and shot all of them down. Air attacks by the Blenheims and Egyptian based Wellingtons gradually damped down French resistance and on 29 June four Blenheims of 11 Squadron placed 250lb bombs in or around the residency of General Denz, the Governor-General.

The conflict in Syria ended on 12 July 1941 and the Allies could turn their attention to the German/Italian Armies in Egypt and Cyrenaica. By the end of October, having learnt many valuable lessons from their recent tragic experiences, the 8th Army became the first Allied Army to have air superiority in their theatre of operations. The Allied air offensive was directed at Axis ports, ships, airfields and fuel dumps, the daylight bombing raids being flown by Blenheims of 11, 14, 45, 55, 84 and 113 Squadrons, plus the Free French 'Lorraine' Squadron.

On 18 November 1941 the 8th Army under the command of General Sir Claude John Eyre Auchinleck GCB GCIE CSI DSO OBE opened their offensive, closely supported by all the Allied air units under their new and far-sighted commander, Air Marshal Arthur William Tedder. The offensive succeeded in driving Rommel's Afrika Korps back to El Agheila by 6 January 1942, being achieved, despite the enemy's superior tanks, due to the Allied air offensive. One of the units which took part in General Auckinleck's offensive was 84 Squadron who, after the disastrous campaign in Greece had been stationed in Iraq. In the August, they received a new Commanding Officer, Wing Commander Boyce, who was given the task of preparing them for the war in the desert.

'Another new arrival was Pilot Officer George Milson, with whom I had flown on 18 Squadron from RAF Oulton during the summer. said 'Dinty' Moore. ' On the posting of George and our observer, Ron Millar, due to a bout of pneumonia I was not allowed to go with them, my place being taken by Flight Sergeant Jones DFM. By the time the campaign in the desert ended, George had been promoted to Acting Flight Lieutenant and awarded the DFC and Ron had been commissioned and awarded the DFM. Further, a mutual friend, Flight Sergeant Bill Proctor, had become their WOp/AG.'

At the time of Wavell's victorious campaign at the beginning of 1941, RAF squadrons were withdrawn to take part in the disastrous campaign in Greece. Once again, early in January 1942, four Blenheim squadrons, 45, 84, 113 and 211, were withdrawn from the desert to fly out to the Far East in a futile gesture as reinforcements to the beleaguered Allied Air Force facing the new enemy, the Japanese. This decision was made at a time when the strength of the Luftwaffe in North Africa, Sicily and Italy was being increased. By virtue of the aerial onslaught launched by the Luftwaffe on Malta, enemy convoys were again sailing across the Mediterranean with little interference, providing Rommel with the reinforcements he sorely needed.

On 21 January Rommel returned to the offensive, driving the 8th Army, deprived of much needed aerial support by the departure of the four Blenheim squadrons to the Far East, in retreat. On 26 May 1942 Rommel launched what was to be his last successful offensive, driving the 8th Army back to El Alamein. By the time the new commander of the 8th Army, General Bernard Montgomery, launched his historic offensive at El Alamein in October 1942, the tide had turned and the Allies were taking their first step on the road to victory.

Chapter 6

Malta - The Modern Crusaders[1]
Flight Lieutenant James W. Moore DFC

'I had no peace of mind when they were out. I could not stay in my office and when they returned I was afraid to ask 'How did it go'. Those aircrew were the flower of our race; all of them had been given a good education in their youth and they were far above average in intelligence, men who knew what they were doing and why it had to be done and men who volunteered to be aircrew in preference to many other less hazardous tasks. Theirs was a calm and conscious courage. To every one of these volunteers the sinking of ships was their crusade and without doubt they were Knights of St. John - the modern Crusaders'.
Air Commodore Hugh Pughe-Lloyd

In April 1941, despite the enormous demands being made of the Blenheims and their crews in the United Kingdom, the Chief of Air Staff, Air Chief Marshal Sir Charles Portal, decided that the feasibility of crews, drawn from 2 Group, operating from the island of Malta against enemy shipping in the Mediterranean should be explored. Should the scheme prove to be feasible, squadrons should be detached from the UK on a rota basis, to operate from the island for five or six weeks before returning to England. Malta is 17 miles long and five miles wide, located only sixty miles from Sicily and 180 miles from the North African Coast. By contrast to its size, it is of immense strategic importance, having a large natural harbour at Valletta, on the route from Gibraltar (1,100 miles to the west) to Alexandria (1,000 miles to the east).The island had been subjected to eight raids by bombers of the Italian Air Force on 10 June 1940, when Mussolini declared war on the allies, raids which became part of a way of life to civilians and servicemen alike. At first there was no fighter cover at all, then four crated Sea Gladiator biplane fighters, awaiting shipment to Alexandria, were found at the docks. These were quickly assembled and brought into service to give combat, one soon being lost. The three remaining Gladiators, who for propaganda reasons became known as *Faith, Hope and Charity*, [pilots who flew the Gladiators, however, preferred to call them 'Freeman, Hardy and Willis'] flew in defence of the island for three months until only *Faith* remained. She carried on alone until joined by Hurricanes from Egypt.

'The flight from Britain was, in itself, difficult for the crews, many of whom were inexperienced. It was a route followed by many crews, posted with their aircraft, for service in the Middle East. The crews would take-off from RAF Portreath near Redruth in Cornwall, in tropicalised long-range Blenheim Mk IVs with long-range petrol tanks fitted in the bomb-bay. en-route, as the main tanks were being emptied, the overload fuel would be pumped by hand into the main tanks, care having to be taken not to pump air into the main tanks system, which would of course have disastrous results. Their route took them over the Scilly isles before turning south across the Bay of Biscay, where they were liable to meet enemy aircraft, to Cap Finisterre off the north-west coast of Spain. They then flew south, parallel to the coast of Portugal, to Cape Vincent where they turned east for the difficult approach to Gibraltar. overall, a flight of 1,500 miles which, without the aid of an automatic pilot, or other 'mod cons' took 8½ hours. Their troubles were not yet over for the runway at Gibraltar - formerly the racecourse - was short and because of the turbulence from the rock, was dangerous. There were a number of wrecked aircraft to testify to the problems encountered by other pilots.

They stayed in Gibraltar, where refuelling was done from four-gallon petrol cans, for suitable weather for the next leg of their flight to Malta. the first leg of their flight, the 1,100 miles to the island, was generally flown at heights of 10,000 feet or more, before returning to sea-level as they approached the Sicilian channel, the stretch of sea between Sicily and Tunisia. At the centre of the channel was the Italian island of Pantellaria, enemy fighters and radar being based both there and in Sicily, as many crews found to their cost. Having survived all these hazards the crews landed their Blenheims at Luqa airfield where they would be based.

On arrival they found themselves subjected to regular bombing raids, food in short supply, poor living conditions and as time went by, the prospect of a very short life. In the case of crews on their way to the Middle East, whose journey was not interrupted, they still had a further 1,000 miles to fly before they reached their destination in Egypt. I hardly need to add that many crews were lost due to enemy action, lack of fuel, mechanical failure or human error on this long and perilous journey.

The officer selected to explore the possibility of Blenheims operating from Malta against Axis shipping was Squadron Leader 'Attie' Atkinson DSO DFC of 2 Group, a highly regarded leader who became a legend to those who flew in these medium bombers. On 31 March 1941 Squadron Leader 'Atty' Atkinson led eight of his crews on 21 Squadron, having been briefed to attack ships off the Dutch Frisian Islands and to open the campaign against 'fringe targets'. 'Attie' found two destroyers. One was bombed from fifty feet, with hits scored on the ship's stern. She slewed round, listing heavily to port as a column of black smoke belched into the sky. Not content with this success, he then led the formation across the islands of the north Dutch coast, saw a German parade, dropped his bombs plumb between the ranks and then chased the regimental cook up a lane. Asked by the Intelligence Officer how he could tell it was a cook, 'Attie' replied soberly that it might have been disguise, but he was wearing a chef's cap and apron. And then his observer commented, 'Dammit, at the height we were flying we could not only tell that it was a cook, we could even tell what the cook was thinking.'

'Attie's report to Intelligence afterwards was typical. 'At Ameland, at about 1400 hours,' he said, 'we sighted what I suppose must have been an after-lunch parade. I alerted my gunner and we sprayed the lot of them. After this, we found a fellow on a gun emplacement, said 'good afternoon' and went on our way.' Their visit had not gone unnoticed, for their presence had attracted a great deal of flak, which, not too surprisingly, accounted for two of the Blenheims. Another successful attack saw 'Attie' being awarded a Bar to the DFC. But he missed the party to celebrate it. On 26 April 'Attie' took-off leading six crews of 21 Squadron on their flight out to Malta, which all of them completed successfully. On their arrival they flew a number of shipping sorties, having their aircraft serviced by naval personnel, losing one aircraft in an air-raid. 'Attie' led the first attack on a convoy to Tripoli and personally sank a 4,000-tonner, while others in the flight sank a destroyer. There were four more attacks on convoys and then the Blenheims came home, flying all the way from the Bay of Biscay to England on one engine. Sea spray had got in the other. Atkinson ran out of fuel and had to make an undignified, but safe, belly landing in a friendly Cornish field. 'Attie' was then posted back to his own original 82 Squadron. The man from Church House who had joined them as Acting Pilot Officer was, at twenty-six, in command of the Squadron. Some of the men who were now with him had escaped from Gembloux, but most of the faces were new. Wing Commander Atkinson flew again to his familiar base at Luqa, taking his Squadron with him.

As Squadron Commander 'Attie' often went out himself after the ships. Ship-sinking was a matter of gambits. Most frequently the big cargo-boats and even the smaller fry for Rommel would be accompanied by a single Italian destroyer. The Blenheims would fly around, looking for an opening, while the destroyer would frantically circle her charge, sending up showers of spray in an effort to get between the attacking Blenheims and the cargo-boat. The game was hard on both sides, ending sometimes in the loss of both Italian ships, guardian and ward and sometimes with the loss of the Blenheims.

On his return, Atkinson reported that the situation in Malta was far from satisfactory, things having been neglected for years. However, he considered the plan feasible to operate there on a squadron, or 'squadron plus' basis. On receipt of Atkinson's report Sir Charles Portal sent for the Senior Air Staff Officer (SASO) of 2 Group, Group Captain Hugh Pughe-Lloyd, to tell him he had been selected to command the detachments of 2 Group in Malta. His brief was 'to sink Axis shipping between Europe and Africa'. It was, in effect, the same task in which the aircrew of 2 Group in the UK were already involved in over the seas off occupied Western Europe.

On his arrival in Malta, Pughe-Lloyd [who enlisted as a private in World War One and stayed on with the British Army to receive a knighthood for his defence of Malta] was horrified to find defences and facilities in a deplorable state, airfields ill-prepared as operational bases. Little thought had obviously been given to the use of the island as a base from which fighter or bomber aircraft could operate. It is to his considerable credit that the aerodrome at Luqa was soon made ready for the arrival of the first detachment of Blenheims.

The first squadron to be detached to the island was 82, commanded by Atkinson, now a Wing Commander, whose presence had been specifically requested by Pughe-Lloyd, now an Air Commodore. The first aircraft to leave England, led by Atkinson, took-off on 4 June, followed a week later by a further nine Blenheims. All of the aircraft carried in addition to their aircrew, two unfortunate ground-crew sitting as comfortable as possible in the well of the aircraft. They all arrived safely, although the last of the crews had to land after dark, using a flarepath which some character, fearful of enemy bombing raids, did his best to extinguish.

Apart from the Hurricanes on Malta there were seven twin-engined Martin Maryland reconnaissance aircraft, a squadron of Wellingtons and a number of Swordfish biplanes of the Fleet Air Arm. The role of the Marylands was to reconnoitre for enemy shipping, keeping a special eye on Naples for signs of sailings or the assembling of convoys for the journey to Africa. On receipt of reports of the movement of enemy shipping, attacks would be launched during the day by Blenheims and Swordfish, with the Wellingtons operating at night.

The enemy convoys from Naples carrying supplies to the Axis Armies in North Africa followed routes which brought them no closer than 140 miles from Malta. Either sailing to the west of Sicily, then directly across to Africa, staying close to the shore until they reached Tripoli, or through the Straits of Messina, then east to Greece before turning south to Benghazi.

South of Pantelleria on 22 June, a biggish convoy escorted by destroyers and enemy fighters was found by six crews of 82 Squadron. The aircrews went into the attack in the manner they had perfected over the North Sea, despite intense anti-aircraft fire and the presence of the fighters. The crew of one Blenheim, Flight Lieutenant T. J. Watkins pilot, Sergeant observer J. S. Sargent and Sergeant WOp/air gunner Eric F. Chandler, dropped their bombs gaining hits on a merchantman. Their aircraft was badly damaged by flak, the explosion of one almost severing Watkins leg. Despite severe pain and shock he managed to right the aircraft, giving Sargent time to come to his aid. Meanwhile Chandler was doing battle with an Italian Fiat CR42 Falco biplane fighter, which he succeeded in shooting down, which earned him a DFM. Showing immense courage Watkins managed to stay conscious during the long flight back to Luqa to give Sargent flying instructions, where miraculously Watkins brought the aircraft safely into land at Luqa and then collapsed. Watkins was awarded an immediate DSO, Sargent and Chandler, who was credited with having shot down an enemy fighter, each received the DFM. The damage to their aircraft was so severe it had to be written off. By a strange twist of fate, three months later, on their return to England, Sargent and Chandler were flying a shipping sweep off the Frisian Islands when their pilot, Flight Lieutenant Bartlett was injured. Sargent flew their aircraft back to base, landing it successfully despite a live bomb on board. As soon as their aircraft came to a stop, Sargent and Chandler leapt out dragging their wounded pilot between them before the bomb exploded.

On 24 June, led by Wing Commander Atkinson, crews on 82 Squadron delivered the first low-level attack on Tripoli harbour, where they bombed the remainder of the convoy that they had attacked two days earlier. That day, it was said, the Squadron really went to town - Tripoli town - at anything from twenty to nought feet. The Wing Commander and two others bombed a 20,000-ton liner and his gunner saw the whole of the top deck blow off.

The squadron continued to operate daily from Luqa, suffering heavy casualties until they could operate no longer. One of their operations worth recalling, was another low-level raid, led once again by Atkinson, on the harbour at Palermo on the north coast of Sicily, which they approached by flying through the Sicilian Channel and coming in from the north. Having dropped their bombs they headed due south across this mountainous island and back to Luqa. The enemy was so surprised that not one shot was fired at the Blenheims, yet the raid was an enormous success. Two ships, one a 10,000 tonner, the other of 5,000 tons had been destroyed; another 10,000 tonner had a broken back, whilst three others had been badly damaged.[2]

Their contribution to the Maltese Campaign completed, the surviving aircrew, despite instructions to the contrary, found their way back to the UK to join their beloved 2 Group by hitching a lift to Gibraltar in a Catalina flying boat and then on by ship.

On 1 July 1941 the second detachment, 17 Blenheims and their crews on 110 Squadron, commanded by Wing Commander Theo 'Joe' Hunt DFC, flew out to Malta, where they wasted no time in getting into action. Their first operation was a low-level attack on three merchantmen in Tripoli harbour, followed on the 13th with the destruction of three more vessels. The next day they switched their attention to Libya, where they bombed a Luftwaffe airfield with some success, followed four days later by a raid on a power station at Tripoli, where Wing Commander 'Joe' Hunt and his crew were shot down into the sea by a CR 42 fighter. Shipping was not neglected, an 8,000 ton merchantman being damaged on the 15th, two ships being destroyed on the 22nd and then four crews bombed and destroyed two more in another visit to Tripoli harbour. In the latter operation the formation leader, Sergeant N. A. C. Cathles, twice hit the sea en-route to the target, which he bombed before he was forced to make a belly-landing in enemy territory. Yet another demonstration of the courage and determination of these young aircrew.

On 28 July, after a short but highly successful attachment, the surviving crews found their way back to the UK, to be replaced by twelve crews on 105 Squadron led by Wing Commander Hughie Edwards VC DFC a matter of a mere 24 days after he had led the epic low-level raid on Bremen. In their first operation six of the crews found a convoy of four merchantmen escorted by a destroyer and Fiat CR 42 fighters, who put up such an effective defence the raid had to be abandoned. The next day three crews found a destroyer escorted convoy close to the island of Lampedusa, which they attacked and lost one of their number to anti-aircraft fire. Apart from flying shipping sweeps the crews were not neglecting land targets such as a barracks at Misura in Libya. In their attacks on shipping they continued to have their successes, as on 7 August, when only two out of a convoy of six ships reached their destination in Africa. One of these, a tanker beached on Lampedusa, where after a second raid, it burnt for days. On the 15th, five crews of 105 Squadron found two escorted tankers, carrying fuel for the Afrika Corps, between Tripoli and Benghazi, which they bombed. One of the tankers exploded whilst the other was very badly damaged, although the Blenheim crews had to pay a high price. The Blenheim piloted by Pilot Officer P. H. Standfast being hit by flak exploded, a second was shot down by machine-gun fire and a third was lost when it collided with the mast of one of the ships and cart wheeled into the sea.105 Squadron were certainly making its presence felt, scoring three hits on two merchantmen on the 28th off the coast of Greece, a shipping sweep so far from Malta it was almost at the limit of their fuel capacity. Then closer to home, they bombed an ammunition factory and a power station at Licata on the south coast of Sicily. On 31 July the command of the squadron had been handed over from Wing Commander Edwards to Wing Commander P. H. A. Simmons, the former returning to the UK for a well deserved 'rest'.

By the end of August it was estimated that 58% of all enemy supplies heading for North Africa had been lost at sea. Those who successfully completed the journey were still not safe in Tripoli harbour, where they were liable to be bombed by day by the Blenheims and at night by the Wellington crews. Understandably, the enemy did not stand idle in the face of this threat to their lifeline to their armed forces in Africa, increasing the anti-aircraft defences on their merchantmen and escorts. The casualty rate for the Blenheim crews was around 12%, an average of one crew per day or one squadron per week. Replacement crews were found by 'press-ganging' unsuspecting crews and their aircraft on their way out to Egypt into service with the squadrons on Malta.

The need to maintain the momentum of attacks on enemy shipping meant that 105 Squadron had to remain in Malta longer than the intended 5-6 weeks. At the end of August 26 Blenheims and their crews of 107 Squadron arrived in Malta to play their part in the campaign. On 17 September three crews flew a low level raid on factories at Licata, whilst at dawn the same day another three crews bombed a large liner in Tripoli harbour and so it continued. On the 22nd in a raid by crews from both squadrons on barracks, ammunition dumps and lorries on the Tripoli-Benghazi road two of the Blenheims collided. The tail was knocked off the aircraft piloted by Wing Commander Don Scivier AFC, which crashed, whereas the other one, piloted by Sergeant Tommy Williams managed to limp back to Luqa. Many convoys were escorted by fighters which, bearing in mind the improved anti-aircraft defences, added to the danger as for example, a formation of six Blenheims found five merchantmen escorted, not only by five destroyers but four Junkers 88 twin-engined fighter-bombers as well. Undaunted the first vie flew into the attack dropping their bombs, followed closely by the second vic led by Wing Commander N. E. W. Pepper DFC. As the latter flew over the convoy the eleven second delay bombs of the first wave exploded, blowing-up Pepper's aircraft. Another, severely damaged did however manage to limp back to Luqa. An indication of the success of the campaign was that the enemy now stopped routing their convoys to the west of Sicily, sending them on the longer journey via the coast of Greece.

On Thursday 4 October 1941 eight crews on 107 Squadron led by Squadron Leader Barnes, set out to bomb the harbour at Zuara on the African coast. The flak from three destroyers in the harbour was so fierce the first vie was beaten off and they came under attack from Fiat CR.42 fighters. The other five Blenheims sought other targets inland, when they too were attacked by fighters, who shot down the Blenheim piloted by Sergeant D. E. Hamlyn. All three crew spent six days in their dinghy before being rescued off the coast of Djerba by an Arab ship, which took them to Tunis and internment. The engagement with the fighters lasted until the Blenheims were fifty miles out to sea on their way back to base. During the night of 7/8 October, a low-level attack in bright moonlight was carried out on a 2,000 ton merchantman off Tripoli, on which two hits were scored causing an explosion.'

On the 11th 107 Squadron found a convoy in the Gulf of Sirte escorted by one twin-engined monoplane. Flying Officer Ronald Arthur Greenhill hit a large motor vessel forward and his aircraft was then seen by Sergeant Harrison to be hit in the belly and crash in the sea as he climbed over the ship. Sergeant Ivor Broom attacked the same vessel and hit it aft and left the vessel in flames with grey smoke pouring from it. He was chased by the escort plane which did not get within firing range. Harrison saw Sergeant Routh attack a small cargo boat, set it on fire and then crash into the sea having been hit by guns from the large motor vessel. Sergeants Leven, Baker and Hopkinson did not make an attack and brought back their bombs. In the afternoon of 11 October a convoy consisting of the steamer *Priaruggia,* the tanker *Fassio,* escorted by the corvette *Partenope*, which left Tripoli at 1600 hours on 10 October, was attacked by three Blenheims in low-level flight. While turning and climbing the Blenheims dropped a series of small bombs and strafed the convoy with machine guns. Of the bombs, one hit *Priaruggia* at the base of the funnel. Almost at the same time, two Blenheims appeared to be hit by the precise fire of *Partenope,* one in a staggering turn trying to touch down on the water, hitting hard and then dived into the sea breaking up. The other, on fire, still managed a half turn and then dived into the sea nose first, vanishing completely. The third Blenheim carried out a wide turn and then continued to remain cruising for some minutes. One of the Blenheims, which prior to crashing, hit the foremast of the *Priaruggia,* bursting into flames and breaking off the mast. The *Priaruggia* must have appeared very badly hit, but the *Fassio* was neither hit nor attacked. The episode shows very clearly the dangers the pilots on Malta exposed themselves to and the brutal and very quick end that awaited most of them. *Fassio* arrived in Benghasi on 13 October. The lost Blenheims were Z7618 and Z9663. While Sergeant Whidden survived the crash, he died of his wounds in hospital shortly after. Their loss was not completely in vain however. *Priaruggia* was badly enough damaged that she had to return in tow to Tripoli after an initial stay at Misurata. When she arrived (still with the same cargo, including ammunition) in Benghazi six weeks later, after the conclusion of repairs, she was bombed on the night of her arrival and all her cargo was lost when she blew up.

'Mid-October saw the arrival of a detachment on 18 Squadron, who were to remain on Malta until the end of the campaign, replacing the surviving personnel on 105 Squadron, who arrived back in the UK on 11 October. The casualty rate was rising at an alarming rate, for instance, the new commander of 107 Squadron was lost on 9 October, followed a few days later by his deputy, Squadron Leader Barnes. By the end of the month the squadron had no commissioned officer pilots left, command falling on the shoulders of Sergeant Ivor Broom, who was awarded an immediate commission. Ivor and his crew of Sergeant 'Bill' North, observer and Sergeant Les Harrison, WOp/AG had been on their way to North Africa when they had been hi-jacked by Hugh Pughe-Lloyd.[3] During the remainder of October, raids were concentrated on Axis targets in North Africa, although Sicily was not forgotten. On the 17th six Blenheims of 18 Squadron with an escort of Hurricanes carried out a successful 'Circus' attack on the enemy's seaplane base at Syracuse, with other low-level operations being directed against factories at Licata and Catania.

The first major success in November occurred on the 5th, when six crews of 18 Squadron found and attacked two 3,000 ton tankers escorted by a destroyer. They had to pay a high price for their success, as two of the Blenheims were shot down. On the 8th six crews from 107 Squadron found a merchantman escorted by a destroyer, a desperate battle ensued with one Blenheim, on being hit by flak crashed into the ship's mast and exploded. Another was hit in the turret, yet despite this, the survivors made a further four attacks without gaining any hits on their target. A follow-up attack was carried out by six crews of ..8 Squadron, who lost two of their number without being able to sink the merchantman. Successful attacks during the same period were carried out in low-level raids on Mellaha airfield, a 4,000 tonner off Cape Kiri and on another convoy of three merchantmen.

About this time a crew arrived in Malta, en-route to Egypt and were 'press-ganged' into service on 107 Squadron. They 'were three inexperienced Sergeants', Ray Noseda RAAF, pilot, Freddie Deeks, observer and Webber, WOp/Air Gunner, who had the good fortune to survive a full tour of operations from Malta before the end of January 1942. I got to know Freddie Deeks when we flew our second tour together on Douglas Bostons on 88 Squadron during 1942-43. Their arrival coincided with a decision by the German High Command to neutralise Malta as a base for Allied shipping and to stop the attacks on their convoys by the bombers of the RAF. The task was given to Luftwaffe Field Marshal Albert Kesselring, who transferred aircraft from the Russian Front to supplement those already in Sicily, Pantellaria and North Africa. So, with a force of 600 bombers and a large number of fighters, the Luftwaffe set about the task of bombing Malta into submission and with only three Hurricane squadrons to oppose them, success seemed highly probable. The courageous resistance of the islanders is now a matter of history, as indicated by the award of the George Cross. The citation reads: 'To honour her brave people I award the George Cross to the Island Fortress of Malta to bear witness to a heroism and devotion that will long be famous in history'.

In his story of air power, Philip Guedalla relates in his book *Middle East 1940-42:* 'Hitherto no more than seventy aircraft had been operating weekly against Malta and they rarely came more than twenty at a time. But in December the weekly number rose to two hundred and the weight of bombs dropped on the island was multiplied by ten. This was doubled in the first eight weeks of1942 and quadrupled in March. By April, as the Axis shipping lanes were crowded with supplies for Rommel's next advance in Libya, the air attacks on Malta mounted to a crescendo and the island's ability to influence events in Africa, which had still been exercised against shipping at Palermo early in March, was practically paralysed. For April saw Malta fighting for its life'.

At the end of November the crew of a Martin Maryland recce' aircraft located a fast new 10,000 ton tanker leaving Naples en-route to Africa escorted by a destroyer. Crews on 18 and 107 Squadrons found and attacked this highly desirable target off Tripoli, following the Blenheims' first attack the tanker's seamen abandoned ship. On the same day four other Blenheims bombed train ferries at San Giorvani, which is the Italian terminus for the ferry from the mainland to Sicily.

The Blenheim losses continued. In bad weather on 8 December 1941 during an attack on shipping off Catania two Blenheims collided and were lost. These were followed three days later during an attack on the harbour at Argostoli when another was shot down. Then on the 12th, two out of six 18 Squadron Blenheims were shot down during an attack on a heavily defended convoy. On the 13th Ivor Broom - now a Pilot Officer - led six Blenheims on 107 Squadron in a further attack on the harbour at Argostoli. The second vic was led by Sergeant E. Crossley on his second detachment to Malta, who is described by Freddie Deeks as one of the many unsung heroes. Sadly, this courageous young pilot and his crew were shot down and killed on 24 December in an attack on shipping in Zuara harbour.

One notable and highly successful raid that took place during the afternoon of 4 January 1942, in which the only serviceable Blenheims totalled ten, from 18 and 107 Squadrons, took part. Due to the winter weather there were only four serviceable Italian airfields in Sicily and the best of these was at Castel Vetrano. The ten bombers crossed the Sicilian coast at low-level, flying up a deep valley on their way to the target. As they drew closer they could see the grounded enemy aircraft silhouetted against the skyline, presenting a perfect target. They flew across the airfield line abreast, bombing and machine-gunning the aircraft, which were lined up wing-tip to wing-tip. At least thirty of these aircraft were destroyed, many others seriously damaged and a great many service personnel killed or injured. The enemy had been taken completely by surprise and the raid provoked no opposition.

That night Wellingtons followed the above attack with another raid, destroying a further fourteen enemy aircraft. Then on 14 January in a shipping strike along the North African coast four Blenheims found and attacked a 4,000 ton motor vessel escorted by a destroyer. The merchantman was damaged, but only one of the bombers returned to Malta.

About this time a detachment on 21 Squadron arrived at Luqa, the same squadron who had supplied the six crews who had made the exploratory flight to Malta in May 1941. Had any of the original six crews arrived they would have found it to be a very different place, with the increased activity of the Axis Air Forces, the airfield being bombed regularly and Blenheims being destroyed on the ground.

On 4 February the new boys' despatched six of their crews to bomb shipping in Palermo harbour, an operation which, without any interference from the enemy, went disastrously wrong. First of all they made the wrong landfall and as they turned to correct this fault, the wingtip of one of the Blenheims touched the sea and it piled straight in. Having missed the original target the remaining five crews dropped their bombs on a goods train and a railway bridge, when they found themselves heading straight for the hills, which were shrouded in cloud. Unable to gain sufficient height to clear the hills they sought in vain for a valley. Tragically, three of the Blenheims crashed into the hillsides, leaving two shattered crews to fly back to Luqa.

Returning to base became increasingly dangerous as German fighters were likely to be waiting for them, as happened on 6 February, when three Blenheims returning to Malta from a shipping sweep, were shot down by Me 109s. There were no survivors. Five days later, three more Blenheims came in for the same treatment although, on this occasion, only one of them was shot down.

During the second half of February the few serviceable Blenheims were engaged on flying shipping sweeps off the Balkan coast, almost at the limit of their fuel endurance, although the bad weather cut down the number of successes. The Blenheim campaign from Malta was brought to an end when, due to the sustained attack on the island, it was no longer feasible to maintain the offensive. All the fuel and supplies which managed to reach the island in the convoys, which were under attack from enemy submarines, surface vessels and bombers, were needed for the defence of Malta and it's naval base of Valletta.

During March the three remaining units, 18, 21 and 107 Squadrons, or what was left of them, departed to be reformed in England with new personnel, the personnel who had served them being absorbed into Middle East units.

What had the Blenheims achieved in waging this very costly campaign? By January 1942 Rommel had only three days of supplies left for his armies and nearly all his oil tankers had been sunk, also the passage of enemy shipping from Italy via the west coast of Sicily had been brought to a halt. As a bonus, the Blenheim and its crews had been largely responsible for persuading the Germans to withdraw Luftwaffe units from the Russian Front for the onslaught on Malta.

Endnotes Chapter 6

1   *Churchill's Light Brigade; The Bristol Blenheim Bomber Crews in Action* by Flight Lieutenant James W. Moore DFC.

2   'Attie' Atkinson died on 22 March, 1950 leaving his wife and three boys and a girl to carry the family torch. *'Attie' Atkinson 'Makes Me Look Like A Bloody Hero'* by Eric Chandler, a wireless operator-air gunner in 2 Group, quoted in *Thanks For the Memory: Unforgettable Characters In Air Warfare 1939-45* by Laddie Lucas (Stanley Paul 1989).

3   Born in Cardiff and raised in the Rhondda Valley, he left school at seventeen having passed the quite difficult Civil Service Entrance Exam. He was posted to the tax office in Banbury, Oxfordshire and by the outbreak of WW2 had been promoted and moved to Ipswich in Suffolk. It was here that he saw and heard the Blenheims of 2 Group passing over his office on their way to the Continent which gave him his first thoughts about joining the struggle against Germany. It was only because of this constant air traffic over his office that he chose the RAF in preference to the either the Army or Navy. He reported for his initial training as an AC2 in August 1940. Unlike the majority of trainees which would follow him, his initial flying training was conducted in Britain, with the Battle of Britain still raging overhead. Chosen to fly twin engined aircraft, he qualified as a pilot, was promoted to Sergeant, converted onto Blenheims and was posted to 114 Squadron in 2 Group at West Raynham in Norfolk. After only 12 operations on 114 he was told to prepare for overseas. Together with six other crews, all skippered by Sergeants he was then advised that as the most experienced, he was to lead the other six to the Middle East via Gibraltar and Malta, although at this stage nobody knew their final destination. He successfully led his flock to Malta at which point fate played a hand. Due to the lack of resources on the island the AOC, AVM Hugh Pughe-Lloyd, had developed the habit of 'high-jacking' aircraft and crews passing through Malta. As a result Ivor Broom found himself retained in Malta, whilst the other six crews continued onto the Far East, eventually being killed or taken prisoner by the Japanese. Ivor Broom then proceeded to take part in offensive operations against targets in Italy, Sicily and North Africa as well as supply conveys to Rommel as part of whichever squadron was detached to Malta at the time (he flew on 105 and 107 during this period). Before long the squadron had suffered such heavy losses that Sergeantt Broom was one of the senior pilots left in the squadron and in Nov 1941 was commissioned by AVM Lloyd to lead the remnants on operations whilst the 'Tour Expired' CO ran things on the ground. Sir Ivor Broom rose to the rank of Air Marshal, having been awarded the KCB CBE DSO DFC* and AFC. He was, until his death on 20 January 2003, a very active participant in the work of the RAFA. He was also President of the Blenheim Society, the members of which have the greatest respect for Sir Ivor and Lady Jess.

Chapter 7

Desert Rescue

D. H. Clarke

250 Squadron spent the entire Second World War operating in or around the Mediterranean, taking part in the battles in the Western Desert and the invasions of Sicily and Italy. The squadron was reformed from K Flight at Aqir on 1 April 1941 and by the end of the month had received enough Tomahawk fighters to become operational. At first the squadron was used to fly defensive patrols over Palestine, but in May 1941 a detachment began to fly offensive sweeps over Syria and in June the squadron moved to North Africa to take part in the fighting in the Western Desert. In February 1942 the squadron was withdrawn for defensive duties, before it converted to the Kittyhawk fighter bomber. It returned to the desert in April, just in time to take part in the disastrous battle of Gazala, which saw the British pushed back to El Alamein. After this the squadron took part in the defensive battles on that line and then the series of Allied victories, beginning at El Alamein, that eventually saw the Germans and Italians cleared out of North Africa. In July 1943 the squadron moved to Malta to support the invasion of Sicily and a few days later moved into the new beachhead. In mid-Sept the squadron moved to Italy and flew fighter-bomber missions to the end of the war, supporting the advancing armies. The squadron was disbanded in August 1945.

'We want you to lead six aircraft fitted with long-range tanks,' Group said over the 'phone 'and 'reccy' the Eyetie landing ground at Hon.' They quoted the map reference and I soon found the small oasis on my chart, situated 200 miles of naked desert south-west of base. Base for a few days was Marble Arch aerodrome: a patch of cleared sand alongside Mussolini's absurdity in stone and marble. 239 Wing, flying Kittyhawk III's[1] on fighter dive-bomber duties, had moved there from Belandah on 18 December 1942, soon after the collapse of yet another of Rommel's ' Lines' - this time at Agheila. As a matter of fact the German defence had not been particularly aggressive and the New Zealanders, who had tried an outflanking movement in the south, barely had a look in. The Germans pulled out in a hurry and did not dig in again until the Buerat Line which was supposed to defend Tripoli. Still, we had found plenty of targets along the coastal road...

'I was 'A' Flight commander of 250 (Sudan) Squadron, a heterogeneous collection of pilots representing a large slice of the fighting allies: from Norway, France, Bombay, Australia, South Africa, Kenya, America, New Zealand, Canada, Singapore and the UK. We were, in truth, an International Squadron - and a very happy one too.

'The only other pilot who has managed to locate Hon,' Group went on pompously, 'is Squadron Leader 'Bobby' Gibbs of 3 Squadron and as you know one of his pilots was shot down yesterday - although he did manage to land and pick him up. So it's about time somebody else...'

'We were pretty matey in the desert and explanations are always more pleasant than direct orders - but it was 24th December and we all had hoped to dodge ops until after Christmas.

'We took off at 1000 and did not return until 1230.

'Well?' Group asked.

'Not much there: four Savoia Marchetti 81's,[2] a Fieseler Storch, a couple of large gliders - at least they looked like gliders - and no more than a couple of dozen tents,' I reported. 'Two or three Bredas fired at us, but they weren't very accurate. I left four 'Kittys' at 6,000 feet and went down to a thousand and made a sketch of the place. I'll send it over to you right away. Top cover couldn't find us because it was very hazy so we came back separately. That's all.'

'Didn't you strafe?' Group demanded apoplectically.

'You said 'reccy',' I retorted.

'There was a brief pause and then the voice said coldly: 'You will report to Group Captain Rosier here at once, Clarke.' Group would not admit that reconnaissance excluded strafing and remained obstinately pig-headed over the point. I was in a cold fury - if they wanted the place strafed why the hell didn't they say so. A 'reccy' was a 'reccy'; a strafe was a strafe...

'All right, Nobby,' Group Captain Rosier said at last. 'But I'd like you to go back today and finish the job.'

'I stumped out of his caravan furiously, for it was only towards the end of that stormy interview I realised that they thought I was suffering from Lack of Moral Fibre. Me!

'I had no lunch. I picked another team of five pilots. At 1315 I slammed myself into the cockpit of Gordon Troke's 'Kitty' (mine had chosen to go U/S - I didn't blame it!) and, still in a seething rage, I repeated the tedious navigation over 200 miles of featureless dun sand.

'Hon looked exactly the same as it had on the first trip: the aircraft had not been moved. I changed over from the belly to main fuel supply, switched on the guns and reflector sight, told the others to echelon starboard and then peeled over viciously - attacking the airfield from south to north. I was still so angry that I didn't bother to weave and I heard the ominous tump! tump-tump-tump! of bullets striking my aircraft as I pulled away.

'Serve you right, Clarke,' I told myself. 'Now take it easy and let Group stew until later.'

'But I was still mad. I looked back at the snaking line of five Kittyhawks as they pulled up to follow me and saw that there was no sign of black smoke from any of the aircraft on the ground.

'I cursed, waited for the others to catch up, then whipped the stick over, jammed on top rudder to fox the surprisingly accurate Breda and skidded down in a second attack from west to east. This time I kept my sights pinned to one S.M. 81; red balls of de Wilde bounced all through it; I nearly rammed the ruddy thing; and still it wouldn't burn!

'And then, as I pulled away with stick and rudder crossed - determined not to be hit by ack-ack this time - I heard Yellow 2 call out, quite casually: ' I'm force-landing 'Nobby': Been hit in the engine.' I looked back to starboard just in time to see Yellow 2 - Sergeant Tubby Palethorpe - hit the sand in a smother of dust about two miles from the aerodrome. That made me swear some more. Of all the damnable luck ... two or three guns and they manage to clobber a kite ... and on Christmas Eve too! And out of the six of us it would have to be Tubby - the largest, fattest, heaviest perisher in the whole squadron!

'I turned back and circled around the pathetic, solitary pranged aircraft at 100 feet, ordering Flying Officer Russell to keep the remaining four aircraft at 2,000 feet in case any 109s were about. I was very relieved when I saw 'Tubby' abandon his cockpit and wave - at least he was unhurt. But to be taken PoW on Christmas Eve...

'Now I liked 'Tubby': he was a genial, good-natured type who never grumbled and did his job well. Apart from that, I blamed all this on to Group and their pigheadedness - and then realised that their answer, if I went back minus one pilot, would probably be: 'Well, if you had strafed on the first trip the surprise would have been complete. Obviously they were waiting for you the second time.' Oh yes, Group would put the onus on to me all right! Moreover the Italians were none too gentle to pilots who had just strafed them.

'Keep your eyes open, Russ,' I ordered. 'I'm going to try to pick him up.'

'I put my wheels down and made two runs along the ground, roughly into wind, at 120 mph to see what the surface was like. It was horrible. Scattered clumps of sun-burned, frost-split rocks lay everywhere and the ground was sprinkled liberally with stones and boulders. From the air it looked like smooth sand - from ground level it looked impossible.

'I picked the most likely run and made a proper approach. I could get no nearer than about half a mile from 'Tubby's Kitty. The three points touched the ground together; I braked as heavily as I could; the oleos and tyres crunched protest... At 60 mph, too late to open up again, I saw the wadi ahead. It was only a shallow one with gently sloping sides and a yellow soft-sand middle. Soft sand! I heaved the stick back and belted the engine. My Kitty plunged down the slope, sagged frighteningly in the floury middle and roared triumphantly up the other side. Then, because I was so far from Tubby and knew that he couldn't possibly run all that distance in the intense heat, I turned my aircraft and repeated the mad charge across the wadi. I taxied towards him, avoiding the worst rocks. It seemed to take an age. Then he was up on my wing: 'Thanks 'Nobby',' he gasped and sweat was pumping from his pores. 'The glycol you're boiling!' There was only one thing to do. I switched off. And in the sudden silence, when the Allison stopped pre-igniting and the propeller blades clunked to a standstill, we heard the shrill whine followed by a CRUMP! One hundred yards to windward the desert exploded in a violent eruption.

'Christ! We're being bombed!'

'We both looked up, but there were only our four Kittys overhead.

'The radio crackled: 'Hallo, 'Nobby'; Russ here. They're shelling you from somewhere. I should hurry up and scramble.' Anxiously, protectively, Russ continued to orbit directly overhead, whilst Tubby and I slung everything removable out of my cockpit: parachute, revolver, lunch-basket, water bottle - we tried to take out the seat too, but we had no tools. It was not until hours later, at the post mortem that it dawned on us that the enemy gunners must have used Russell's aircraft to get our range.

'Tubby and I tried half a dozen ways of sitting in the cockpit. Bravely casual at first, we became desperate as the shells continued to burst all around us. Eventually, Tubby sat on the parachute-less seat and I sat on his left knee facing half to starboard, with my left leg cramped back and my right foot bent to the right as I had to strain my leg round the control column. I gave half a squirt on the Ki-glass and energised. The glycol temperature still showed 135°. An Allison was always the very devil to start when hot and at the most there was enough juice in the battery for three tries. Another shell exploded: Crump! I engaged. The airscrew jerked. Black smoke dribbled from the exhausts. The heavy flywheel of the inertia starter slowed. Then, at the last second, the engine fired and blasted the smoke into oblivion and cold air into the radiator. The temperature dropped suddenly to 110° - still terribly hot. I taxied as far from the wadi as possible, turned into wind, closed the hood, checked the trim and pitch, noted the glycol was up to 120° already, yelled 'OK?' over my shoulder and then opened the throttle smoothly to full power: 54 inches of boost.

'We ran straight for about 100 yards. At 50 mph the tail was up. Then the port wheel suddenly lurched - probably into a shell-hole, although we never really knew. The aircraft swung violently to port. The starboard wing hit the ground and ploughed like a knife into the rocks, stones and sand. My lateral control of the stick - especially to the left - was negligible, so was the movement of my right leg. I tried to work the starboard brake with my toes to prevent the swing, tried to pick up the wing with port aileron. It was impossible. In all, we swung through nearly 180°. I sat and watched the starboard wing disintegrate. Eventually the engine clawed us off the ground. We took off on one wheel and a wing - losing four feet of the tip and most of the aileron in the process.

'As we lifted sluggishly, another wadi dropped away ahead of us and we sank into it. We almost cleared the rocky far side. Almost. The overstrained undercart struck it heavily and when I retracted the wheels the port red light did not come on - neither would it show green. We discovered later that it was nearly torn from the wing by the blow and that all the way back to Marble Arch it just dangled underneath like a loose first tooth ready to come out.

'I had some difficulty in trimming her straight and level, but she flew surprisingly well on one aileron. Russ and the rest of the boys fell into protective formation, but we couldn't talk because I had taken my helmet off. Russ pulled ahead and jettisoned his long-range tank and I was grateful for his reminder. Obviously we would have to make a belly landing and I had clean forgotten the streamlined 44-gallon tank slung in the bomb rack. I jerked the toggle and let it go. I spent the rest of the trip back brooding with Tubby (for we could talk with the hood shut) on how the deceleration of a belly-flop would affect us without safety straps. From time to time we inspected the panels on the starboard wing, most of which seemed to be loose - the fantastic wrenching strain during the take-off having popped most of the rivets. It seemed more than likely that the slipstream would rip off the flapping wing covering before we had a chance of breaking our necks with deceleration. But we made it! Never before was old Musso's monument such a pleasant sight.

'I flew a gentle, wide circuit. I approached at a low level, put the flaps down, pitch in coarse and switched off the fuel, switched off the ignition, braced my left hand against the cockpit rim by the reflector sight. Tubby jammed one foot against the instrument panel, his right hand against the starboard switch box and clasped his left arm round my middle. It was quite a performance. I eased back on the stick, back... back ... She hit, bounced slightly, then grounded with a tearing and rending of tortured metal and a juddering of violent deceleration which

86

drove Tubby and me forward and up, so that I bashed my head (but not too hard) against the closed hood and my left arm bent under the load. The dust drifted clear. We were safe and quite unhurt. The hissing, spitting engine crackled as it began to cool.

'Tubby wound back the hood hurriedly. 'Let's get out of here!

'We scrambled out and sat on the port mainplane. Tubby offered me a cigarette and we lit up. I looked at the familiar tents and aircraft and sand, the blue sky, the dusty grey camel-thorn, even the white absurdity of Marble Arch - suddenly all these things looked different, as though I had been away for a long, long time. I felt a wonderful contentment.

'And the next day was Christmas...'

Endnotes Chapter 7

1   In 1943, the scarcity of Packard Merlin engines necessitated that the Allison engine be reintroduced yet again into the P-40 production line. The result was the P-40M Warhawk version. The P-40M was essentially similar to the P-40K-20-CU, apart from the use of the Allison V-1710-18 engine, rated at 1,200hp for takeoff and 1125 hp at 17,300 feet. The P-40M could be distinguished from the P-40K by the introduction of a cooling grill forward of the exhaust stubs. The P-40M was built solely for Lend-Lease, the contract being approved on August 24, 1942. The first P-40M appeared in November, 1942. Most of them went to the RAF, the RAAF and the RNZAF as the Kittyhawk III. The type served with British Commonwealth forces in the Far East. A number were operated in Italy by No. 5 Squadron of the South African Air Force.

2   The Savoia-Marchetti SM.81 'Pipistrello' (bat) was the first three-engine bomber/transport aircraft serving in the Regia Aeronautica. When it appeared in 1935, represented a real step ahead in Italian military aviation: it was fast, well armed and had a long range. It proved effective during the war with Ethiopia and the Spanish Civil War. Despite being too slow to remain competitive as a bomber in the latest years of World War II, it was one of the most flexible, reliable and important aircraft of the Regia Aeronautica from 1935-1944 and adapted to second-line duties in performing a wide range of tasks.

Chapter 8

'The Widow Maker'

Jack Millin

My introduction to the South African Air Force and the American B-26 Martin Marauder - known to some as the 'Flying Prostitute' - or 'The Widow Maker' - was at the Shandur Operational Training Unit in Egypt. Later in the service, still alive though still with the Marauder, I had the unusual experience of carrying bombs to Italian northern airfields, taxiing to a grassy area and then dropping the bombs! The bombs weren't fused! This was immediately after the German surrender and the idea was that the bombs - fused this time - would be going on a further journey. It was a hurried move to forestall any move by Tito to occupy part of Northern Italy. Although there were many losses during training, most crews, after completing a successful OTU, I did eventually fall in love with the sleek and beautiful Marauder, even if she was a lady of doubtful repute.

'I arrived to Egypt for training via the Air Crew Receiving Centre, London, in April 1943; Initial Training Wing, Number 2 Radio School at Yatesbury, Number 8 Gunnery School at Evanton, the *Monarch of Bermuda* to Port Said and pre-OTU in Jerusalem. On arrival at Shandur I and nine other WOp/AGs were taken to a hangar and told find SAAF crews who needed one. The good news was that my captain was a 29-year-old married man with a family, that he had been instructing in South Africa and that the observer was an ex-infantry soldier who had survived Tobruk before volunteering for aircrew. With such maturity and experience we had great assets in the survival stakes.

When the B-26 appeared in 1940 it was said to be the most advanced bomber in its class. It could claim many firsts - four-bladed props, weapon pods, all-Plexiglass nose, power-operated turrets and rubber safety-sealing tanks. A total of 5,266 B-26 Marauders were built. They were operational in the Pacific, North Africa and Europe as well as Italy. Early models had a top speed of 323 mph, a cruising speed of 258 mph and a range of 1,200 miles. The crew of six had at their disposal 11.5-inch Browning machine guns, a bomb load of 4,000lb - and a landing speed of 135 mph! Later models, after modifications and extra armour plate, only had a top speed of 282 mph. Unfortunately the early Marauder was too advanced except for the very best pilots and mechanics. A spate of fatal accidents led to the rumours of Marauders being unsafe to fly. Some statistics put matters into perspective. A total of 521 B-26 Marauders were purchased, equipping 2 Squadron RAF and 5 Squadron SAAF. Of these 154, that is 35%, were lost. Only 55 were accounted for by enemy action, the other 99 were accidents!

It appears that some crew members were a bit hair-raising. I remember well, while at OTU, having to squeeze through the bomb bay between two bomb racks when approaching the target. This meant carrying my chest parachute while manoeuvring along a nine-inch wide cat-walk, holding on to a two-rope handrail. When I was right in the middle, at 12,000 feet, the bomb doors were suddenly opened, a 'special treat' for me planned by the rest of the crew.

I recall the 0530 calls for 6 am PT sessions, arranged for that time because of the high day-time temperatures in Egypt. After a while we conspired to give it a miss. At 0615 all of us still abed had our names taken.

On Sunday, our 'day off', we were lectured on keeping fit and detailed to walk the two-mile runway picking up empty cartridge cases and ammo belt gun links which had dropped out of landing aircraft. Eventually, we thought the job was completed. The South African CO inspected the runway in his jeep and sent us back again. Nor was that all. After a walk right across a desert airfield for lunch we were presented with overalls, 45-gallon drums of paraffin and long brushes and told to wash and clean our Marauders - in the heat of the blazing afternoon sun. No one missed PT again!

After 22 months and 22 days in the Service, I joined 12 Squadron SAAF at Jesi, near Ancona, in February 1945 to take part in the last stages of the Italian campaign.[1] All the operations were in daylight, flown in two boxes of six or three boxes of four formation, against communications targets and ammunition dumps in Northern Italy and South Austria, usually at 12,000 or 13,000 feet. During the last major battle the Squadron attacked Po river bridges and troop concentrations, bombing only 100 yards ahead of 'T' markers laid by British Army units.

My last flying duty as a WOp/AG was with the Flight Commander, transporting passengers to Rome and Naples. The Commander had the distinction of shooting down a Me 109 with the four front guns of a B-26, an exploit which won him the DFC. In July 1945 I returned from the SAAF to the RAF.

I and many of my colleagues were transferred from flying to

ground duties. I became a Motor Transport driver, tackling anything from a 15 cwt pickup to a 10-ton diesel, transporting equipment from Naples to Rome, Bari etc.

In March 1946 this was relieved by a three-week home leave in the UK. When I got back to Italy I was greeted by 'Don't unpack - your early class B release has come through'. This was to allow me to return to the building trade, 12 to 18 months before my release group.[2]

Endnotes Chapter 8

1   12 Squadron was formed in December 1939. On 16 June 1940 it flew the first SAAF bombing raid against Italian forces in Abysinna when it attacked the town of Moyale using Junkers Ju 86 bombers. 12 Squadron later saw combat during the Second Battle of El Alamein operating Boston light bombers. Following the end of the war in Europe the squadron flew South African personnel home until it was disbanded.

Chapter 9

A Wimpy Pilot In Italy

Jack Challinor

Jack Challinor volunteered to join the RAF when he was 18 in 1941 and was posted to Canada where he did pilot training. In 1943 he was sent to Italy for an operational tour on Wellingtons. Conditions in Italy were very poor. His crew of five were housed in one tent about 15 x 10 feet long with no groundsheets. There were no showers and toilets were empty oil drums. There was only Marsala wine to drink and the food was very basic rations e.g. bacon from a tin which was 90% fat, eggs and bread. They managed to rig up some 'beds' using bomb fin protectors which enabled them to stow their kit bags underneath them. Most of the squadron was made up of Aussies. Challinor's crew were Jimmy Lane, navigator; John Howell, bomb aimer; Bert Lambert - WOp/AG; and David Clarke - rear gunner. There were no co-pilots in those days.

'The following four examples were the type of operations we were tasked with.

1. On 1 July 1944 six aircraft were despatched to drop mines in the River Danube at 200 feet south of Belgrade at night. The Germans were using the river to despatch supplies by barge to their front line positions and the blocking of the river could stop or delay their plans. This type of operation could only be successfully carried out during a moon period, when the river could be seen and pilots could line up for a successful run into the target. This operation was successful. There was no opposition and all aircraft returned to base safely. On 30 July the operation was repeated, but this time the Germans were ready for us, having positioned 88 mm guns on either side of the river plus a Hawser (a thick metal cable) across the river. At 200 feet the aircraft had no chance and the first two were shot down. Seeing this I dropped my mines early and, remembering something my instructor told me, I slammed down 15 degrees of flap just before I reached the enemy positions and at the speed I was running in at, the aircraft went up like a lift and I got away with it. Sometime later at a rest camp I met the pilot of the first aircraft who had been shot down. He had got out of the aircraft, swam to the riverbank and was eventually picked up by a partisan group who helped him return to his unit in Italy, via Turkey.

'2. On 19 April 1944 having attacked a target at Piombino, Northern Italy, I was turning for home when David Clarke, the rear gunner, shouted 'Junkers 88 approaching from starboard high, shall I open fire?' For a split second I thought 'could it be one of ours?' and then decided to tell the rear gunner to open fire. He immediately replied that he had hit the enemy and fire was seen coming from the cockpit area. As he did not see the Junkers 88 hit the sea, we could only count this 'kill' as a probable. However, it really was a feather in David's hat.

3. Oil wells were one of the main targets and at the de-briefing the intelligence officer could not understand how we had, what in effect was, a double exposure of the target which showed two identical lines of oil wells very close together. Further examination showed another aircraft had obtained exactly the same photograph. It was deduced that we must have both been running into the target at exactly the same height, speed and heading probably only a few feet apart, wingtip to wingtip and had not seen each other, which probably was the explanation - no lights were displayed on the aircraft for obvious reasons. How close can you get, one touch and we would all have had it!

'4. About this time the squadron received some 5,000lb bombs. They were so large that the bomb doors had to be removed and a single bomb was strapped to the aircraft with a cable. I had the doubtful honour of being the first to drop one, the target being the Ploesti oil refinery, close to Bucharest in Romania. A large raid was organised in the direction of Bucharest. About fifty miles from that target I was briefed to break off on my own, taking the enemy by surprise and bomb Ploesti with this super bomb. I dropped the bomb from about 8,000 feet and was completely taken by surprise when the blast from the bomb blew my aircraft vertically upwards with a crack like thunder. I managed to regain control and return to base not knowing the result of the raid, due to cloud over the target. You see nobody knew the effects of this new weapon in our theatre of operations at that time. It was all trial and error.

'After we completed forty sorties we could go home. The relief that we all felt when the wheels touched the runway safely for the last time was incredible and as I rolled to stop and turned into the Dispersal Area the whole crew cheered. I remember thanking the ground crew who had serviced the aeroplanes so conscientiously, they also cheered us. I had seen many an airman cry if 'his' aircraft did not return.

'We packed our kit bags and were transported to the railway station in Naples. On arrival a young Army officer who was the RTO (Rail Travel Officer) issued me with two tins of bully beef and three packets of biscuits, which were just like dog biscuits - five to a pack. These rations were for the five of us. He explained that our journey would last about three hours, but for security reasons he could not reveal our destination.

'When the train arrived I could not believe it - we were herded into cattle trucks which had not been cleaned of straw and cattle dung. Soldiers from the front line of all nationalities were already aboard. We thought for three hours we could put up with the awful conditions, but little did we know that this journey was to take three days, the destination being Taranto, which was in fact about three hours by train. What we eventually discovered from the train driver, an Italian, was that the train had the lowest priority and as he arrived at each halt, or small station, the engine was uncoupled and used to shunt trucks from one siding to another, sometimes for hours. The routing took us along the coast for much of the way, where we endeavoured to keep clean, by stripping off and going for a swim. Food now became a problem because sharing two tins of bully beef and fifteen biscuits between five did not go far. Eventually Jimmy Lane and I went in search of food when we arrived at Salerno Station. This had been the scene of the allied landings and the entire town was in ruins. The population had fled northwards, the place was dead. On our way back to the train an old woman appeared and sold us one egg for three cigarettes. The problem was how to cook it. I remembered a desert survival film I had seen and suggested we bury it in the sand. After fifteen minutes or so we dug it up and halved it. It was cooked to perfection (one hard-boiled egg), we did not have the heart to tell the others. For the rest of the journey we had to survive on our canteens of water, which we had fortunately filled in Naples. On the second day I started to itch very badly all over my chest and arms. My right arm became very swollen and in general I did not feel at all well.

'Eventually we arrived at the port of Taranto and were taken aboard a naval vessel which I think was a destroyer. Altogether I suppose there were about 200 of us and it was clear to the Medics that we were all lousy. We had to stay on deck, our clothes were taken away and de-loused and we lined up around the deck for medical inspection. I was told I had septic scabs and my arm was infected with a horsefly bite. The treatment was simple, when my turn came a matlot (Navy term for a sailor) Medical Orderly said 'Sorry made but I've got to open up those sores. Shall I do it, or do you want to do it?' I let him do it. I held onto an overhead rail, while he used what I can best describe as a scrubbing brush, to open up the sores and then with what looked like a bucket of whitewash he brushed the open sores with a large soft brush. Next came my arm which was treated with a poultice of boiling paste which was slapped onto my arm. That was the worst part. How I didn't cry out I don't know, but in front of all the others you just couldn't. I have to say the Navy were fantastic. Some of us had a hammock, but most had to sleep on deck. Fortunately it was a warm night. The food was excellent. After a few days at sea I felt better, the itching stopped and my arm healed.

'We docked at Alexandria and were transported to a transit camp at Heliopolis, near Cairo. It was here that my commission came through.

'I arrived home in need of a long leave to recover from the responsibilities and experiences of the previous year. While on leave I learnt I had been awarded the DFM.'

Chapter 10

The 'Goldfish Gang'[1]

With the entry of Italy into the war, Swordfish based in the Mediterranean area came into prominence. Swordfish of 767 Training Squadron, based in the south of France, attacked Genoa on 14 June 1940, using French bombs borrowed for the occasion. This was the first British air raid on Italy. Shortly afterwards this intrepid squadron divided up, one half going to Malta, where it became 830 Squadron, on 22 June 1940. On the night of 30 June/1 July it made its first operation from Malta, bombing oil-tanks at Augusta. From then onwards Malta-based Swordfish never ceased to be a thorn in the side of the enemy. Although the force never at any time exceeded 27 aircraft, it sank an average of 50,000 tons of shipping every month for nine months, the peak being 98,000 tons in one month. In 1942, joined by Albacores, the Fleet Air Arm torpedo force at Malta sank 30 ships in 36 night attacks, expending 67 torpedoes and losing only three aircraft.
British Naval Aircraft since 1912 by Owen Thetford (Putnam 1958)

Many famous flights have been made from that piece of Mediterranean rock which was awarded the George Cross. Spitfires and Hurricanes based on Malta won glory in defence of the island and later bombers based on it paved the way for the victorious advance on the shores of Sicily and later the Italian mainland. But to the Maltese there was an almost romantic glamour attached to a squadron of Fleet Air Arm Swordfish torpedo-bombers [830 Naval Air Squadron] based on the island. The cumbersome biplanes, with their low speeds, were like aircraft from another age and were affectionately alluded to in Malta, as elsewhere, as 'the Stringbags.' The crews of this particular squadron of 'Stringbags' were known in Valletta as the 'Goldfish Gang'. They helped to make history.[2]

The old-type Swordfish had one very great quality - one could take liberties with it. With its low speed it could be employed on missions, which would merely spell disaster for a streamlined monoplane. One such mission fell to a 'Stringbag' of the 'Goldfish Gang'.

A secret envoy had to be flown to North Africa shortly before the landings of the British and American troops. The envoy's mission was so important that he had to be landed in Algeria, complete with the means of taking himself to a certain rendezvous. Upon his reaching that rendezvous depended much of the success of the forthcoming landing operations. To accomplish his mission it was decided that one of Malta's 'Goldfish Gang' should fly the envoy to Algeria and deposit him with supplies and a bicycle. The supplies were to be contained in two large suitcases. Accordingly the gallant old Swordfish was briefed.

The bicycle was strapped to one side of the aircraft's fuselage and the two suitcases to the other, to balance the additional weight. Extra petrol tanks were fitted to the plane, but it was calculated that even with these, there would not be enough fuel for the pilot to make the return flight, so spare cans of petrol were stored inside the aircraft.

In addition, because of the extra loading of the Swordfish, the pilot selected for the run was told he would have to make the trip with only an observer. He would have no escort. In short, he would have to fly the passenger to the secret landing-place in Algeria and then, having set down the passenger and luggage, he would have to refuel his aircraft and fly back to base.

Furthermore, he would have to fly on a route that took him close to the enemy-held islands of Lampedusa and Pantellaria. On both those islands there were enemy fighter bases.

The trip looked very much like a one-way flight. The only advantage the pilot might have would be cloud cover and from reports that was highly dubious. Without concealing clouds it was a slender chance indeed that the pilot would be able to avoid the routine patrols of Italian Macchi and German Messerschmitt fighters.

'It is absolutely vital that you should land your passenger safely,' the pilot was told. 'You've got to set him down here - somehow.'

The pilot looked at the tiny spot near the Algerian coast indicated on a chart and his thoughts can perhaps best be imagined. What he said was, 'Very good, sir,' saluted and went to prepare his aircraft.

A few hours later the very full and bulging Stringbag took off. The wind whined mockingly through its stays as the pilot circled his base and then set course south-west across the waters of the sea Mussolini was still claiming as an Italian lake. Over the open sea cloud was patchy and approaching Lampedusa the sky was almost clear, like the Mediterranean skies in a tourist's handbook. The biplane, dead on course, flew close to the islands occupied by Axis troops and airmen and one can believe that the pilot handled the controls with his fingers crossed.

Brave men are said to have then own luck. Certainly that pilot deserved to be lucky. He sighted the Algerian coastline with its bright fringe of sandy dunes and still had the sky to himself. Not a Macchi nor a Messerschmitt had appeared to shoot the intrepid invader into the white-curling waves. The Swordfish arrived at the tiny speck marked on the chart dead on time, grounded and the passenger alighted. Bicycle and suitcases were unstrapped and passenger and pilot shook hands. The man whose part in the drama being played behind the scenes of one of the war's great amphibious operations mounted his cycle, wobbled a little and then pedalled away.

The pilot and observer began the business of refuelling the petrol tanks and then took off from that lonely spot in what was virtually enemy country. The Swordfish got back to base safely, after completing one of the war's most memorable flights.

But that same Swordfish was later called upon to repeat the extraordinary performance and on that occasion the Goldfish did not return to its bowl. It came down in a swamp and sank while pilot and observer struggled to free themselves. They were taken prisoner by the Vichy French authorities, but fortunately their internment was only of short duration. The invasion they had so gallantly helped to speed saw them freed and returned at length to the welcoming mess of the 'Goldfish Gang'.[3]

Endnotes Chapter 10

1   Adapted from *A Goldfish Leaves The Bowl* by Leonard Gribble (1908-1985), a prolific English writer. He served in the Press and Censorship Division of the Ministry of Information in London, 1940-45, was a founding member of the Crime Writers Association in 1953 and also wrote Westerns and books on criminology and other subjects. Gribble also wrote as Sterry Browning, James Gannett, Leo Grex, Louis Grey, Piers Marlowe, Dexter Muir and Bruce Sanders. As Leonard Gribble his series character was Superintendent Anthony Slade. Despite his volumous output he probably remains best known for his football based mysteries, namely *The Arsenal Stadium Mystery (1929)* and *They Kidnapped Stanley Matthews* (September 1950).

2   830 Naval Air Squadron was formed in Malta in July 1940. During 1940–41 the squadron carried out attacks against the Axis supply effort in the Mediterranean. These included torpedo attacks against merchant ships and their Royal Italian Navy warship escorts and also bomb attacks on port installations in Sicily and Libya. In July 1941 the squadron began operations with ASV RDF airborne radar to locate ships. Operations were mostly by night, with some dusk bombing sorties to Sicily.

3   By March 1942 830 Naval Air Squadron was so depleted that it merged with 828 Naval Air Squadron and continued operations. By March 1943 however, losses were such that the composite squadron ceased to exist. In May 1943 830 Squadron was reformed in its own right at Lee-on-Solent as a torpedo-bomber reconnaissance squadron operating Barracuda IIs. Most of the personnel at this time were New Zealanders. After completing training, in March 1944 the squadron embarked upon HMS *Furious* and subsequently participated in Operation 'Tungsten', a dive bombing attack on the German battleship *Tirpitz*. Throughout May to October the squadron alternated between the *Furious* and *Formidable* and continued to carry out operations against the *Tirpitz*. In October 1944 the squadron was absorbed by 827 Naval Air Squadron and ceased to exist.

Above: A Wimpy crew on 40 Squadron in Italy getting ready to board their Wellington.
Below: Bombs dropped by a 70 Squadron Liberator hit 'V for Victor' on 37 Squadron during a raid on the shipyards at Manfalcone, Italy on 16 March 1945. Although the bombs had not fallen far enough to become 'live' the perspex in Wally Lewis's mid-upper turret and the port inner propeller were both ripped away, leaving a large hole in the fuselage behind Squadron Leader L. Saxby, the pilot and hitting Flight Sergeant Cliff Hurst, the WOP, in the back, leaving him unconscious. 'V for Victor' limped home to Tortorella, more than 300 miles away and landed safely.

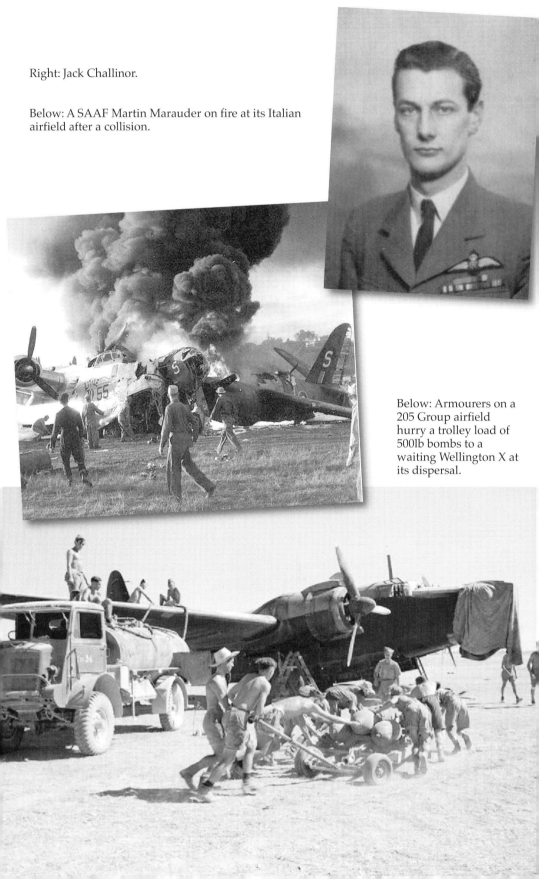

Right: Jack Challinor.

Below: A SAAF Martin Marauder on fire at its Italian airfield after a collision.

Below: Armourers on a 205 Group airfield hurry a trolley load of 500lb bombs to a waiting Wellington X at its dispersal.

Above: Liberators of 205 Group over the burning target at Budapest.

Below: A RAF 205 Group Wellington crew in Italy arriving at their dispersal in a jeep.

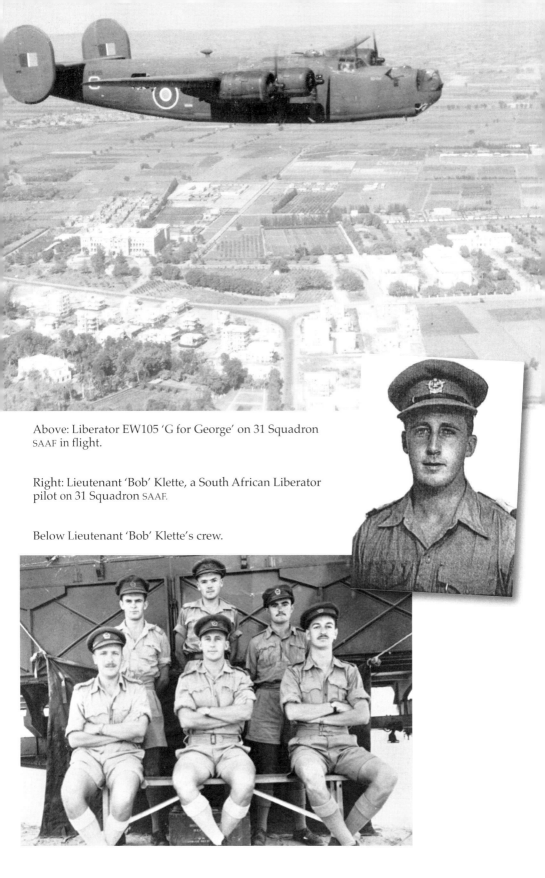

Above: Liberator EW105 'G for George' on 31 Squadron SAAF in flight.

Right: Lieutenant 'Bob' Klette, a South African Liberator pilot on 31 Squadron SAAF.

Below Lieutenant 'Bob' Klette's crew.

Above left: Bryan Jones, Lieutenant 'Bob' Klette's observer.
Above right: Warrant Officer Frank Langford, the 23-year old tail gunner on Captain William E. 'Bill' Senn's crew.

Centre, left: General Tadeusz Komorowski Bór.
Centre, right: Brigadier James ('Jimmy') Thom Durrant CB DFC SAAF.

Left: Captain Jacobus 'Jack' Ludewicus van Eyssen SAAF with friends.

Above: Young members of the Armia Krajowa - AK (Polish Home Army) putting on a brave face during the tragedy played out during the Warsaw Uprising.

Below: Armia Krajowa members jubilantly marching along a Warsaw street with a container of supplies dropped by aircraft of 205 Group.

Above: SAAF
Liberator at dispersal.

Right: Briefing the
crews.

Below, left: Lieutenant Charles Stewart Searle Franklin SAAF, 2nd pilot on Liberator KH152/F.

Below, right: Sergeant Ronald T. Pither RAFVR, air gunner; the only survivor on Liberator
EW250.

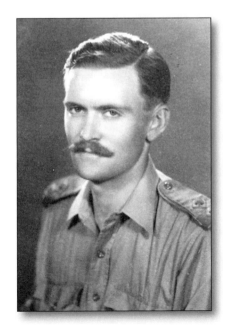

Above: Lieutenant Grattan Chesney Hooey and his crew on Liberator KG836 on 31 Squadron SAAF were killed on the night of 15/16 August 1944 when their aircraft crashed after a wingtip hit a building in Warsaw Central Square while making an airdrop at Plac Krasiński.

Below: Living conditions at Foggia Main.

Right: Lieutenant Edward Theodore 'Ted' Strever, a South African seconded to 39 Squadron RAF on Malta in the early summer of 1942.

Centre: The three-engined Cant (Z.506-B) captured in flight by 'Ted' Strever's crew.

Below: Savoia-Marchetti SM.79 Sparviero ('Sparrowhawk') three-engined Italian medium bomber with a wood-and-metal structure, being bombed up on Sicily for another raid by the Regia Aeronautica on Malta.

Above: Bristol Blenheim I L6670 UQ-R on 211 Squadron RAF preparing to taxi at Menidi/Tatoi, Greece c1941.

Centre: Air Vice-Marshal Sir John Henry D'Albiac.

Below: Pith helmeted personnel on 27 Squadron inspect the damage to a Blenheim IF.

Martin Maryland 'O' on 21 Squadron SAAF flies over the target as bombs explode among poorly dispersed enemy vehicles of the 15th and 21st Panzer Divisions east of Sidi Rezegh, where they had assembled with the intention of breaking through the British positions at Bir el Gubi.

Above: Gloster Gladiators on 83 Squadron.

Below: 'Dinty' Moore (left); Flight Lieutenant George W. Milson and Pilot
Officer Ron Millar RNZAF on 18 Squadron pictured at Blickling Hall, Norfolk
before the crew broke up and Milson and Millar were posted overseas to
Burma. 'Dinty' Moore did not go with them owing to a bout of pneumonia.
(Jim Moore Coll)

Above: Blenheim IVs on 18 Squadron photographed from the mid-upper turret of the leading aircraft head back for Luqa, Malta at low level after bombing a target in the port of Locri, Italy.

Right: Group Captain Hugh Pughe-Lloyd who commanded the detachments of 2 Group on Malta pictured with a Beaufighter in March 1944.

Above: RAF officers try on their 'Bombay Bowlers' or topees prior to going overseas.

Left: In India at the beginning of March 1942 the RAF's most modern aircraft were a handful of Curtis Mohawks (pictured) and three Indian Air Force squadrons - equipped with obsolete Hawker Hart biplane fighters and a few Lysanders.

Left: Lieutenant Colonel Tateo Katō, JAAF.

Below: A Nakajima Ki-43 being waved off by Japanese girls.

Above: A Nakajima Ki-43 of the 64th Semtai concealed under a tree.

Below: A Nakajima Ki-43 Hayabusa ('Oscar').

Chapter 11

Miracle In The Desert[1]

The target was Tobruk. Flying Officer John King, an observer on board a Wellington of 104 Squadron, watched the town appear on the horizon with mixed feelings. This, at the end of 1941, was his thirteenth operational flight. He wasn't superstitious - but thirteen did have an unfortunate reputation... King was a conscientious officer - even to the extent of leaving his personal valuables behind when on 'ops.' Just before take-off he had handed his watch to the Station Adjutant with his usual cheerful smile. 'Just in case, Adj' he had said. The Adjutant had laughed. 'I'll be here in the morning to hand it back,' he had replied. But when morning came, the Adjutant was there and King was not. Over Tobruk his Wellington had run into heavy and accurate flak. The port engine was hit and stopped. The pilot made several desperate attempts to feather the propeller, but in vain. The blades windmilled around creating a terrific drag which the remaining engine found it difficult to counteract. There was nothing left but to turn home - and hope
Desert Flight by Leslie Hunt. Born in Blandford, Dorset, on 19 July 1922, John King went to Blandford Grammar School until 1938, then left to work in a local government office. Early in 1939, wanting more than a sheltered desk, he volunteered for the Fleet Air Arm but was still waiting for call-up at the outbreak of war, so he joined the RAF instead and trained as an observer in Canada.

John King handed his watch to the adjutant just before the Wellington 'P for Peter' hauled herself off the hard-packed Kabrit sand and set course over the Canal for Tobruk. It was the first time he had left his watch behind; he felt silly trying to explain why and the adjutant had laughed indulgently and said that a lot of people felt like that before their thirteenth trip. At 2,000 feet under a thin moon they could see the line where pale sand rimmed the sea and it was like looking at a big map. South of Sidi Barrani 'One-Eyed-Joe' the searchlight woke up and waved his long white finger round the black sky in the same spot as usual; he had never found anyone yet but when they saw 'One-Eyed-Joe' they always knew where they were. King murmured, 'Thanks Jerry' and checked his pin-point on his map. Five minutes before ETA[2] he left his map table and crawled down to the bombsight.

It was just as he yelled 'Bombs gone' that 'P for Peter' shuddered as something thumped her and Wills was jinking and diving as they ran for the far darkness. In three minutes the searchlights had given them up and the flashes of the flak were a long way back. King had given Wills his course home and was arguing with Jackson, the second pilot, about the coffee thermos when the smooth note of the port engine started breaking up into roughness and sharp bangs. Wills said something about over-heating. The bangs got louder, shaking the plane like a rolling mill and when the temperature ran right off the clock Wills cut the engine and feathered before it seized.

Then the other engine was overheating. He throttled back to ease her and the altimeter needle started to slide slowly round the wrong way. He throttled on and the engine started running rough. Once more he throttled back - the engine cleared and the altimeter needle started sliding back again. They threw out the guns, the ammunition trays, the bombsight and anything else loose they could find and the needle kept unwinding.

'Can't make it, blokes,' Wills said over the intercom.

He ran in from the sea over the desert and they were so low that King could see the rocks of the coast. He said, 'Watch the escarpment, Willy. It's about a thousand feet high round here.'

'OK' said Wills and turned east inside the escarpment towards Alamein. In a few minutes he saw the Libyan wire slide under the wing about five hundred feet below. 'We're in Egypt anyway,' he said. Hartley, the wireless operator, was tapping out a position message to base.

Wills said, 'Take up crash positions' and King crawled on to the 'dead man's bed,' took a grip on a stowage bracket on the bulkhead and hung on grimly.

It seemed a long time before the jolt came - not a very heavy jolt - there was a grinding and rending and then everything was still and quiet and King smelled the thick roughness of dust in his nostrils.

Through a tear in the side of the fuselage he saw a glare near the port engine, yelled 'Fire,' grabbed an extinguisher, smashed open the emergency escape panel and jumped out. Bodies came tumbling after and he said, standing by the wing, 'It's all right. You left the landing light on, Willy.' Ahead of the plane the glare lit a sheet of flat sand spotted with stumpy camel-thorn bushes and in the backwash of the light he saw that the Wellington had her buckled nose well down and her tail slanting into the air. He said, 'Who's here? Are we all OK?'

A scream came from the tail and they swung round in fright and saw a shape twisting on the ground. King yelled, 'It's Jock' and ran up to it with the others. Barr, the durable little Scottish rear gunner, was rolling over on to his knees and they knew in a while from the salty language that he was not badly hurt. He had turned his turret to the beam and stepped out of the doors, discovering only as he fell that the tail was hoisted about eight feet off the ground. They hauled him to his feet and he was all right in a minute.

Wills switched off the tell-tale landing light and the six of them stood uncertainly in the black silence of the desert. Someone said, 'Where are we, Johnny, d'you know?' King climbed back to his map table and came out with his astro-sextant and a torch. His hand was shaking so much he had to rest the sextant on the wing, took his sight and plotted it from his tables.

'According to me we're just south of the coast between Solium and Buq-Buq' he said. 'That puts us about three hundred miles from the bomb line at Alamein. If we can get that far we can probably do a quick scuttle by night into the Qattara Depression and outflank the line.'

'I'm not walking that before breakfast,' Jackson announced. Facetiously he yelled: 'Taxi! Taxi!'

'That's about our only chance,' Barr said. 'We'll have to knock off some Jerry transport and drive back; which way's the road?'

Wills thought they had passed over the road shortly before the crash so they should be between the road and the escarpment.

'Fair enough,' King said. 'We'll have to wait till dawn to see what the form is so we might as well relax.'

'Good show,' murmured the blithe Jackson. 'Let's get stuck into some grub and coffee.'

They ate some of their sandwiches and lay on the sand, resting their heads on parachute packs. None of them was relaxed enough to sleep, though it was warm and peaceful and a million stars glowed softly over their heads.

'Good thing it's summer,' Jackson said, but Barr grunted - 'You won't think so at noon tomorrow.'

At dawn they saw the bald escarpment rising off the desert about two miles south. To the north, about a mile away, they could make out the thin black line of the bitumen road, the only road that traversed the twelve hundred miles of sand between Alexandria and Tripoli. The road was bare - no sign of a car or truck for miles - and they knew that for the time being they were fairly safe where they were. Wrecked aircraft were common in the desert and no lonely truck rolling along the desert road was likely to turn off and bounce over the camel-thorn to have a look at another one.

The road was so bare of cover it would be risky trying to stop a car by day. They decided to walk to the road at nightfall and when a truck or car came along by itself one man would step into the road as though thumbing a lift. When the driver pulled up, not dreaming that way out here the hitch-hiker was an enemy; the others would jump forward with the revolvers.

'No shooting unless we have to,' King said. 'They can play at that, too and we're out on a limb here.'

Looking over his maps that morning he found there was a waterhole marked about a mile back towards the escarpment from where he judged them to be. He and Wills walked out to find it and tramped for hours without seeing a sign of it. Back at the plane Hartley and the carefree Jackson were sleeping peacefully and Barr was watching the road. Two trucks and two cars had gone by, he reported and there had been many miles between them.

At dusk they walked to the road. King waited by the side, Jackson and Hartley spread out a hundred yards on each side of him to whistle if a suitable car approached (they would not risk covered trucks) and Wills, Ted the front gunner and Barr waited behind King. Barr was handling his revolver in a very businesslike way.

It was a long and frustrating wait. Several times the headlights came gleaming along the road and King tensed himself, but no whistle came and the lights went speeding past. A couple of them were cars, obviously just the kind they were waiting for. He walked irritatedly along to both Jackson and Hartley but they both swore they had whistled. He told them to come nearer so he could hear.

Next time the headlights neared he heard the whistle all right but by that time the car was shooting past. He walked down and chivvied Jackson again but Jackson said he could not whistle any sooner because he could not tell in the glare of the headlights whether a vehicle was suitable till it was passing him. On the long straight road the vehicles were all rolling fast.

The night seemed endless, the longest King could remember. A few more cars and lorries passed before they could move and as dawn glowed in the east he called the others and they walked despondently back to the aircraft. They ate some bully and biscuits, got a little sleep and around noon tough little Barr got to his feet and said briskly: 'What about another crack at the road?'

King demurred: 'It's not worth it by day, Jock. Not enough cover... not unless we have to. We'll try it again tonight.'

'There're some rocks up along the road. They're good enough cover,' Barr insisted. 'Let's have a go. We'll never bloody well do it by night.'

It was a spirited argument but in the end King and Wills over-ruled him and went off towards the escarpment to look for the waterhole again. It was no good; they walked for miles, saw only sand, stones and camel-thorn and walked dispiritedly back to the plane. They were staggered to find it deserted; called out and looked into the torn fuselage but the others were gone.

'Either the Jerries have been or they've gone off to the road,' Wills said grimly.

'They wouldn't try the road on their own,' King said. 'Jock might be that crazy but the others aren't.' He added a moment later, 'If it was the Jerries they might be coming back for us.'

They walked round the plane trying to see if there were any vehicle tracks and it was King who saw the German car in a dust cloud moving towards them across the desert from the road. He yelled to Wills: 'Into the plane, quick' and they ran for it, crawled through the hatch and hid down near the tail.

The noise of an engine came up to the plane; they heard tyres on the stony ground and then the engine stopped.

King was trembling. If they had not been seen running for the plane he thought they had an even chance of getting away with it.

Footsteps grated on the sand and a voice just outside the fuselage by the tail, almost next to his ear, said: 'Where the hell are Johnny and Willy! They ought've been back by this.'

Startled relief ran through him like an electric current and he yelled, 'Jock! Jock! We're in here.'

He crawled excitedly up the fuselage, stuck his head out of the hatch and saw a Volkswagen in Afrika Korps camouflage by the wing. Barr, Jackson, Ted and Hartley were grinning smugly with revolvers in their hands and beside the Volkswagen stood a sheepish German officer and two German soldiers.

'What d'you think of her?'

Barr grinned. 'How did you get her?'

'On the road. Piece of cake.' He told them how they had hidden behind the rocks and how he had walked out to thumb a lift. It had gone perfectly. The car had pulled up, he had shoved his revolver under their noses and the others came out and did the same. The officer was a doctor Barr added and spoke a little English.

They were the first Germans King had seen in the war and he looked at them fascinated. All of them wore drill slacks like himself, canvas boots and little peaked caps like skiing caps and he had to admit they did not look bad types at all. Frightened he was going to be shot, the doctor was eager to be friendly and kept saying that they were not to worry about him because he accepted the situation. He seemed genuinely sorry that no one was wounded and in need of his services.

King was delighted to find that the car had ration bags, jerry cans of water and petrol and a spade ; also a couple of empty jerry cans which Wills filled with petrol from the smashed bomber's tanks. They transferred what food they had left, a landing compass, the sextant and a few other things.

'Now what'll we do with the Jerries?' Barr asked. The doctor looked worried.

'We can't shoot 'em' Jackson said. 'Take their boots.'

The doctor looked relieved and bent to his laces.

Barr got behind the wheel and the other five squeezed aboard, King beside Barr, two on the back seat and two sitting on the back over the seat. Barr hoped pessimistically that the springs would hold. He fiddled experimentally with the gears for a while, said, 'Here we go,' and the Volkswagen jerked forward. They left the doctor and the other two Germans standing by the wing and Jackson said cheerfully after a while, 'I'll bet that bastard isn't smiling now. If he ever catches up with us he'll operate on us and we'll never be the same again.'

Barr drove east, parallel to the road but well over towards the escarpment. King had the map on his knee looking for detail to pin-point their position. The sand was flat and smooth for a while, apart from the camel-thorn, but then they stopped on the lip of a wadi that cut down from the escarpment and Barr looked dismayed at the steep, stony depth of it. He steered the Volkswagen along beside the wadi and in less than half a mile came to a spot where the banks were broken where army engineers had cut a rough road down into it and across. Easing the car down he revved up the other side and then, nervous of the springs under the heavy load, kept her moving across the sand at about twelve miles an hour, trying to steer between the clumps of camel-thorn.

King was trying to work out how they should go about out-flanking the bomb-line. About forty miles from the coast the Alamein Line stopped at the Qattara Depression, a plain of endless sand dunes, soft, drifting and trackless. Cars could not drive there; men could not fight there. It was a barren No Man's land, watched only from the air. He suggested they should leave the car on the edge of the Depression about five miles behind the line and try a fast night walk around the flank. The others said,' Good show. Good show,' and were cheerfully singing a rude song as they bounced over the desert when they came to a single strand of barbed wire running on posts across the sand in front of them. A board hung on one of the posts; Barr drove towards it and they saw on it a roughly painted skull and crossbones and the words, Achtung Minen.

He turned and drove along the wire looking for the end of the minefield and had gone several hundred yards with no end in sight when King jerked his head to one side and shouted, 'Stop. Stop! For God's sake pull up, Jock.'

Barr, startled, braked the car. King, pointing down at the sand, said,

'Look at that, will you!'

The others saw the little flat, circular thing half hidden under the sand; it looked like grey painted metal and was about six inches across.

Wills said in a stricken voice. 'We're on the wrong side of the fence. This is the minefield.'

For a while there was silence and no one moved.

'There's another one over there,' Barr said, pointing on the other side, ahead of the car.

King wondered aloud how many more there were still covered by the sand. They all wondered that and guessed that most of the mines were still uncovered.

'Well, we can't spend the rest of our lives here,' Barr grunted. 'Better stick in the car.' The wire strand was about four yards away; he swung the wheel, let out his clutch and, revving hard, they plunged towards the wire and burst through.

On the other side they stopped and King got out and walked gingerly over to one of the signboards. It said Achtung. Minen on both sides and he walked back and said disgustedly, 'What a clottish bloody thing to do.'

At dusk he estimated that they had done about forty miles. That night it grew cold and they wrapped themselves in parachute silk and slept huddled together.

In the morning they came to a couple more wadis but found tracks broken across them as before. The desert was more broken now with low ridges running down like spines from the escarpment to the sea. The car kept going up over the ridges and down into the hollows and Jackson said he was going to be seasick any moment.

Pulling over one of the ridges they almost ran into the middle of a group of men squatting on the sand. Barr braked sharply and they saw with relief that the men were Arabs - six of them, with three camels on their haunches nearby. Nearly all the desert Senussi were friendly.

'Ask 'em if they've seen any Jerries around,' King suggested. 'Maybe they can tell us where we are, too.'

The Arabs gazed without particular interest. King jumped down and an old Arab with a short, grizzled beard got off his haunches. 'Saida' King said and the old Arab nodded gravely and intoned 'Saida.' King could see a flea crawling on his neck above the dirty gelabia and, keeping his distance, held out the map and tried to ask in sign language where they were. The old man looked at the map blankly. King, Wills and Barr in turn tried to ask if any Germans or Italians were about but the old man continued to look blank. Some of the other Arabs came and stood around and Jackson said curiously, 'Look, half these types seem to have lost their left hands.'

Only then King noticed the dirty bandages round the wrists and remembered someone telling him that Arabs punished cut-throats and robbers by chopping off a hand. He told the others and Barr said, 'Come on. No future in these customers. Let's get going.' They got back in the car, keeping their hands near their revolvers and drove off.

That day was a scorcher and the desert shimmered in heat-haze so that at times sheets of it seemed to lift and float eerily above the sand, retreating before them as they drove on and then dissolving. Disembodied peaks lifted over the ridges of the escarpment, changing shape weirdly as the car moved along. Several times King would have sworn he saw little lakes shining on the sand ahead; they looked so real but they always vanished as the car came near.

In the early afternoon a vague cluster of buildings shimmered to the north and King estimated that if it was not another mirage it was probably Mersa Matruh. Barr swung the car south to skirt the Stuka landing grounds at Bagush.

Here the escarpment ran deep inland, much lower and turning east at the foot of it the car ran into a rough patch where the tyres scrabbled over thousands of sharp little stones. A sharp bang came from one of the front tyres and Barr braked quickly; their first puncture. The Volkswagen had a good tool kit and they were on their way again in half an hour. Five minutes later the other front tyre went. This time the repair was done faster but they did not like the look of the tyres. All of them were worn and the canvas was showing on both of the front ones.

At dusk King took a sight and estimated that they were between Matruh and Fuka and about ten miles south of the coast. That night it was so cold that he lay awake for hours, shivering and in the early hours of the morning, when morale is lowest, began feeling that they would never make it. So far they had not seen a single enemy and he wondered how long their luck would hold. From now on they would be running into dangerous areas.

In the morning they kept running across more stony patches and by noon, when they stopped for bully beef and biscuits, they had had three more punctures. Shortly after moving off again they had another one and this time there was a great rent in the tube. Barr threw it away and packed parachute silk inside the tyre instead. It was better than running on the rim, but only just.

Somewhere south-east of Fuka they stopped at dusk and rostered each man to take a turn as sentry through the night. Around midnight the man who was to have woken King for his turn fell asleep instead and in the morning they were shaken to find a set of heavy tyre marks ten yards from them. King was positive they had not been there the previous night.

The other front tyre blew out that morning and they had to pack this one, too, with parachute silk. As they moved off again Jackson said cheerfully, 'Well, at least we can't get any more punctures in front,' but Barr growled that it was the springs they had to worry about now. The car was juddering badly; he dropped to about eight miles an hour to nurse her along and had a hard time steering between the worst ruts in the stony ground. The day's run was less than fifty miles, King estimating when it was dark enough for a sight that they were somewhere south of Daba, the German fighter base. (They all knew Daba. The squadron had been based there a few weeks earlier - before the retreat to Alamein.)

In the morning they had gone about two miles when one of the front springs snapped with a sharp crack. They got out and had a look, but all Barr could do was put the car into low gear and keep her moving at walking speed, flinching all the time as the front of the car thumped hard on the axle. Grinding up a long slope to a ridge there was another crack and the bonnet flopped on the sand between the splayed wheels and they knew that the axle had gone.

'She's had it this time,' grunted King, looking at the snapped metal. 'Looks as though we walk the rest of the way.' He spread his map on his knee and put his finger on the spot where he guessed they were. 'About twenty, twenty-five miles to the bomb-line and about fifteen miles from the coast.' He ran his finger diagonally down to the end of the blue-pencilled bomb-line and added: 'And a damn long way from the Qattara Depression.'

'We've had the Depression,' Wills put in grimly.

'Why?' Barr demanded.

'Because it's about sixty miles down into the Depression and round into our blokes' lines,' Wills said. 'If we have to walk, we've got to do it in one night. If we get stuck out on the bundoo on our own by day down near the lines we'll get picked up for certain.'

'What about walking through the German lines?' Hartley wanted to know.

'It's been done before,' King said.

'Maybe they'll be asleep,' suggested Jackson, the optimist.

'Maybe they won't,' said Barr. 'And what about the minefields on the other side if we do get through the Jerries?'

'We're going to have to risk those whichever way we go,' said King. 'That's been done before too.'

It was too hot and too risky to walk by day - that was clear. They sat by the car to wait for the cover and the coolness of night. King and Barr walked to the top of the ridge and dropped flat on the ground when they got there. Two miles away six tanks were trundling north across the sand, dragging thick trails of dust. They watched them vanish, not so sorry now that the axle had broken, because if they had carried on they would have been roughly where the tanks passed.

Back at the car, they decided to leave everything behind but water-bottles. It was not going to be easy walking over desert in flying boots. The ration bag was still nearly half full and they hacked open the bully-beef tins and gorged themselves.

The moment the sun vanished they started walking, climbing to the top of the ridge and seeing miles of bare desert ahead. King was carrying his landing compass; he took a bearing due east, the shortest way to the line and they walked briskly down the other side. It was dark in ten minutes, but King kept them on track by the luminous dial of the compass. Around their feet the pale sand was fairly visible, but after a few yards it merged into the blackness.

For the first hour and a half it was fairly easy going. The sand was flat and not too soft and when they felt they had made about five miles they rested for ten minutes, taking off their fur-lined boots to let their hot feet cool.

At the end of the next hour Barr and Hartley were beginning to limp and they rested again. King asked anxiously if the two thought they could make it and Barr grunted, 'We've damn well got to make it... we've only got tonight to make it in.'

They had been walking again for about fifteen minutes when someone said sharply, 'Look at that!' The darkness a few miles ahead was suddenly nickering with sharp flashes and many seconds later the dull thump of the guns reached them. 'That's it,' Wills said soberly. They stopped and looked at the flashes for a while and King felt nervous excitement tingling through him. He said, 'Well, we know where we are.'

Barr commented dryly, 'They don't look very sleepy.'

'What are they - ours or theirs?' Jackson wondered.

'If they're ours we'd be pretty well in the front line now,' King considered. 'They must be Jerry.'

'I dunno' muttered Barr. 'You can't see ten yards in this darkness. We could be right in the middle of the Jerry line now.'

'If they were ours we'd be in the middle of a lot of thumping big shell bursts,' Wills remarked sensibly. 'They're Jerry. Come on, let's get weaving.'

They moved ahead again, keeping close together and looking

warily around them, particularly ahead, but the night was thick and silent. Barr's feet were hurting him a lot; he kept fairly quiet about it, but even in the gloom they could see he was limping painfully. He tried taking his boots off and walking in his bare feet, but the ground was stony and that was even worse. Wills had a knife on him, so Barr slit the heels of his boots where they rubbed him most and after that found he could walk a little more easily.

Little by little the muffled rumbling of the guns hardened into heavier, more explicit explosions and the flashes were getting nearer. Occasionally a flare splashed into brilliant light low in the sky and they knew that that was where the line was. King was steering by the stars now, keeping Altair on his right, Polaris on his left and walking at right angles between them. Without warning the flashes and thumps of the guns stopped and the front was dark and silent.

After another hour they saw a dark shape ahead and to one side and sank silently to the sand. Barr crawled a little closer to it and identified it as the covered top of a truck parked in a dug-out pen, with the sand heaped along the sides as cover from bombing. They detoured around it and headed on, but now they were going very slowly and no one was even whispering.

They passed two or three more trucks and in the back of one saw the glowing end of a cigarette. A little later, voices were mumbling off to the right. King found he was walking with his shoulders hunched, flicking his eyes about furtively. His mouth was dry and he recognised that symptom and the shivery feeling all through him as the way he felt before take-off on a raid, though this was worse. He felt like a blind man walking near a precipice. They were either in or very near the line now. Perhaps only a mile away were British troops, but in between, almost certainly, lay a minefield... a thick one. He had been putting off thinking about the mines, but it had to catch up with you in the end. He did not know whether he was more frightened of the Germans or the minefields.

In front of them the line of a low ridge cut against the sky that was a shade less black than the ground. They were moving up the slope when King sank to the ground with a gentle 'Hsss.' Then the others saw the two dark shapes on the ridge that looked like men. Quietly they moved off at an angle and as they reached the ridge found a haversack and some pieces of metal equipment. With a shattering noise a motor bike started up about fifty yards behind them and moved off somewhere.

Barr whispered, 'Look, let's walk as though we belonged here. They won't dream we're British.' He had his revolver in his hand.

'All right,' King muttered. 'Come on.' He took his own revolver out and they walked down the slope.

They passed another truck parked in a pit-shelter, then another and another. A tent loomed out of the darkness, then two more and in one of them a man was snoring. Veering slightly, they walked boldly on. Apart from the soft crunch of their boots on the sand the desert was eerily silent.

Abruptly a sharp voice shouted about ten yards away and King's nerves jumped. They sank down and froze. The voice shouted again, obviously at them and King thought he caught the word 'Halt!'

He said incredulously, thrilled, hardly believing they had come to the British lines, 'Are you English?'

A bright orange flash and a bang came from the direction of the voice and they lay flat and terrified. There was another flash and bang. For a few seconds it was silent and then all around they heard movement and the mutter of voices. King aimed at the spot where the shots had come from. Barr, doing the same, was whispering, 'Let's dive for cover.' King was drawing his legs up, bracing himself to jump and run when he saw dark shapes all round and knew they were trapped. One of the crew shouted in a strained voice, 'For God's sake, stop shooting. We're British.'

A crisp voice came out of the darkness, *Hande Hoch!* It was too quick and confusing to remember feeling. They had their hands up and as the dark shapes moved nearer they stood up, dropping their revolvers on the sand. A hooded torch shone briefly on them and they heard German voices.

Men were prodding them in the back and they walked about a hundred yards till they stumbled into a hole in the sand like a very wide slit trench. They sat in it with shadowy figures around them. A soldier arrived who spoke some halting English and they told him they were shot-down airmen. The soldier went away and they waited, shivering, huddled together for hours till the sun came and they saw they were in an area pitted with slit trenches. Two German soldiers were guarding them; others were walking casually about nearby, but a hundred yards to the east some soldiers were crouching to keep under the ridge. King asked one where the Tommies were and the man pointed east and said, 'Half kilometre.'

'Less than half a mile,' King translated bitterly. 'We damn near made it.'

The German who spoke English came back and told them amiably that the soldier who had first hailed them in the night had thought they were German and was warning them that they were heading for the minefield a hundred metres ahead. He said confidently that they would all have been blown up. Another German brought them tinned meat and biscuits and about nine o'clock a truck with an Italian driver and soldiers pulled up and the Germans pushed them over the tailboard. The truck rolled north across the sand and fifteen minutes later swung west along the coast road. Out of the back they could see a ridge held by British troops and silently watched it grow smaller.

It was only a quarter of an hour later that the truck turned off the road by a barbed-wire enclosure and as the Italians were nudging them through the gate King knew he had been there before. It was beside one of the Daba landing grounds and a few hundred yards away he recognised the spot where the squadron mess tent had been. They looked at it through the barbed wire, muttering pungently.

The cage was a square of hot sand surrounded by thick barbed wire. About twenty British soldiers were already in it, looking deadbeat. Most had been trapped in the retreat and many had dysentery and sores. About noon an Italian threw them a little tinned meat and some biscuits, but it was water they wanted more than anything.

Hours later another Italian came with jerry cans of water, but when he saw the airmen he started screaming at them and would give them nothing to drink. An army lieutenant in the cage who spoke a little Italian translated: 'He says he's been strafed by the RAF and no water for you. You'd better have some of ours.'

The night was bitterly cold again, but by ten in the morning the sun was blazing hot. At noon they were given a little water but no food.

An enormous lorry pulled up by the gate and the guards screamed at the crew of 'P for Peter' to come out. At rifle point they climbed over the tailboard and the army lieutenant and an army sergeant were put in with them. Four nondescript Italian soldiers climbed in and they were rolling fast along the road westwards again. There was little traffic on the road; a convoy of lorries shot past from the other direction, one or two Volkswagens and, strangely enough, several captured jeeps. It was annoying to see the Germans driving them.

Barr grunted, 'This is no damn good. We've got to do something fast or we've had it,' and that started the escape talk. They edged away from the guards, who were squatting by the tailboard and tried to talk naturally, breaking into rather false laughter now and then to hide the conspiracy, though none of the guards seemed to understand English and in any case the screaming of the tyres over the bitumen drowned their voices.

It took something less than a minute to decide that the obvious course was to rush the guards, capture the truck and head south-east over the desert once more for the Qattara Depression. The best time would probably be when the lorry pulled off the road for the night.

'What if they stop at some camp?' Barr demanded. 'Let's jump 'em now.'

'We're not likely to find any camp along here,' the lieutenant said. 'If we go for 'em now we'll probably have to shoot it out with the driver and guard in front. We can't get at them from here.'

'I'm game.' Barr was eager.

'It's not as simple as that,' the lieutenant said. 'There's something in the rules of war that, if you're captured and use violence to escape, they can shoot you or something if they get you again. I'd say there's a fair chance we'll be caught again, so if we have to use rough stuff let's keep shooting out of it. It might save our skins.'

Barr rather reluctantly agreed. King said seriously, 'If anyone wants to pull out of this thing he'd better say so now.'

No one said anything. They sat fairly silently while the lorry bowled fast and noisily along the road, hour after hour. They must have been doing over 40 mph, King thought and he found that the waiting, rolling farther and farther away from the lines, frayed his nerves. The road seemed deserted - that was reassuring - but the sun was getting low and they must be nearly two hundred miles from the line now. He started worrying about if and when and especially where, the lorry would stop for the night and had almost convinced himself gloomily that they were carrying on to some camp when the lorry started slowing and turned and stopped about fifteen yards into the desert

Everyone got out and two of the guards stood over the prisoners with rifles while the others put their guns down and lit a petrol fire on the sand. King and the lieutenant lounged by the side of the truck trying to seem listless. Even Barr was contriving to look timid and defeated. One of the soldiers after a while slung his rifle over his shoulder and, like a sheep, the other did the same. The drivers and the other two guards left some food cooking on the fire and wandered back to the lorry.

The army sergeant, a thick-jawed old sweat, had been edging craftily nearer the two guards with rifles. One of the guards put a cigarette in his mouth and offered one to the other man. He lit a match and as the other leaned towards it the army sergeant jumped and yelled 'Now.' He grabbed the shoulders of the man with the match, slung him to the ground and the quiet scene exploded into action. King had dived for the other armed guard; Barr, with a yell and his teeth bared had gone for the group of four with Jones and Jackson. The lieutenant had dived for the pile of guns. King had his man pinned and Wills was tearing the rifle off his shoulder. The other one was shrieking on the ground with the sergeant's knee in his back.

There was a swirl of bodies round Barr, Italians were dropping rapidly and then, as suddenly as it had started, it was over. King, the lieutenant and the sergeant had rifles and the Italians were lying on the sand looking terrified. Two of them were moaning, Bambini. Bambini.

'What'll we do with them?' the sergeant asked.

'We can't leave 'em here,' the lieutenant said. 'They'll raise a hell of an alarm. We'll have to take 'em with us. Come on; let's get going before anyone arrives.'

They prodded the Italians with their own rifles towards the lorry and the sergeant was nudging the driver back behind the wheel when King and Barr in the same moment spotted the two lorries coming down the road towards them. King yelled, 'Get 'em out of sight.' They hustled the Italians round to the side of the lorry farthest from the road and the lieutenant, swinging his rifle at their chests, hissed at them to keep quiet. King and Barr lit cigarettes and sat against the wheel of the lorry, trying to look natural. The dusk was fairly deep now and there was not much chance of their uniforms giving them away. The lorries were a hundred yards away and King saw, with a stab of fright, that they were pulling up. One after the other they braked to a stop fifteen yards from him. He was thinking crazily, 'If they speak in Italian I'll try and talk German and if they speak in German I'll try and talk Italian.'

No sound came from the lorries and the seconds dragged. The front one suddenly revved up and started again and both of them rolled on along the road.

The lieutenant was encouraging the Italians to climb hastily over the tailboard by some boot and butt work. The others climbed in after them and the truck bumped south away from the road. Not till they were well out in the desert and cloaked in the darkness did King feel he could relax. They slept out there in the truck, two of them staying awake at a time to cover the Italians, who gradually stopped their terrified pleadings as they realised they were not going to be shot.

At dawn they examined the lorry and found it was carrying only half a jerry can of water, several jerry cans of petrol, but no food except a tin of meat and a little bread.

The lieutenant said that their best chance of avoiding the enemy was to go up to the top of the escarpment and turn east there. King said immediately, 'Don't forget we haven't got a compass now. We'll have to navigate by the sun.'

They bumped slowly over rough ground along the foot of the escarpment for an hour till they found a spot where the stony bed of a wadi led up to the top in a long slope. It was a hard climb even for the powerful truck and when they reached the top steam was hissing out of the radiator cap. King dropped down to have a look at it and it was then he found the radiator was leaking. The water was well down in it and they tried to plug the leaks with strips torn off their shirts, but some water still seemed to be seeping from hidden spots.

'Well, press on and hope we find a well,' Barr grunted.

For the first half-hour's run east along the top of the escarpment the ground was flat and firm and then they topped a small rise and saw spreading sand that lay in a great basin that ran for miles. They moved down to cross it and the lorry started ploughing through the soft sand that silted up the floor of the basin. It moved jerkily, wheels spinning in the sand and the inevitable happened quite soon; she stuck fast, axle-deep.

There were boards in the back of the lorry, obviously for this emergency. They all jumped out - Italians included - dug the wheels out and put the boards in front of them. Barr took the wheel, gave the lorry plenty of throttle and she jerked out; he kept her moving to stop her sinking into the sand again while the others grabbed the boards, chased madly after the lorry, threw the boards aboard and scrambled over the tailboard. In five minutes they were axle-deep again. That was the pattern of the morning. They were bogged five times and around noon when they came thankfully out of the thick sand the engine was boiling hard.

They waited for the engine to cool but that took a long time because the sun was beating down with midsummer strength and any metal parts were blisteringly hot to touch. There was no question of topping the radiator off with their half-jerry can of water. They needed it themselves too much. King proposed a mouthful of water each, feeling that he could drink a jerry can easily by himself. In the afternoon they ran into more sand and were bogged several times again, so that at dusk King estimated they had made only about twenty-five miles all day. At that rate he hardly needed to tell the others that the trip would take about ten days. With a mouthful, morning and evening, he thought the water might last three days.

They huddled under the truck to try and keep warm that night and moved off at first light to get the benefit of the cooler hours. Barr found the sand firmer now and by noon they had made about thirty-five miles. They ate the last of their food then and in the afternoon - more sand; they were bogged again and as they came on to harder ground, King, sitting on a tarpaulin on the cab roof with his shirt covering his head, sighted a lorry ahead.

It seemed to be half on its side and they guessed - rightly - that it was a derelict. Barr drove up to it; King jumped off and ran to the bonnet, tore off the radiator cap and cheered madly when he saw the radiator nearly full of rusty water. They drained it, filled their own radiator and had a little over to put in a jerry can.

Half an hour later King sighted an untidy mess on the desert and, driving up to it, saw that it had been a food dump. Tins of vegetables and meat lay scattered on the ground but when they dived triumphantly on them they saw with over-whelming bitterness that every tin was punctured and the food destroyed.

'You always do that when you have to leave your stuff,' the lieutenant said. 'I don't think I could ever bear to do it again.' Wills would not give up the search. He went rooting around in the faint hope of finding an unopened tin and under a pile of tins (every one punctured) found two boxes of dried prunes. Grabbing a handful each they chewed them, though they were like leather and they could hardly swallow them because their throats were so dry. King thought they had made over fifty miles by dusk and guessed they had well over a hundred miles to go.

Next morning was flat, soft sand again, shimmering in heat so that they kept seeing the maddening mirages of lakes that vanished as they went up to them. Twice more they were bogged and King could see as they worked to dig the lorry out that they were all slowing up visibly. His mouth was like an old boot; he tried to stop thinking about water, but could not and it was becoming an obsession. He thought it ironic that sweating to dig the lorry out was draining more moisture from their bodies, though he noticed now that little sweat was coming out of him. The jerry can was nearly empty.

That morning he saw what looked like a mark on the desert ahead and as they came nearer it began to look like one of the posts that mark a water-hole. In the heat haze his eyes, aching from days of glare, could not be sure and he went through agony as they got nearer and nearer until he saw it was a water-hole and gave a croaking cheer. Barr drove for it. King jumped off with a jerry can and ran, followed by the others. He flopped down by the rocky rim of the water-hole and looked stunned at the black sludge below. 'It's oil,' the lieutenant said quietly. 'May have been done by our blokes in the retreat.'

They went back and climbed into the lorry and lay there silently as it moved off again. Jackson was first to speak, saying, 'It's a great life if you don't weaken' and King looked at him a little sourly. Jackson grinned and winked back with a little sideways nod of his head; it was not much of a grin, more of a grimace on one side, but it was a good effort and oddly encouraging. It struck King how alike they all looked, burned nearly black by the days of the sun, scruffy with beard stubble and tangled hair and with the fine sand caked at the corners of their eyes and mouths and in the nostrils. His lips were dry and cracking painfully. The army sergeant was still keeping a rifle by him but the Italians huddled apathetically in a corner of the truck.

At noon they stopped, had a mouthful of water and lay in the shade under the lorry until Barr said, ' No good hanging around here. Let's get cracking again.' King climbed back on top of the cab and the effort and the sun beating on him made his head swim and his eyes hurt. As Barr was getting in behind the wheel King shouted, ' Just a minute, Jock, I can see some water over there.' He knew it could be only another mirage but it looked so real about two hundred yards off to the right that he started getting down from the cab.

The lieutenant said, 'Take it easy, Johnny. We might come to a well soon,' but King had dropped down from the lorry and was plodding over the sand. He heard someone saying wearily. 'Don't be a bloody fool. Come back,' but kept doggedly on. A detached corner of his mind knew it was stupid, but the rest was a woolly obsession about water.

Even when he was ten yards from the pool and it had not vanished he still did not really believe it. He had to get down on his knees and dip his hands in it before his mind cleared and he turned round and started shouting. They thought he was crazy until he threw some water in the air and they saw it sparkle and came running across. There was a lot of shouting and they lay on their bellies by the edge, splashed their faces in it and sucked it up. The lieutenant said, 'Don't drink it too fast.'

The pool lay in a shallow saucer of sand about twenty yards across and the water was a milky colour from the sand grains in suspension. After stirring it up round the rim they kept moving about to clearer patches, dipping their heads in. Barr went back and drove the truck over and they filled all the empty jerry cans and the radiator, then took their clothes off and lay in it. Instead of being warm under the sun the water was surprisingly cool and they never found out where it came from or how it happened to be there. The only possible explanation seemed to be that it came up through some spring in the rocky layers under the sand. As far as they were concerned it was a miracle, an explanation which the Italians seemed to accept devoutly.

They did not stay long by the pool; everyone was keen to move and so elated and restored by the miracle that they felt that luck or some guardian angel was going to see them safe.

After so long in the empty desert King was feeling that they would go through without seeing an enemy. Only later he realised it was wishful thinking, shying away from the fear of what would happen if they were caught. The cowed Italians in the back of the truck would doubtless exaggerate what little violence there had been to excuse their own carelessness.

The lorry bogged in the sand two or three times more that afternoon, but no one minded so much now except the Italians who were elbowed out of the truck to help (rather lackadaisically) with the digging out.

That night they really began to feel hunger for the first time and King felt pinpricks of doubt sapping his new confidence. He had been praying for days that they would run into a stretch of hard smooth sand but it did not look likely now. He and Barr talked about moving down off the escarpment again but it would have meant running north towards Fuka, doubling their chances of meeting enemy patrols, so they shelved the idea.

More soft dunes in the morning and Barr flogged her across them in low gear. She ground up a long, eroded slope where the ground was hard and stony, dipped into more dunes and bogged again. They scrabbled the sand away, jammed the boards under the driving wheels and when Barr pressed the starter the engine turned gratingly but did not fire.

He tried again and again and again, but there was only the metallic whining while the others stood round looking at the bonnet, willing it to start. King called, 'Watch out for the battery. We can't push her here.'

Barr swung out of the cab and hoisted the bonnet and he, the lieutenant and the Italian driver poked about vainly trying to find out what was wrong. He tried the starter again but she would not fire.

'How far are we from the bomb-line?' the lieutenant asked and King said in a strained silence he thought about ninety miles. The butterflies were awake in his stomach again. Jackson said, 'Taxi!' but his voice sounded half-hearted.

'She's got to start,' Barr said flatly and went back to the engine. An hour later he looked up and shrugged.

They lay under the lorry and chewed some prunes. Afterwards all the mechanically-minded ones started systematically taking the engine down, laying the pieces on a tarpaulin. It felt better to be doing something. No one had started to talk about the alternatives yet. In a way, there were no alternatives.

Wills suddenly said, 'Hullo. Look at that!' He stood up and stared across the desert and the others looked and saw a cloud of dust.

'MT of some sort,' said the lieutenant.

King ran to the top of a hillock of sand a few yards from the lorry. 'There are two of 'em, whatever they are,' he said and a minute later added grimly, 'They're coming this way.' He could see the two dark shapes in front of the dust trails and thought at first that they were tanks but they seemed to be moving too nimbly. 'Jeeps,' he said at last. 'They've seen us all right. Heading straight for us.'

'Get under the lorry,' Barr yelled. 'We might be able to knock 'em off.' He had one of the rifles and was jabbing the Italians into movement. The jeeps were coming up fast. King could see men in them; realised how exposed he was on the hillock and dropped down behind it. He had a wild idea he might be able to start a diversion and wished he had brought one of the rifles with him.

He could see the lorry round the side of the hillock, but not the jeeps, though from the sound he knew the jeeps must be less than a hundred yards away and his insides felt in a knot. An Italian under the lorry started screaming for help and suddenly the tearing clatter of machine-guns shocked the ears.

Bullets were whanging against the truck and he pressed himself instinctively against the hillock. A lull, then two more quick bursts of machine-gun fire. Hoarse shouts came from the lorry and edging round the hillock he saw the others crawling out from under it with their hands up and one of the Italians waving a dirty white handkerchief.

God, should he stay out and die of thirst or join them and a voice came from one of the jeeps saying, 'What'll we do with this bloody lot?' It spoke in English.

A moment of stunned silence was broken by a babble of voices. Barr was shouting. 'Hey, are you English?'

'Don't move,' a voice said. 'Who are you?'

'English... RAF... we're escaping,' Barr shouted. The babble broke out again and people started shouting wildly. King cautiously lifted his head above the sand and saw four British soldiers by the jeeps shaking hands with the others. He walked down the sand over to them. A burly man with captain's pips was explaining that they were a party of the Long Range Desert Group. King had heard a lot about their brazen sorties far into enemy territory.

Wills had an angry red bullet score across his back; he had taken his shirt off and one of the soldiers was dabbing some stuff on it. He was the only casualty.

'You're pretty lucky,' the captain was saying. 'This wouldn't happen again in a million times. You're a hundred miles behind the line here. We only came out to look for a German officer who's escaped from us. We had him at our base so if we don't find him we'll have to pack up, or he'll give us away.'

King asked where on earth they had come from and Jellicoe, the captain, pointed behind and said vaguely. 'A couple of miles back there.' He added seriously, 'Don't be too happy. You're not very safe out here with us, but we'll do our best for you. You'd better come back with us. That lorry won't go again.'

King turned and saw the lorry's cab and bonnet riddled with bullet holes.

Jellicoe tossed the Italians a packet of iron rations and the rest of them crammed somehow into the jeeps. After bumping several miles over the desert out of sight of the Italians, they turned inland, coming to rugged, hard country where the jeeps left no tracks. Near a clump of rocks the two jeeps stopped, but King could see no signs of life anywhere. Jellicoe, beside the driver, was looking at another escarpment that rose steep and bare like a cliff out of the desert half a mile ahead. He murmured, 'All right. Next point.' The jeep moved off to the left a hundred yards and stopped again. In a few seconds Jellicoe said, 'OK' and the jeeps moved on and stopped in another hundred yards. 'All clear,' Jellicoe said and the jeeps moved on towards the cliff.

They were still fifty yards from the cliff and King was wondering what it was all about when he saw the face of the cliff at the base wrinkle and a part of it rose in the air, showing a dark space behind. He was looking at it goggle-eyed and Jellicoe was laughing as the two jeeps rolled into the cave and the sand-camouflage netting dropped behind them like a theatre curtain.

A very big man with a moustache, drill shorts and desert boots was there and Jellicoe introduced them to Colonel Stirling, leader of the Group. Nearly everyone in the Middle East had heard about Stirling but few people seemed to know him.[3]

Behind the netting quite a lot of light filtered through and they could see that the cave was actually a wide, long space under an overhang of the cliff and there were another dozen soldiers and a lorry there. Stirling was saying wryly that it was not a very healthy spot at that moment.

'We'll try and get you back,' he said, 'but the Jerries have broken our supply route through the Depression and now that this Jerry has escaped we may have to evacuate this. Meantime we've got plenty of food, so relax and do just what we tell you.'

King and the others did not move out of the cave for two days, though they were quite happy to lie there in the shade eating bully beef and pickled onions. The cave, the men and the operations fascinated them. The jeeps went out before dusk and in the morning they watched them coming back, stopping for a few seconds by the pile of rock half a mile away, turning to stop at the next check point and then the next and moving on to the cave.

Nearly every time the machine guns had to be cleaned. King gathered that the airfields around Fuka were the favourite hunting grounds.

Late on the third day Stirling said, 'You're flying home to-night... I hope.' He would not tell them how, but later motioned them into the truck and Jellicoe drove them out into the desert. At dusk they were moving along the smooth bed of a wadi that cut down to the flat coastal desert from the heights of the escarpment. By the time it was dark Jellicoe was heading confidently across the bare sand, steering by compass. About forty minutes later he stopped and some of the soldiers who had come in the truck spread out in the darkness with rags and tins of petrol.

It must have been two hours before they heard aircraft engines and soon the sound was circling somewhere overhead. Jellicoe flashed a torch and a line of flares sprang up along the sand where the soldiers had gone.

'Stick together and move smartly when I tell you to,' Jellicoe was saying. 'It's not healthy to waste time on these junkets.'

They saw the big transport low, running up to the flare-path and then it was trundling over the sand, braking hard. They were running towards it as it turned at the end of the lights; a door in the side opened and one by one they were jumping through it like trained dogs going through a hoop. The engines blared and King felt the familiar bump and rumble of take-off; the propellers changed pitch and he knew they were flying.

He was lying between Jackson and Wills on some blankets on the floor feeling cold and restless. There was nothing to see out of the windows except blackness, but after half an hour he guessed they had crossed the line and leaned over and told Jackson.

'Yeah,' Jackson said. 'This junket's just about saved my bacon. I've got twelve days' pay coming.'

King's first operational tour ended in July 1942 without further incident. Less than a year later, on Tuesday 4/5 May 1943, Flight Lieutenant King was the navigator on Halifax JB915 on 78 Squadron at Linton-on-Ouse; one of 596 bombers sent to raid Dortmund. On the eve of the thirteenth trip of his second tour of operations he felt the old premonition again. He gave his watch once more to the adjutant, talked a mess WAAF into bringing him two extra dinners and three hours later a fighter set them on fire over the Dutch border.[4] This time he got out by parachute, lost his flying boots on the way down and landed in a field. He had to get a pair of boots - that was the first thing - and then contact the Dutch Organisation. After an hour padding about in his socks he saw a white farmhouse, took the plunge and knocked on the door. A man opened it. 'Are you Dutch?' King asked.

'Ja, ja,' the farmer said and it was not till the German police arrived an hour later that he discovered that the farmer thought he had said 'Deutsch.'

He learned a lot more German behind barbed wire. In Stalag Luft III, King worked on the famous 'X' Organisation, the escape society in the camp, though (perhaps luckily) he did not draw a 'ticket' for the mass break-out of March 1944 when the Gestapo murdered fifty out of 76 escaping Air Force officers. Freed eventually by the liberating armies, he left the RAF in 1945 and married Diane, a Blandford girl whom he had known since he was a schoolboy. He became a teacher and the father of two daughters, but after four years of quiet country life went back to the Air Force and was a navigator (and adjutant) on 25 Squadron, flying jet night fighters from a base in Kent. He was granted a permanent commission as from 1 April 1952. On 21 May he was in a Lancaster which caught fire in the air. The pilot tried to get down on West Malling airfield, but at one minute past midnight, half a mile short of the runway, the plane crashed into an orchard and King and three others were killed.

Endnotes Chapter 11

1   *Escape - Or Die* by Paul Brickhill.
2   Estimated Time of Arrival.
3   Colonel Sir Archibald David Stirling DSO OBE (15 November 1915-4 November 1990) was a Scottish laird, mountaineer, British Army officer and the founder of the Special Air Service.
4   JB915 crashed near Ahaus. Squadron Leader J. H. B. Chapple and four of the crew were taken prisoner. One crewmember was killed.

Chapter 12

The Setting of the Rising Sun

Even in 1945 the bomber forces in Burma were very much in the same position as Bomber Command in the early days, full of vigour and high hopes but as yet still small and weak and a little uncertain, yet having much of the gallant spirit of those early Whitley and Hampden boys. Let me tell a little of some of those early Far East bomber sorties, as it was told me by a Blenheim navigator. In the days when four-engined bombers were hitting at Germany, a lone squadron of Blenheims flew out to Rangoon. As soon as they arrived at their new base, they were assembled and welcomed with stirring words and encouraged by assurances that now they would be operating under ideal conditions and, of course, always with fighter cover. This was excellent news to the Blenheim boys who had just come from the discomfort of the desert, where fighter cover was an unheard-of luxury. The celebrations that followed were rudely interrupted by news of immediate 'ops.' The briefing was simple. A forward aerodrome was surrounded by Japs and was to be evacuated by air. A white sheet laid out on the airfield would indicate that it was safe to land. And, of course, fighter cover would be provided throughout the attack. 'Fighter cover' was duly provided, one lone Mohawk. Luckily, this force was doubled by the arrival of a gentleman known as 'Handlebars' in honour of his vast mustachios. He insisted on coming along in a Tomahawk. And as it turned out, this 'fighter cover' was more than equal to its task. The whole force flew out peacefully to the aerodrome and circled it, but there was no white sheet. Then suddenly seventeen Jap fighters, Zeros, came screaming at them out of the sun. The Japs had captured the airfield and were sitting up aloft waiting for the relief. The Jap fighters were terrific in their dash and determination. Yet the only aircraft that was hurt had his aerial pushed off by a Zero which did an inverted loop and attacked him head-on, flying upside-down at a phenomenal speed. Meanwhile, the 'fighter cover' who could by no means compete with these fantastic aerobatics, but knew how to shoot, hacked down seven of the Zeros before following the bombers home. They all landed safely, that is, all but 'Handlebars'. He was missing and they were afraid he had 'had it'. However, a few hours later he turned up. He had lobbed down at another forward aerodrome, refuelled and collected some more bullets and gone back to shoot up what was left of the seventeen Zeros parked on the airfield perimeter.

Wing Commander E. W. 'Bill' Anderson OBE DFC AFC. **Anderson was a schoolmaster in peacetime and joined the RAF in 1940 as a Pilot Officer in administration. The death of an air crew friend led him to volunteer for flying and, despite 'advancing age' and a suspect right eye, he managed to pass on to training in Canada and then on to bomber operations on 9 Squadron at Honington. He soon discovered another inherent 'weakness' - he was air-sick every time he flew. He went on to make a name for himself as a wing commander and a Master Bomber in the Path Finder Force.[1]**

60 Squadron moved to Burma in February 1941. After the outbreak of war against Japan the squadron fought in Malaya. Blenheim Is L4912 and L4915 remained in Burma and they were destroyed on 20 and 21 January 1942 respectively. L4912 had been damaged beyond repair during a sortie in Burma and L4915 was destroyed by enemy bombing. When the war against Japan broke out on 8 December 1941 60 Squadron was ordered to attack Japanese shipping near Kota Baru. L4913 was shot down by Japanese anti-aircraft fire over the Gulf of Šiam while attacking the 9,794 gross ton freighter *Awagisan Maru*, which was commissioned by the Imperial Japanese Navy to transport troops. Along with its sister ships *Ayatosan Maru* and *Sakura Maru*, it was carrying around 5,000 troops during the landings at Kota Bharu. The pilot of L4913, Flight Lieutenant William Bowden, survived the crash and was the first allied airman captured by the Japanese. He was imprisoned at the Zentsuji PoW Camp where he remained until late June 1945. He was then transferred to Tokyo 12D Camp at Mitsushima where he was eventually freed in September 1945. *Awazisan Maru* was bombed by a Lockheed Hudson of 1 Squadron RAAF, set afire and was abandoned to drift. It is believed that the freighter sunk or was subsequently torpedoed by the Dutch submarine K-XII. The invasion of Malaya preceded the attack on Pearl Harbor by an hour and a half, making it the first Japanese campaign of World War II, likely making the *Awazisan Maru* the very first casualty in the war.

On 24 December 1941 the remnant of the squadron's ground crew and a few of its air crew, having lost all their aircraft in action, sailed from Singapore on the SS *Darvel* to Burma. They arrived in Rangoon on 1 January 1942 and were joined on 7 January 1942 by 113 Squadron and a couple of 45 Squadron's Blenheim Mk IVs. 60 Squadron's spare aircrew were assigned to 113 Squadron as needed. Because the three squadrons lacked both aircraft and supplies they were seldom able to put more than seven aircraft up at one time, so they tended to operate as one. 60 Squadron's Blenheim aircrews manned 113 Squadron's

Blenheims for the first bombing raid on Bangkok and participated again in the second one later in January. The Squadron suffered heavily at the hands of the advancing Japanese forces and was declared non-operational and moved to Asansol, West Bengal along with 45 and 113 Squadrons. Once in India the Squadron was re-equipped with Blenheim IVs.

On 22 May 1942 nine Blenheims on 60 Squadron at Asansol flew to Dum Dum for a strike against the Japanese airfield at Akyab in Burma. Initially it was planned that six bombers would fly up-river to attack targets there, while three others would attack the airfield. In the event, only the latter three finally prepared for take-off, but one suffered engine trouble and did not get away, while a second returned early with other technical problems. Only Blenheim IV Z9808 of 60 Squadron flown by Warrant Officer Martin H. 'Paddy' Huggard managed to reach the target. The Blenheim dropped its bomb from low-level and sped off out over the Bay of Bengal at wave-top height and was attacked by three Ki-43 Hayabusa ('Peregrine Falcon') 'Oscar' fighters from 64 Sentai. Despite their element of surprise the Blenheim crew had spotted a number of 64th Sentai Ki-43s scrambling after them as they flew over Akyab. First off in pursuit of the enemy bomber was ten-victory ace Sergeant Major Yoshito Yasuda, who soon caught up with the Blenheim and dived in to attack. Fortunately for the three-man Blenheim crew (Sergeant Jack Howitt was the third member, serving as navigator), their turret gunner, Flight Sergeant 'Jock' McLuckie proved to be a crack shot, despite having never before fired his guns in anger. He hit Yasuda's 'Oscar' on its first pass and the JAAF pilot was forced to return to Akyab.

Captain Masuzo Otani then took up the attack, which lasted for 35 minutes but he too fell victim to a well-aimed burst from the Vickers 'K' gun and had to retire back to Burma. Having survived an estimated 25 attacks, McLuckie finally scored hits on the lead fighter flown by Japanese ace (18 victories) Lieutenant Colonel Tateo Katō, who commanded the Sentai. As Katō pulled up after making his first diving pass on the Blenheims, McLuckie raked the fighter's exposed belly with a long burst. The Ki-43 started to burn and crashed into the sea. Realising that he would never make it back to Akyab, Katō half-looped his stricken 'Oscar' and purposely dove into the sea - he had advised his pilots on numerous occasions in the past to perform just such a manoeuvre if hit badly over the water. The two Japanese pilots reported the terrible news (they also reported that Katō has shot down the bomber, which obviously not true). The Blenheim returned to India unscathed by the Japanese attacks.

Katō was posthumously promoted two steps in rank to Major

General and was honoured by a special State Shinto ceremony at Tokyo's Yasukuni Shrine as a 'god of war' in mid-October 1942.

Katō was born and raised in present-day Asahikawa, Hokkaidō. His father Sergeant Tetsuzo Katō was killed in the Russo-Japanese War. He graduated from the 37th class of the Imperial Japanese Army Academy in 1925 and enrolled in the Tokorozawa Flying School two years later. In May 1927 he was posted to the 6th Hiko Rentai (flight regiment) in Pyongyang, Korea. His flying skill with the Kawasaki Ko-4 biplane fighter (a licence-built Nieuport-Delage NiD 29) was shown to be so outstanding that he was selected to become a flight instructor at Tokorozawa in 1928. In 1932, Katō was promoted to head instructor at the Akeno Flying School, the premier air academy for the Imperial Japanese Army Air Force. In 1936 Katō became commander of the 5th Rentai and with the outbreak of the Second Sino-Japanese War in 1937 he became commander of the 2nd Daitai, equipped with Kawasaki Ki-10 'Perry' biplane fighters, which quickly achieved air superiority over northern China. Katō claimed nine Chinese fighters during his rotation, making him the top-scoring Army pilot in China during the period 1937-41.

Katō returned to Japan in 1939 to attend the Army Staff College and was assigned to the headquarters staff of the Imperial Japanese Army General Staff. He also visited Europe on assignment together with General Hisaichi Terauchi and inspected the Luftwaffe in Germany. During this period he was also promoted to major. In 1941, with the start of the Pacific War, Katō was again given a combat command – this time as commander of the 64th Sentai, based at Guangzhou, China and equipped with the latest Nakajima Ki-43 Hayabusa fighters. His unit participated in the early stages of the war, especially distinguishing itself during the Battle of Malaya. The 64th Sentai was based at Dương Đông airfield on Phú Quốc, Viêtnam's largest island to provide cover for the Japanese invasion fleet bound for Malaya and to attack ground targets in Malaya and Burma. The 64th Sentai had its first combat experience against the Flying Tigers on 25 December 1941, escorting a bomber raid on Rangoon. Under Katō's command, the unit recorded over 260 aerial victories over Allied aircraft. He disallowed individual victory credits for the sake of teamwork. Katō was promoted to Lieutenant Colonel in February 1942. Katō's heroism had considerable propaganda value and the Japanese government sponsored a film entitled *Katō Hayabusa Sento-tai* glorifying his life story.

On 30 March 1943 an English Argentinean from Estancia Dos Hermanos, Los Pinos, Richard 'Ricardo' Campbell Lindsell, who had joined the RCAF, was appointed Squadron Leader. Lindsell had been educated at Stowe School in England. By the time he joined 60 Squadron its Blenheims had flown numerous missions against the Japanese in Burma and were reaching the end of their useful operational life and needed replacing. In May the Squadron was stood down while replacement aircraft were sought. By August the decision had been made to re-equip the Squadron with Hawker Hurricane IIc fighter-bombers. Training was commenced in August at Madras and by November the Hurricanes were providing escort duties. In January 1944 the Squadron began ground attack missions and troop support against the Japanese in Burma. During one month in 1944 the Squadron completed 728 sorties and also received considerable praise for the accuracy of its bombing by allied ground troops. For their efforts and his leadership Lindsell was awarded the DFC. In May 1945 the Hurricanes were replaced by Thunderbolt fighters. These remained in service with the Squadron until 1946.

'The Jap fighters in those days were a peculiar mixture' says 'Bill' Anderson. 'They would stay out of range of the Blenheim machine guns and lob cannon-shells hopefully at them. They would not come in to mix it. Yet if they were shot down, they would parachute to earth with Tommy-guns blazing, spraying bullets in all directions and fight to the bitter end. On every sortie the bombers would be shadowed and nibbled at, but they only lost one aircraft. He crash-landed and the Japs shot up the wreckage but the gunner escaped. He set off into the jungle, met a local chieftain and tactfully presented him with his Irvine jacket, one of those magnificent, wool-lined, leather jerkins. The worthy potentate was so delighted that he dressed the lad up as a Burmese and drove him on a bullock cart to safety through the Japanese lines.

After a time, the big Japanese push began and it was a case of evacuating one aerodrome after another. The Blenheims did a lot of useful work, however. Once they caught a regiment of Japs making whoopee in a native village and riding elephants up and down the streets. Once they caught a fleet of boats and the river ran red. But gradually they were forced back. And the tale is told how once, while the squadron commander was in conference with General Alexander, the Japs surrounded the camp. The Blenheims were made ready to take the general and his staff to safety, but he would have none of it. They were soldiers and they had Tommy-guns and a car and they would shoot their way out. And shoot their way out they did.

The Blenheim boys had plenty of fighter cover by now and they needed it, for the Japs put in all they could to knock out the bombers. This fighter cover was the AVG, the American Volunteer Group, a collection of sportsmen who toured the countryside accompanied by a sinister celestial who apparently paid them 400 dollars out of his cash-box - yes, just like that - every time they downed a Jap aircraft. Later on, some Hurricane boys came along, too and then a peculiar phenomenon developed. The AVG types would now notch thirty Zeroes whereas previously their scores had only been 15, but the Hurricane boys would only bag a couple. It is said by some curious coincidence that there were always plenty of dollars flowing in the RAF, as well as in the AVG mess! After the Americans had gone the Hurricane boys' bag apparently went up with a most remarkable bang!

But the Japs kept pegging away at the Blenheim airfields. Their Mitsubishi bombers, fitted with an automatic revolving gun in the tail that sprayed bullets around in all directions, would come over in formation. One special type would fire off a red cartridge and all the spectators promptly went to earth, for that was the signal for the formation to drop. This leader was not always at the head of the flock and if he could be shot down the other Mitsubishis were liable to wander about in a lost fashion until they, too, were put out of their misery.

Yet, slowly but surely, the Blenheims were getting broken up. At last, only one was left. And this aircraft was flown safely back to Calcutta. I learned much of this tale from the navigator of that last Blenheim. He wore a wound stripe which he had earned in the very early days of the war when a cannon-shell burst in his face over St. Nazaire. He was lucky, for his was the only aircraft of the squadron to return that day. He had no other decoration though he had done about a hundred sorties. Indeed, he told me that the only man who was decorated on the squadron during those troublesome times was the squadron cook. This worthy had already proved himself in the desert, for one day, hearing the clatter of guns, he had left his pots and pans, gone outside in a huff and shot down a Me 110. The exploit which was to earn him the Military Medal was even more remarkable. The Japs were advancing up a road a few miles away and looking out of his cookhouse door, he saw a party of Ghurkhas marching smartly but in quite the wrong direction. The cook was horrified and stopped the Corporal Ghurkha in charge, who explained that they had lost Sahib Father, an officer and were going to look for another, whereupon the cook, assuring them that he was indeed the father of all the sahibs and officers, led them back into battle. At least, he tried to lead them, only they insisted on forming a shield round him with their bodies lest they should lose their newly-acquired progenitor and strategist. So they went cheerfully back to the fighting and set about the Japs.

But at last the tide of war turned in the Far East, as it had turned two years before in Europe. The bomber force was to be built up as had been Bomber Command in England, to hammer away with the Americans at the Jap cities. And now that I had finished the polar flight, I was wanted to go out and to lend a hand. I didn't tell Mary for I knew how it would hurt her. Besides, I argued, it might never happen.

'From Greenland's icy mountains, From India's coral strand.' But the atomic bomb saved me, as it saved millions of other men.

Endnotes Chapter 12

1   *Pathfinders* by Wing Commander Bill Anderson OBE DFC AFC (Jarrolds London 1946).

Chapter 13

The Forgotten Air Force

When Britain declared war on Germany in September 1939 urgent operational requirements in other theatres of war made it impossible to reinforce or modernize the pre-war air force in India. Until Japan's involvement in the war in December 1941 the Royal Navy had protected India's 3,000 mile coastline and her armies had defended her land frontiers and maintained internal stability. As a result, when Air Chief Marshal Sir Richard Peirse arrived in India at the beginning of March 1942 he discovered the RAF had no more than four squadrons. The most modern aircraft were a handful of Curtis Mohawks and three Indian Air Force squadrons - equipped with obsolete Hawker Hart biplane fighters and a few Lysanders. In Burma the four fighter; three bomber and two Army Co-operation squadrons lacked the necessary repair and maintenance facilities and the only early warning system was maintained from inadequate observer posts. Early Japanese advances overwhelmed both air and ground forces and the sadly depleted squadrons were forced to retreat with the 14th Army to Indian hinterland. As the war progressed British material personnel were reserved mainly for the Home front and the 14th Army sardonically named itself 'The Forgotten Army'. The Air Force squadrons which supported and supplied it might justly have been called the 'Forgotten Air Force' as they too seemed always at the end of any list of priorities. Fortunately no further Japanese attacks were launched on India or Ceylon before the 1942 Monsoon giving the Allies the opportunity of building up their depleted squadrons.

In January 1942 159 and 160 Squadrons reformed at Molesworth and Thurleigh respectively and were equipped with Liberator Mark IIs. At the end of January 1942 159 Squadron's ground personnel embarked for the Far East. Its Liberators flew out via the Middle East in June but became involved in long range bombing raids from Palestine and Egypt until September. 160 Squadron was given training on Liberators by 86 Squadron before flying to Nutts Corner, Northern Ireland in May 1942 for a short period of anti-submarine patrols with Coastal Command before flying on to the Middle East in June. Their passage to India was halted while five Liberators provided air cover for convoys desperately needed for the relief of Malta. This was followed by bombing raids on Tobruk and others targets in the Mediterranean area. In January 1943 its personnel was combined with that of 159 Squadron, remaining in the Middle East and became 178 Squadron. On 15 January 1943 160 Squadron was reorganized in Ceylon as a Liberator general reconnaissance unit. For the rest of the war it operated under the auspices of Headquarters 222 Group and later Area Headquarters Ceylon. In addition to patrols and shipping escort duties 160 Squadron flew long-range photographic reconnaissance missions over Sumatra and the Nicobar Islands.

During the first two weeks of October 1942 the first 159 Squadron Liberator IIs flew to India touching down at Salbani. Hacked out of the jungle, Salbani provided adequate accommodation for the heavy B-24 bombers but precious little else! Living quarters were primitive. Leather turned green overnight during the monsoon and each morning, before dressing, boots and clothing had to be carefully checked for lurking scorpions. Operations over the first few months were all made at night and rarely extended to more than five aircraft and sometimes only two. RAF Liberator crews sought targets at Akyab Island, Maungdaw, Buthidaung, Schwebo and the Mandalay and Rangoon areas. Later operations extended as far as Bangkok involving an air time of twelve or more hours. Losses in general were not high compared to Europe. This was because the Japanese normally held their aircraft back from the forward airfields in Burma unless they were mounting a specific offensive. Also, a high proportion of the Liberator's flying time on operations was spent over the waters of the Bay of Bengal and thus safe from ground fire. On the other hand the chances of getting home or surviving from a crashed aircraft were slim as far as operations over Burma were concerned.

Crews numbered about seven men for night operations, including a first and second pilot. Later flight engineers were posted to the squadrons supposedly in place of the second pilot. However both the second pilot and flight engineer were carried in the Liberators. This proved very unpopular with the crews, especially in view of the long distances flown. Towards the end of the Japanese campaign, additional gunners were carried on daylight operations increasing the crew to anything up to ten and even eleven. Serviceability was quite good, magneto drops and oleo legs being the main exceptions. Most major servicing was carried out at the maintenance unit at Drigh Road, Karachi. Later Liberator models arrived from the United States with many minor items of equipment missing and flight crews had to improvise, as Ronald French, a fitter on 159 Squadron, recalls: 'We had little or no equipment and even had to make trestles and stands out of bamboo.' Another fitter on 159 Squadron, Flight Sergeant Stanley Burgess, recalls those early days in the Squadron: 'Morale was low at the time. There was no mail from home and we could not get any spares for the aircraft. Even so we managed to get about four out of six Liberators ready for operations to Ramree and Akyab. Later Wing Commander James Blackburn took command of the squadron and injected new life. We received Mark VI Liberators and later Mark VIIs and started a gradual build-up of spares and a regular supply of beer. At times the squadron flew with American Liberators on operations. They could never understand how we managed to take off with such heavy loads of fuel and bombs.'[1]

On 10 May 1943 354 Squadron was formed at Drigh Road, Karachi. At first the Squadron was to operate in a general reconnaissance role carrying out long range photographic reconnaissance but owing to the vulnerability of the single Liberator to enemy fighters, already experienced by 160 Squadron, its role was changed to convoy escort and anti-submarine duty in the Bay of Bengal. The first convoy escort was carried out on 4 October 1943 from Cuttack, where 354 assembled in August that year. By the time the Squadron moved to Minneriya, Ceylon, in October 1944, about 236 sorties had been carried out without the loss of a single ship from the convoys covered. Another important part of the Squadron's role was the 'Maxim' anti-shipping patrols off the Arakan coast from the Mayu River to the mouth of the Irrawaddy. Liberators flew their first patrol on 11 December 1943 and continued daily without a single operational failure until 28 May 1944 when the monsoon prevented further operations. These patrols, which were of an average duration of twelve hours, were instrumental in preventing the Japanese from supplying their forces in the Arakan by means of large merchant vessels. Numerous small craft which the enemy was forced to use were sunk or damaged.

Allied offensive operations began in Burma in the spring of 1943. With the coming of the monsoon in June the Japanese practically ceased operations, withdrawing their units for training, rest and re-equipment. Although the 14th Army failed in its objective to secure forward positions in the Arakan and hold them during the monsoon, air supremacy was maintained throughout the fighting and direct support was given to the troops. The small number of Liberators and Wellingtons available were afflicted with icing in the air and occasional cyclones on the ground. These storms were so fierce as to lift a Liberator at dispersal bodily into the air. But Wellington and Liberator operations continued despite the appalling weather, disrupting the enemy's communications to such an extent that he was forced to move the bulk of his troops and supplies at night.

After the 1943 monsoon a re-organization of the Allied air forces was undertaken. On 18 August the Liberators in South East Asia were supplemented by the arrival of 355 Squadron, which was formed at

Salbani. Its motto, *Liberamus per caerula* ('We liberate through tropical skies'), could not have been more appropriate. 355 Squadron flew its first mission of the war on the night of 19/20 November when three Liberators bombed the central railway station at Mandalay. That same month South East Asia Command, which had officially been created at the Quebec Conference, came into being and in December British and American Air Forces in that theatre were combined to form a single operational whole. Air Chief Marshal Sir Richard Peirse was appointed Allied Air Commander-in-Chief under the direction of the Supreme Commander, Admiral Lord Louis Mountbatten. Responsibility for the prosecution of the air war against the Japanese from Eastern India was vested in the new Eastern Air Command with the American Major-General George E. Stratemeyer as Air Commander. The Command was staffed jointly by British and American officers and controlled all RAF and USAAF squadrons in Assam and Bengal.

Early in March 1944 the Japanese crossed the Chindwin River and advanced on Imphal. But by mid-June 1944 the Japanese had been routed, defeated by Lieutenant General 'Bill' Slim's 14th Army, supported by SEAC squadrons of Liberators, Wellingtons, fighters and transport aircraft. The shattered remnants of the Japanese army retreated across the Chindwin leaving behind 30,000 dead. With the battles of Kohima and Imphal resolved the Allied High Command was able to resume its strategic offensive. The Americans wanted to open the road to China from Burma and mobilize the Chinese armies against the Japanese occupation forces. However, Slim wanted to force the Japanese to stand and fight in central Burma where he believed the 14th Army could destroy them. He was ultimately proved right and went on to take Rangoon, another of his objectives.

The British, Ghurkha and Indian land forces were cheered by their victories but the hot steamy jungles and monsoon rains took their toll. The RAF and American 10th Air Force squadrons encountered similar problems. Just as the ground forces had to hack their way through the undergrowth, Indian coolies had to carve out improvised landing strips from the paddy fields in the Delta region. Although the runways were often of a high standard the construction of the dispersals left much to be desired. They should have been constructed with three layers of brick but the Indians were usually satisfied with just mud and as a result crews arrived in the early morning to find most of their Liberators completely bogged down.

But when the weather held and the dispersals were baked dry the Liberators took off from the RSP matting runways to seek their shipping targets in the warm waters of the Indian Ocean. The Allies had intercepted the Japanese codes and the British 'Y' service was responsible for passing on the intercepted information to the SEAC squadrons. Reports filtered through confirming the exact location of the Japanese ships and the Liberators sank them, almost at will. Meanwhile 'Earthquake' or 'Major' operations were flown involving ten to twelve squadrons of RAF and American aircraft in support of General Slim's armies in the jungle offensive.

On 27 July 1944 356 Squadron flew its first bombing raid of the war. Seven Liberators were dispatched to bomb Yêu in Viêtnam but one accidentally released all its bombs on the run-up to the target and the other six did not bomb because of cloud. Instead they flew on to Kongyi, accompanied by the Liberator without bombs and hit an enemy supply dump. In August 215 Squadron at Jessore, India began converting from Wellingtons to Liberators. 215 Squadron had arrived in India in early 1942 and was at first engaged in supply dropping flights during the aftermath of the retreat from Burma. In August coastal patrols began along the east coast of India. In October airborne forces training began and it was in March 1943 before the squadron undertook bombing missions over Burma. Wellingtons were withdrawn from operations on 23 June 1944 and 215 moved back to Kolar for Liberator conversion training. Operations were resumed on 1 October by both day and night and in April the squadron's role was changed to transport duties, Liberators being replaced Dakotas.[2] In September 1944 99 Squadron, which was in the process of moving from Jessore to Digri and which had been operating against the Japanese since November 1942, also began replacing its ageing two-engined Wellingtons with Liberators. Its long-overdue conversion (the Squadron had been flying Wellington aircraft since October 1938) meant that it could now strike at targets in Thailand and Malaya.

In October 354 Squadron flew to Minneriya, Ceylon to take up anti-submarine patrols in the shark-infested waters of the Bay of Bengal. Upon their arrival it was discovered that the facilities existing would not permit the employment of all the Squadron aircraft and one flight was subsequently dispatched to Kankesanturai in Ceylon. During their stay in Ceylon 354 Squadron flew fifty-seven anti-submarine patrols over the shipping lanes of the Bay of Bengal, losing two Liberators, by which time submarine activity in the Indian Ocean had completely ceased. The Liberators had played a very important part in protecting the supply lines to the Burma front and driving the enemy submarines from the area.

By now the Liberator was one of the finest aircraft available for Burmese operations. One drawback had been the relatively small bomb load the Liberators could carry over the vast distances to their target. On operations involving distances of between 1,000 and 1,100 miles the maximum bomb load was considered to be only 3,000lb. But Wing Commander James Blackburn, Commanding Officer of 159 Squadron from July to December 1944, experimented with fuel consumption and soon dramatically increased the bomb load. The improvement was commended by the Americans and soon the example was followed by units throughout the Strategic Air Force. Eventually, round trips to targets as distant as the Kra Isthmus (2,300 miles), the Malay Peninsula (2,800 miles) and the approaches to Penang harbour (3,000 miles) were made carrying vastly increased bomb loads.

Eric Burchmore, who joined 159 Squadron at Digri in Bengal as the Engineer Officer (Maintenance Officer), recalls:

'Re-equipping of the squadron was imminent, the object being to replace earlier Marks with Mark VI (B-24J) aircraft. It was unfortunate that the configuration of the aircraft was such that, bearing in mind, the distances to targets weapon loads were not large; for example, only 4,000lb of bombs could be carried to Bangkok. The new squadron commander was a very experienced Liberator pilot from the Middle East, with many new ideas for improving the performance of our aircraft in relation to the threats from the Japanese defences both in transit and over the targets. There were serious risks to be taken by the aircrews, but nevertheless I was instructed to proceed on weight saving measures. Most significant of these were: Removal of the mid-position gun-turrets, removal of all armour plating, removal of heat exchangers in the turbo-blower systems, a very limited amount of ammunition for any remaining guns. In addition to weight saving I was instructed to carry out some trials with a view to authorizing an increase in the maximum permissible all-up-weight, which as I recall, was 56,000lbs. Before long we were operating at 65,000lbs with no ill effects on either structure or engines. The bomb-loads became 8,000lbs to Bangkok and 12,000lbs to Rangoon for example.[3]

'We were the only Liberator squadron in the campaign operating on that basis all the time. It was therefore natural that we should be chosen to attempt a most audacious raid requiring great skill and daring. The situation was that in October 1944 intelligence reported the presence in Penang Harbour of a Japanese fleet. This was a golden opportunity to attack it and the solution was to mine the harbour which meant an eighteen-hour round-trip of 3,000 miles. Calculations showed that with a full fuel load, including the bomb bay overload tanks, 4 x 1,100lb US mines could be carried, provided that we could have access to a 3,000 yard runway at least and that the aircraft would withstand an all-up-weight of about 68,000lbs. The operation would be risky from the start with a chance that the aircraft would not actually get off the ground. But the go-ahead was given. We prepared the whole squadron of sixteen aircraft and moved them to a US base about 70 miles away with only a light fuel load, but with the mines loaded unarmed; the operation was to take place starting at dawn the following day. I can well remember the terrific hospitality we had overnight.'

John Hardeman, rear-gunner on 'Z for Zebra' flown by Warrant Officer Bartter recalls:

'We took off from Digri the day before the actual operation and flew to an advance landing ground close to Calcutta. It was occupied by the Americans as evidenced by B-29s parked everywhere. We were going to take off at a vastly overloaded weight and this was the reason for flying to the advance landing strip which had a longer runway than Digri. After taking on a full fuel load we were in the region of 5,000lbs overweight. The Americans were naturally inquisitive but we were not allowed to tell even them where we were going.'

On the night of 27 October at the briefing immediately prior to take-off Wing Commander Blackburn said that as they had never attempted such a take-off before he was going first and if he did not make it all other crews could choose what to do. 'This was a very emotional time for us ground crews with such close ties to our aircrews,' continues Eric Burchmore. 'Our US hosts were aware that something special was about to happen and they were present in large numbers. So, the CO taxied out to the end of the runway and away he went hugging it for 3,000 yards with no sign of lift-off; all we then saw was a great cloud of dust as he went over the overshoot area and suddenly he appeared climbing ever so slowly. The cheering was unbelievable as each aircraft did the same. After a superb breakfast we packed our equipment and made the road journey back to base. We knew that with the best of luck it would be twenty hours before we saw anyone return and that turned out to be the longest twenty hours of my life, as there was to be radio silence until the first aircraft was near base. We simply had nothing to do as every machine was on the raid.'

One of the crew members on this operation was John Hardeman on Liberator 'Z for Zebra' flown by Warrant Officer Bartter. 'We flew with a skeleton crew which meant a reduction in gunners (I being the only gunner on board). Apart from the skipper we flew a wireless operator, a navigator and a bomb aimer only, to save weight. All armament, save my rear turret guns, was removed and so was the armour plate with every effort to make the Liberator as light as possible. The front bomb bays were filled with bomb-bay tanks while the remaining bomb-bays were filled with about half a dozen 'non-sweepable' bakelite mines. Wing Commander Blackburn, who earned the highest respect of all the crews on 159 Squadron, took off first. If, when he was airborne, a green Very was fired then it would be safe for the rest of us to take off. We had to get a maximum run without 'going through the gate' and climb at a very gradual rate. The Squadron watched the Wing Commander take off with bated breath. Sighs of relief went up as he became airborne. He fired the green light and off we went. During take-off I was up front in the flight deck. A rear gunner's job was to take charge of the auxiliary power unit located directly underneath the flight deck. Fortunately, the take-off was just as usual. But the extreme range of our mission was such that we had to perform a climbing rate that was unbelievably economical; so much so that we hardly noticed the ascent. There was certainly no strain imposed on the aircraft and we got rid of our excess fuel as quickly as we could to save more weight. We climbed very, very, gradually until we reached something like 20,000 feet. Bartter immediately throttled back and just dipped the nose so that we had in effect, a descent rate, more or less equivalent to the climbing rate. We reached about fifty feet and levelled off for the mine-laying operation. The mines had a very bad habit of breaking up if they were dropped from a very high altitude and if they were dropped too low they had a bad habit of bouncing rather after the style of the Dam-buster bombs!

'We arrived at Penang at night quite amazed with ourselves because no one had ever flown this far south before. It was quite obvious from the illumination of Georgetown and other villages on Penang Island that the Japanese were certainly not expecting visitors. Lighthouses were clearly seen and we had no trouble in determining our target or our mining direction. There were no fighters or flak - nothing! It was complete and utter surprise. We carried out our mining operation as though it was a conventional exercise, using our prescribed compass bearing. Our homeward trip was a replica of the outward journey except that we were that much lighter, possibly climbing that little bit faster. We flew straight back to base and not the advance landing ground, where we were debriefed.'

'Around midnight' recalls Eric Burchmore 'we were told that they were not far away from us and one by one they appeared and landed - all sixteen of them. The raid had been a complete surprise and a success; a message of congratulations was received from General Arnold and I seem to remember it contained the claim that it was the longest raid of the war by a bomber.'

The mining operation, flown entirely over water, was carried out copybook fashion with an exceptional degree of navigational skill. Wing Commander Blackburn had prepared the operation right down to the last detail, including laying on 'air sea rescue' - a half-submerged submarine - in the event that any Liberator got into difficulties! The following day a Royal Navy carrier-borne aircraft brought back photographic evidence of shipping scuttled in the Penang approaches confirming the Liberators' accuracy.

'The great punch line', adds Eric Burchmore 'was that every one of the sixteen aircraft was fit to be turned round without any work other than routine being needed.'

The success of this raid led, on 26 November to a second mining operation by Wing Commander Blackburn's crews in the approaches to Penang. It was a carbon copy of the first except that this time the Japanese were expecting the Liberators and fired on them. (159 Squadron's expertise in mine-laying operations continued and in January 1945 sixteen Liberators carried out a further mine-laying mission in the approaches to Penang). Blackburn was also encouraged to think in terms of a raid on Singapore; he asked Eric Burchmore to consider putting two 50-gallon drums somewhere in the aircraft, to give the necessary fuel for such a trip. 'Circumstances of his promotion (and mine) overtook the idea' recalls Burchmore 'and I am bound to say that I was not enamoured of it. Finally, 159 Squadron became famous for its ability to put up all sixteen aircraft each operation, largely because we felt the maintenance requirements in many cases were unnecessary: for example I think it was laid down that each 25 flying hours the aircraft should be jacked-up and the undercarriage checked for operation; it was our view that it was all right last time it landed so it was a waste of time checking it on jacks. I had reason to believe that none of the aircraft suffered any ill-effects from what we did in overloading them.'

'Eastern Bengal is an unfriendly place at the best of times' recalls Frank Tinsdale on 356 Squadron 'and 1944 was not a good time to be there! In fact, it was considered downright hostile by the personnel of 356 Squadron, which, together with 355 made up 184 Wing, South East Asia Command (SEAC). Their Liberator bombers ranged far and wide over Burma and Malaya attacking the enemy wherever he was to be found. Take-off one particular morning in late 1944 was proceeding as it had done on many previous occasions when the Liberators of 184 Wing had gone to war. In the dispersal bays, ground crews were making final adjustments. Petrol tanks were being topped-up to give maximum flight time and already several of the aircraft were being guided out of their bays onto the perimeter track leading to the runway approach. In the cockpits of the waiting aircraft, the crews were being cooked under the perspex windows. Even the open hatches did little to alleviate the sweltering heat and discomfort suffered by the aircrews in their escape suits and parachute harness. All around were the squeal of brakes and the very distinctive noise of Pratt & Whitney Twin Wasp aero engines.

'A green light flashed from the Control tent and the leading Liberator shook as the pilots pushed the throttles forward, holding the aircraft steady on the brakes. As the propellers screamed to full speed, the brakes were released, the bomber lifted its nose as if checking the path ahead then slowly, ever so slowly, it began its run down the long concrete track and over the notorious 'hump' where nature had prevented the contractors from levelling the ground entirely. Soon the aircraft had gathered speed enough to lift it from the face of India and it flew into the sunlight to circle slowly while it waited for the rest of the Wing to follow.

'The take-off proceeded. Bomber followed bomber in quick succession. Ground crews, their tasks temporarily completed watched the aircraft leave and they were joined by others including aircrews who, for one reason or another were not on operations that day. An aircraft of 'A' Flight, 356 Squadron, turned on to the runway and as the green light flashed, lurched towards to follow its fellows into the Asian sky. The din of its engines merged into the general clamour and the watching men waited for its reappearance beyond the hump as it became airborne. Soon, the B-24 could be seen, wallowing slightly as it struggled for height, the big wheels of the undercarriage folding into the wings as the crew trimmed the bomber for the climb to the formation circling above. And then it seemed as if all the noise had stilled. As if time itself had ceased to exist. The watching air and ground crews stared in horror. Imperceptible to the uninitiated but immediately discernible to those who knew the B-24, the sound of the engines had taken on a different and disturbing note. Out of phase with the other three engines, the No. 2, port inner engine had 'runaway'. The constant speed unit (CSU) was no longer controlling the engine speed as it should have done. Now the engine revolutions were increasing in pitch to a high scream which would soon cause the motor to seize up and wrench itself out of the wing mountings. All eyes were on the stricken aeroplane as it continued its efforts to gain height. The propeller of the No. 2 engine stowed and stopped as the pilot switched off the engine and 'feathered' the airscrew, turning the propeller blades so that they presented a sharp edge to the on-rushing air. The Liberator was about 600 feet above the ground and the tension among the onlookers began to ease as it seemed the heavily-laden aircraft was, after all, going to be able to maintain height long enough to allow the crew to jettison their bomb toad. They would then be able to circle the base for two or three hours to use up fuel before landing safely.

'Attention switched to the next aircraft on the runway and then a shout drew everyone's eyes back to the sky above the end of the concrete strip. Incredibly, the aircraft with the dead engine, instead of continuing straight ahead, was banking left into the wing with only one motor to support it. In helpless dread, the horrified watchers saw the disabled Liberator dip into an ever-steeper angle until the whole aircraft was silhouetted in plan against the burning, metallic sky. For what seemed an eternity, the B-24 slid down the arc of the sky until there was a sudden burst of violent, thick bright flame and then, even as the roar of the impact reached the ears of the onlookers, a monstrous column of heavy black smoke with an inferno at the base rose into the cloudless skies.

'A semblance of normality returned. Aircraft turned into line. Another Liberator rolled down the runway to rise through the smoke billowing from the funeral pyre. It made a wide circle and joined formation with the rest of the Wing already airborne and at last, the gaggle of heavy bombers turned towards their rendezvous in Burma. The charred remains of the crew of the crashed Liberator were removed for burial and the task of investigating the loss of the 'A' Flight aircraft was begun. Although it took some time to confirm the results, it was known that some oil supplies had become contaminated, possibly through sabotage in India. What was discovered however was that main oil filters were suffering premature collapse under the density of carbon particles and indeed, this had been the case in the engine of the lost Liberator. Minute specks of matter had reached the main oil stream and one of these, almost invisible to the naked eye had lodged under the valve of the CSU, holding it open and thus preventing it from controlling the maximum engine speed. The scene on the flight deck of the doomed bomber was easy to imagine. The crew huddled forward for take-off. The intense heat and humidity, the tension which attended every operational departure and then, the awful realisation that what had hitherto been only a nightmare fantasy had become reality. Hindsight might enable some to claim that the disaster could have been averted but hindsight is only available to survivors!'

Later, when all the aircraft had returned from the operation and happily without further loss, the CO of 356 Squadron called his pilots together to consider what might be done to avert another tragedy in the event of another engine 'runaway'. After much discussion, it was decided that it might be possible to keep an engine functioning with sufficient power to continue the take-off by using the 'feathering' mechanism of the propeller to control the engine speed.

Flight Lieutenant Frank A. Dismore had served in the RAF for two years as a flying instructor before being granted his wish to serve on an operational unit. Being only too aware of the hazards facing a pilot when the unexpected happens, it was only natural that he should immediately set about practising the emergency procedure with his co-pilot. Of course, no one expected Dismore's aircraft, 'Y-Yogi' of 'B' Flight to experience failure of any kind. After all, Yogi was the veteran bomber of 356 Squadron with more operations to its credit than any other B-24 Liberator in SEAC. Instructions had gone out calling for all main oil filters to be inspected after twenty flying hours instead of the previous thirty. 'Yogi' had only flown eight hours since the last check and so when orders came for yet another foray into Burma, no one in the crew gave any serious thought to the possibility of engine failure. Anyway, no other failures had been reported in either the British or American B-24 squadrons since the loss of the 'A' Flight 'Lib' some months earlier. Yogi got her name from the mascot displayed on the port side of the nose. A gently-dozing figure, clad only in a loincloth sat on a magic carpet. Beneath the carpet hung a huge bomb, the release hook connected to a string leading from 'Yogi's big toe! Alongside the figure, 38 bomb symbols showed the extent of the operations carried out by 'Y-Yogi' and the B-24 was loved by air and ground crews alike as an old warhorse which would always return safely from the battle. 'Yogi' would eventually complete 49 long missions over enemy territory before she was scrapped, including one trip, with Dismore at the controls which was, at the time, the longest operation carried out by any RAF bomber in World War Two.

'Yogi' taxied into position at the start of the runway. Sweat poured from the crew huddled below the flight deck as they waited for takeoff. The initial run-up of the engines was completed and the noise and vibration increased again as the four engines were opened-up to maximum power. The green light was given and with a brief 'here we go' from Dismore, Liberator EW177 began her 39th operation against the Japanese.

In the cockpit, the two pilots and the flight engineer worked hard to keep the heavy bomber on a straight course as it thundered down the strip. Laden to the limit with five tons of high explosive and incendiary bombs, with ammunition for the ten machine guns and the weight of the eleven crewmen, the ungainly aeroplane seemed reluctant to leave the earth for its natural habitat of the air. Speed increased until the word was given to the captain that take-off was committed. Now, there was no alternative but to become airborne but as Dismore began to pull the control column to lift the Liberator off the ground, so came the ominous signs that all was not well. Like its unfortunate predecessor No 2 engine was beginning to run wild. The revolutions were climbing up the clock. Cylinder head temperatures were rising as fast and all the evidence showed that a critical condition had been reached just as all available power was required to ensure that the overloaded Liberator could climb into the Bengal sky. It was now that Frank Dismore's foresight in practising the 'feathering' technique paid-off. Immediately, on the command, the left hand of co-pilot Bill Sykes flew to the weathering button under the bright red flap. A firm push and the propeller blades began to turn to the 'coarse' position, presenting their broadest face to the air. The engine speed began to fall under the greater load and Bill operated the switch again to move the blades towards fine pitch. Once again they began to turn, offering the thinner edge and so the engine speed began to rise. Once again, Bill, his eyes glued to the revolution counter, pressed the red button. And so the take-off, fraught with danger, progressed, 'feather-defeather', 'feather-defeather'. By using the hydraulic pump feeding oil to the pistons in the propeller gear case, Sykes was operating a crude, but effective 'constant-speed-unit' of his own making. His efforts and Dismore's skill paid-off and slowly, the aircraft left the ground. At sufficient height, the bomb-load was dropped on 'safe' and the B-24 circled for three hours using up fuel so that they could make a safe landing. At last, with a dead engine, Yogi returned to earth and the faulty engine was opened up.

'Remarkable and commendable as the efforts of the two pilots had been in saving the aircraft and its crew, their achievement is all the more praiseworthy as the failure occurred during total darkness. In spite of the hazards of a departure in the black of an Indian night, the pilots of Yogi had shown skill and coolness of a high order and their success gave confidence to some of the less-experienced crews on all Liberator squadrons. Thanks to Frank Dismore and Bill Sykes, a technique for coping with runaway engines was proved but at the same time, orders were flashed to the Engineering Officers on all B-24 squadrons and contaminated oil was sought out and removed from all stocks. Soon, the matter was all but forgotten as more and more sorties were flown over the already retreating Japanese.[4]

By 1945 160 Squadron a Liberator maritime reconnaissance unit in Ceylon commanded by Wing Commander John Stacey was gradually extending its mining or 'Nutting' sorties southwards along the Malayan coast. Although Singapore was 1,600 miles from Ceylon, the mining of Singapore harbour could cause considerable disruption to Japanese shipping. Stacey found that Blackburn's pioneering fuel conserving techniques were particularly advantageous when applied to the Liberator V, the maritime version of the B-24D which was lighter, faster and consequently handled better than later marks. Now Stacey planned to use eight of them to reach Singapore. Having received permission from Command he ordered top turrets and all equipment not essential to the operation, including even the Elsan chemical toilet, to be removed. Each aircraft carried 3,280 US gallons of fuel, 400 of which was in two forward bomb-bay tanks and 75 in a Catalina overload tank slung above them, while the rear bay held three 1,000lb magnetic mines.

The operation was dispatched during the afternoon of 26 March.

Weather could hardly have been worse as vast storm clouds rising to more than 20,000 feet covered much of the Bay of Bengal. Flying just below the cloud base and a few hundred feet above the ocean, rain and gales slowed progress to a point where the force was an hour late on its flight plan when only half-way to the target. The weather cleared for the run into the target area and seven of the Liberators deposited their mines in the Johore Strait separating Malaya from Singapore. The eighth aircraft had so diminished its fuel in battling through the storm that the pilot was forced to abandon the attempt to reach Singapore and instead unloaded over a secondary target area. Storms had to be penetrated on the return flight but all Liberators returned safely to base. The average flight time was 21 hours 30 minutes for the round trip of 3,460 miles with one aircraft taking 22 hours 6 minutes. Approximately 17 hours of the flight had been through rain and clouds on which Stacey commented, 'I have never seen so much lightning in my life'.[5] '

On 26 November 1944 99 Squadron had flown its first Liberator operation of the war when twelve aircraft bombed the railway station and marshalling yards at Pyininana, Burma. Ron Davies, a ball-turret gunner on 99 Squadron, recalls some experiences flying on Liberator operations. 'Each operation lasted anything from six to sixteen hours. Sometimes we flew so low that Indians used to throw rocks at us because we upset their bullocks pulling their carts. On one occasion the nose cone was shattered when we sheared the top of a palm tree.

Many of 99 Squadron's operations were against the Burma railway, the Liberators going in at low level after the PoWs, who were being forced to build it, had dispersed. Railway bridges were frequent targets and often bombed from zero feet, as Ron Davies recalls:

'On 13 December we took off at 0730 hours for the Kyaikkatha railway bridge. Flying in the ball turret at zero feet (as far as the altimeter was concerned) I had a good view from underneath, skimming the tree tops. We ran into a clearing, the railway station was ahead and the target just beyond. I could see the signs on the platform quite clearly. Then we were on to the bridge but we were a little early. Mud and debris were still in the air from the previous aircraft's bombs, there being two seconds' delay on the bombs to allow us to get clear. We dropped our bombs and ended up with mud plastering the sighting window of the ball turret. On the way out, while still in formation, we met up with Japanese fighters, one of which was destroyed and one damaged.'

Mine-laying operations were again undertaken on 29 December when Liberators on 159 Squadron laid mines in the river approaches to Rangoon. John Hardeman flew his twenty-fourth and final operation of the war that day when he was selected as rear gunner for one of the six Liberators which took part.

'I flew with Flight Lieutenant Hall in Liberator 'Y for Yoke'. Much to my chagrin I was selected to fly with what was a special crew for this operation which meant I was parted from my normal crew who now flew with Warrant Officer Sinclair. My skipper, Warrant Officer Bartter, had already completed his tour, having flown a 'blooding operation' before becoming operational. I protested about not being able to fly with my regular crew but the decision was final.

'It was a well-planned operation with a diversionary raid laid on at high altitude to soak up any fighter opposition. We six flew at low-level over the Golden Pagoda, which was our initial point for the mining operation. At timed intervals each Liberator dropped a string of mines almost on the Pagoda's doorstep, all the way along the river and almost up to Elephant Point at the river's mouth. We flew position number five in the dropping order. All six aircraft dropped their mines and headed straight out to sea for home. We had completed our drop according to plan without meeting any opposition. It appeared to be a carbon copy of the first raid on Penang, except the lights of Rangoon were out. We were also very surprised at the absence of flak. It immediately brought to my mind the possibility that night fighters were around. Hardly had I warned the rest of the crew when I spotted an aircraft astern and slightly high. Although the moon was shining it was a dark night and I was unable to identify it. I warned the pilot that an unidentified aircraft was flying in the seven o'clock high position. Then all hell let loose from the ground. At a predetermined time the Japanese had switched on every available searchlight and had opened up every damn gun they had in the place. An inferno erupted on what was a peaceful night. Right in the middle of it all I saw the aircraft again. It was not a night fighter but another Liberator and it had been hit. It caught fire, keeled over and went in with one big explosion. It was only on our return about 100 miles from base, when we broke radio silence and the call signs came through, that I realized I had witnessed the destruction of my crew with whom I had flown twenty-three operations. It was a very sad day and I broke the news to 'Bing' Bartter the day after, explaining that there was no hope of any survivors.'

On New Year's Day 1945 during a daylight raid on the Bangkok-Chiengasi railway a Liberator B.VIII KH274/H on 215 Squadron piloted by Squadron Leader Clive Vernon Beadon was seriously damaged by flak and set on fire. Eventually, after three hours the fire was extinguished and the 1,000 mile flight home accomplished successfully. Sergeant Arthur David Harding RAFVR the 24-year old rear gunner, of Plaistow, Essex was killed. Beadon, who completed three tours of operational duty, two of which were in the Far Eastern theatre of war, was awarded the DFC in 1945.

Towards the end of the war five RAF Liberator squadrons in the Far East were operating against the Japanese in daylight but the enemy was equipped with only primitive radar equipment. None the less the RAF decided that a special flight should be formed to monitor enemy W/T and R/T transmissions and plot his radar stations. A special ELINT (Electronic Intelligence) flight was activated under the control of 159 Squadron and began operations in September 1944. ELINT missions were carried out until early January 1945 when the Special Flight began dropping leaflets. On the night of 31 January 1945 Flight Sergeant Stanley James Woodbridge RAFVR, a 23-year old wireless operator on 159 Squadron was personally selected by his Squadron Commander to fly on an important operation to pinpoint the location of certain Japanese radar installations in the areas of Yogange Isle, Rangoon Rover, Bassein, Ywangyaung, Meiktila, Ywathet, Moulmein, Bangkok, Tavoy and Diamond Isle. The nine crew on BZ938 'W for *Wottawitch!!'* on C Flight (Special Flight) was skippered by Squadron Leader James Wilson Bradley. Born of English Quaker medical missionaries in China, Bradley was educated in England including Cambridge University, worked in San Francisco briefly before the war, possibly in real estate, before joining the RAF. He had over 2,000 flying hours, both as a pilot instructor and operational flying in India and Burma. Having completed a tour of operations, Bradley was recalled to fly specialized operations of radar detection. 'Stan' Woodbridge was born in Chelsea, London on 29 August 1921, the son of James Henry and May Ashman Woodbridge. In later life 'Stan' had married Florence Edith Woodbridge of Chingford, Essex.

The operation was successfully completed and the Liberator was turning for home at 3.10 am when it suddenly developed engine trouble and Bradley gave the order to bail out. Incredibly, six of the nine crew members managed to parachute into the same area and reunite on the ground. Flying Officer William James John Lowery, wireless operator, Flight Sergeant Leslie Adams, air gunner and Warrant Officer Anthony Roland Williams RAAF wireless operator-air gunner, were never seen again and perished in the crash, which occurred near the village of Letpanbin on the coast not far from Rangoon. The six survivors started to trek towards the coast in the hope of finding a boat and putting out to sea where Air Sea Rescue might be able to locate them as Flight Sergeant Woodbridge had managed to send a last minute SOS. The Bay of Bengal was combed repeatedly for four days.

Meanwhile the airmen came upon a small village and offered the head man a large sum if he would get them a small boat. He agreed and told them to hide. For two hours the six men waited, confident that they would soon be back with their friends in the squadron. But when the headman returned he brought with him a force of Japanese soldiers.

The six airmen were conveyed down the Irrawaddy River to the Bassein district where they were handed over to the Japanese 55th Engineering Regiment. Lieutenant Colonel Murayama, the regiment's Commanding Officer instructed Lieutenant Okami, his civil defence officer, to question the six British airmen. James Bradley was the first to be interrogated. He produced a document on which was written, in Japanese, an extract from the Geneva Convention stating that prisoners of war need only tell their captors their name, rank and serial number. Japan was ostensibly a signatory of the convention, although it had been no respecter of the rights of those prisoners who were forced to build the Burma railway. When the skipper refused to reveal the name of his base he was severely beaten for half an hour. Flying Officer Allan Graham Jeffrey, navigator, was then questioned but was not beaten because the interrogator was only interested in learning the identity of the special wireless-operator. All four NCOs were beaten, but when the interrogator recognized that Woodbridge was the special wireless operator, it was he who bore the brunt of the tortures. Woodbridge was asked to reveal his codes and wavelengths, to give technical details of the equipment carried in the Liberator and tell what link he had with operators on the ground who were responsible for providing details of Japanese targets. Woodbridge steadfastly refused to reveal one scrap of information to his captors. After the first interrogations, Bradley and Jeffrey were taken away in the middle of the night to Japanese headquarters in Rangoon for a more detailed interrogation. When the British overran Rangoon these two officers were found in gaol and released. But the fate of the other four airmen - Flight Sergeants 'Stan' Woodbridge; Leslie Bellingan, second pilot; John Derek Woodage, wireless operator and Robert James Snelling, flight engineer - was sealed on 7 February 1945.

The beatings began again and continued for four hours. Fists, bamboo canes and swords in their sheaths were used on the badly bruised Woodbridge. One of the soldiers, a ju-jitsu expert, threw the gallant airman around for some considerable time and at intervals another officer, Lieutenant Kanno, encouraged his soldiers to kick the defenceless airman where he lay. Eventually Kanno's patience was exhausted with the realization that no amount of torture would force the courageous airman to speak. Woodbridge was then told he was to meet the same fate as his colleagues who had already been executed.

As Stanley Woodbridge reached the spot where his three fellow crew members had been executed he paid a silent tribute to them. They had been forced to dig their own grave, a trench about two and a half feet deep and long enough to take four, not three bodies. After digging the trench all three men were made to stand in line, then a Japanese officer, Lieutenant Matsui, invited his soldiers to kick and beat them. The airmen were then brought to the edge of the trench, blindfolded and forced to squat. Matsui ordered two prisoners to be beheaded and then Kanno ordered a corporal to behead the third airman. All the bodies were subjected to bayoneting. Woodbridge was beheaded by one of Kanno's fellow officers, Lieutenant Okami and pushed into the grave. He died defiant.[6]

Liberator aircrew later carried .38 Smith and Wesson revolvers so that they could make their own 'ultimate decision'.

Early in January 1945 354 Squadron returned to Cuttack to carry out anti-shipping operations in the Andaman Islands area off the southern Burmese and Tenasserin coasts. Numerous shipping lane patrols were flown to enable fuel consumption tests to be carried out. In February anti-shipping operations were resumed and during the month 354 flew eighteen sorties and five Japanese vessels were sunk. These attacks created a serious problem for the Japanese and with the continuous attacks by Eastern Air Command on the Burma- Šiam railway the use of the sea route from Singapore to Rangoon became vital to the enemy.

The Allies had no such problem and new crews continued to arrive on the Liberator squadrons. Among them was Tom Henthorne who joined 99 Squadron as a co-pilot.

'My first operation was on 5 February when we bombed Japanese munitions hidden in the jungle at Madaya. There was no opposition but three days later when we hit Japanese concentrations at Yenanyaung we were met by intense flak. Our Liberator was slightly damaged. On 11 February the Squadron destroyed Japanese supply dumps at Rangoon without damage to the famous Shwe Dragon Pagoda nearby. There was a lot of flak but it didn't seem to worry the Japanese fighters, who attacked regardless. Three of them were shot down.'

The Liberators on 99 Squadron continued making sorties on supply dumps throughout the remainder of February, often leaving a pall of smoke over blazing Japanese fuel dumps. Flak was often light and 99 Squadron Liberators rarely encountered any fighter opposition. On 2 March the target they sought was the No. 1 railway yards at Bangkok. Tom Henthorne recalls:

'This was one of the few night sorties we made and it turned out to be very successful. The entire target area was left in a mass of flames. Only a few searchlights tried to find us but there was little flak and only one fighter, which got on our tail for a few seconds but soon veered off. Two days later we made a second night attack, this time on the Central railway yards at Bangkok. Later in the month, on 27 March, I returned to operations with a daylight sortie against Japanese supply dumps at Bangkok and two days later, against the Japanese Headquarters in Rangoon.'

By the end of March 1945 the decisive battle for central Burma had been won and Slim was eager to advance on Rangoon. At this point the Chinese and American forces were suddenly withdrawn. It proved a severe setback but was worsened by the unexpected decision to use the USAAF element of the air transport force to ferry the troops out. The entire mobility of the 14th Army depended on this force and the US Chiefs of Staff only relented after appeals from Admiral Lord Louis Mountbatten and Chiefs of Staff in London. The Americans put back the order for evacuation until 1 June or when Rangoon finally fell, whichever was the sooner. The British chiefs need not have worried. Japanese reinforcements which tried to infiltrate from the west were checked by resistance groups and by a technique developed by Wingate's Chindits; clandestine ground observers with radio sets calling for air strikes by RAF Liberators. On the night of 26 March Liberator VI KH391 on 357 Squadron, piloted by Squadron Leader Tom Lee carried out a supply drop deep in enemy held southern Malaya. The operation was of 22 hours 45 minutes' duration. The Squadron specialised in such delivery operations to organised behind-the-lines resistance in Burma, Malaya and Indo-China. Using stripped down Mk.VIs with extra bomb-bay fuel tanks many of its operations exceeded twenty hours in the air.

On 24 April seven Liberators on 160 Squadron carried out another 'Nutting' mission. BZ830/T piloted by Canadian Flight Lieutenant Percy Waddy strafed a Japanese trawler, evaded ack-ack and fighters, covered 3,520 miles and was in the air for 22 hours ten minutes. On the night of 30-31 May four Liberators on 160 Squadron flying at 1,000 feet and as low as 500 feet when in range of enemy radar, sowed a dozen Mk 36 mines around Singapore. New duration records were established when Flight Lieutenant Roy Schroeder's crew on BZ867/P were airborne for 22 hours and 22 minutes and Flight Lieutenant Leo Davidson piloting FL991/F was airborne for just two minutes' less.

At the end of April crossover patrols were flown by Liberators in the Andaman Sea to prevent a Japanese naval force located at Singapore from interfering with Operation 'Dracula', the seaborne operations against Rangoon. But on 1 May, the day before the 'Dracula' force was to land, a reconnaissance Mosquito flying over Rangoon saw painted on the roof of a gaol known to contain Allied PoWs, the words *Japs Gone. Extract Digit,* which in RAF parlance meant 'pull your finger out!' Tom Henthorne was among those on 99 Squadron who successfully bombed coastal gun batteries that day unaware that the Japanese had pulled out.

On 2 May during an attack on Japanese gun positions in the Rangoon area, a Liberator on 355 Squadron ditched in the Bay of Bengal after an engine caught fire. Among those lost was the first RAF Fighter Command VC of the war, Wing Commander Eric James Brindley Nicolson, who was flying as an observer. His body was not recovered.[7]

On 22 May at 0655 hours Graham 'Mac' Baxter's crew on 99 Squadron at Dhubulia, about sixty miles north of Calcutta, took off on their first Far East Operation. This crew had flown Lancasters on 622 Squadron in 1944. Leslie Parsons, the navigator, who had joined the crew in March that year and had completed a tour of 31 ops recalled:

'Our mission on 22 May was to attack a stretch of railway south of Moulmein with delayed action high explosive bombs. Any train we saw on this railway was to be bombed and we were to do this at very low altitude (about 200 feet). At the briefing I was given details of the route to be taken, time to be at the target, speed to fly at, weather forecast and wind etc. From this information I was able to construct a flight plan and draft a map of the area over which we were to fly. Having completed all the necessary calculations I joined the other members of our crew at the general briefing. By this time it was about 0615 hours and we were taken out to the aircraft by lorry, climbed on board, carried out a series of tests on the aircraft and at 0655 hours we took off.

'It was just getting light as we headed south over the Delta of the great River Ganges. I had the impression that there were dozens and dozens of small rivers entering the sea. The land was extremely low-lying and there were plenty of fishing boats around. We headed out over the Bay of Bengal. I can remember the sky everywhere was full of dark low clouds, with a cloud base of about 2,500 feet. You could sometimes see violent thunder storms where the clouds and rain came down to sea level. We took great care to keep away from these and flew in clear air just below the clouds. After four hours flying over this most depressing water we hit land at the south-west tip of Burma. We then headed across more sea for another hour to the target at Moulmein. As we approached the coast there was a yell of excitement when we saw an engine with three coaches heading northwards. The driver of the train must have realised he was about to be attacked because he stopped in a deep cutting to get the maximum protection.

'It was a most exciting moment as we swung into the bombing run, bomb doors open. Down the bombs went in a cluster around the train. Judging by the steam and smoke coming out of the locomotive it seemed likely that we had made at least one direct hit, but because of the delayed action fuses we did not see the actual bombs explode. We turned round and swept back along the seashore with all guns blazing in an attempt to destroy the carriages. Although the action had only lasted a few minutes, I told the skipper that our instructions were to head back out to sea before any Japanese fighters appeared. 'OK', he said, 'we will just do one more run and then go home'. Once again the gunners started to open fire. Suddenly, I was horrified to see a man of about thirty with dark Burmese-looking skin, dressed in a pair of baggy brown trousers race from behind a sand dune and throw himself down into the railway cutting. He was probably just a local man walking along the beach and he must have been absolutely terrified by the enormous aircraft flying at 200 feet at about 200 mph. From the navigator's position in the nose of the aircraft I had a grandstand view of what was going on. I have always prayed that he was unharmed.

'The total trip there and back was about eleven hours and we said we thought the trip was satisfactory. However, the Debriefing Officer told us that the Japanese were very skilful at repairing bomb damage and that he expected them to have the railway operational soon. It was no surprise therefore, to find ourselves on another trip to Moulmein five days later. Our instructions were to disrupt the railway line should it have been repaired. On this occasion we did not find any trains but we blew up more stretches of the line. This happened again on the following day, so in one week we caused considerable destruction to the Japanese supply lines.

'On one of these trips we were flying at our usual height just below the clouds when Frank Ramsey our Rear Gunner reported another Liberator about a quarter of a mile behind us flying very low over the water, saying, 'I don't like the look of this, he is much too low...' Suddenly, he shouted that the Liberator had plunged into the sea and had sunk very quickly. There was nothing we could do. There was no hope of mounting a rescue as we were about half way across the Bay of Bengal. We were badly shaken and took it as a lesson not to fly too close to the water, realising that a sudden down current of air could quickly force an aircraft into the sea. Movements of air in the tropics could be extremely violent, especially during the Monsoon.

'Some idea of the pressure maintained on the Japanese can be gauged from the fact that following the three attacks on Moulmein we were ordered to bomb shipping near the port of Satahib. This port was important because it helped to supply the city of Bangkok. It was a fourteen-hour trip, half of which was in darkness. We flew the same route to Moulmein and then a further two hours over to the Gulf of Šiam. Past Moulmein, the monsoon clouds broke up and we had a beautiful sunlit view of jungle-clad hills and the sea below. Satahib was clearly visible and we could see the ships in the harbour. Frank Carter the bomb aimer took up his position.

'I'm fed up sitting down here all the time,' I told him, 'I've been here for seven hours. I am going up onto the flight deck with the pilots while you do the bombing.' I crawled back through the small passageway and stood up on the flight deck. It was possible to see the harbour clearly. There was moderate anti-aircraft fire but nothing like the flak we had experienced in Germany. We were flying at about 15,000 feet as we started our bombing run. 'Bomb doors open,' said the Bomb Aimer and up came the roller bomb doors. I turned round, stepped to the edge of the bomb bay and looked down. The sea was clearly visible through the open bomb bay and as we approached the shipping, down went the bombs. It was a most peculiar feeling, observing the sea from this height, but since then I have realised that I must have been mad to stand there, because if the aircraft had been thrown around by gunfire or air currents I could have easily gone out with the bombs! Thank goodness this did not happen. Frank Carter claimed that he had hit a ship in the harbour and this was confirmed later by Intelligence reports.

'By the end of May 1945 the Japanese Army, which in 1944 had reached the border of India, had been driven back into Southern Burma. The British 14th Army was in fact near to Rangoon, the Burmese capital. It was clear that the next operation was to drive the Japanese from Malaysia and Singapore. It was no surprise, therefore, to be told that our next job was to disrupt railway communications between Bangkok and Singapore. We were given the target of bombing the railway bridge at Sindhasani, a small village on the east side of Malaysia, a sixteen-hour return flight, the longest we had done so far. I have already mentioned that the monsoon season, with its heavy cloud and tremendous rain had already begun and this got steadily worse. As monsoon clouds can rise to 30,000 feet, there was no way that a piston-engined aircraft could climb 'above the weather' as is possible with modern jet-powered aircraft. We had to fly underneath the clouds or through the middle of them.

'We took off on 5 June for Malaysia during a heavy storm on 'K'. All aircraft had an identification letter and in addition, a British aircraft usually had a bomb painted on its nose for every completed operation. The Liberators we flew in were old American aircraft and as well as bombs they painted huge pictures of famous people, mainly film stars of the 1930s. A popular film at the time was King Kong, the story of a huge gorilla that created havoc and terror in New York. It was no surprise, therefore, to find that Liberator 'K' had a replica of King Kong painted on its nose.

'As we headed out over the Bay of Bengal the clouds and rain were at about sea level and it was much too dangerous to fly underneath them. We had already seen how a low flying Liberator could be sucked into the water, so we decided to fly at about 15,000 feet through the weather. The rain cascaded down in sheets and we could see nothing above, below, or ahead. After flying for some four hours in these conditions I calculated we must be somewhere near the southern Burmese coast. Suddenly, without the slightest warning, the Liberator plunged downwards into a tremendous dive. About thirty seconds later it was flung upwards at a similar speed. It was then spun round in a tight circle and equally suddenly was flung out of the cloud. We emerged into bright sunshine and below us, by some miracle we could see the coasts of Burma and Malaysia. I realised that we must have unwittingly flown into a cumulonimbus cloud due to the zero-visibility conditions. These clouds have very powerful up and down currents which are easily capable of breaking the wings off an aeroplane. They can rise to 30,000 feet or more, with a huge 'anvil' on top. I do not suppose that the whole incident lasted more than 45 seconds but we were all badly shaken and thoroughly frightened. During the previous two years of flying we had faced all manner of hazards, but nothing equals the sheer force of nature. We flew on for about ten minutes to get away from the storm, realising how lucky we had been to survive. Each one of us went over his own part of the aircraft to check for damage. The bombs were still in position, the compasses were working and the engines seemed OK, so we decided to carry on to the target which was some three hours away. With the improved weather we were able to fly at a lower level and we had no problem finding the railway bridge which was successfully attacked with delayed-action bombs.

'It was about 1330 hours when we started our eight-hour return flight. Near the equator it gets dark at 1800 hours, so much of the homeward trip would be in darkness over the sea and we knew that there would be more storms to face. After two hours flying over the Malaysian jungle I could see the skipper and co-pilot having a discussion, looking anxious. Rather than talk over the intercom I decided to crawl to the flight deck to find out what was going on. 'You chaps look worried. Have we got a problem?' I enquired.

'We've got problems with the oil pressure on No. 2 port engine,' the skipper replied 'and we're concerned that it could catch fire. I'm afraid we are going to have to switch it off and feather it.'

'The consequence of this would be that the aircraft could barely climb and would also lose speed. The prospect of a safe return to India looked remote. I crawled back to my navigational position and did some calculations which confirmed how difficult it was going to be. While I was doing this I remembered reading in the Indian papers several days earlier that the 14th British Army had advanced to a position near the airfield of Mingladon near Rangoon. This was the only airfield in the area which might be big enough to take a four-engined bomber. I said to the skipper that we should head for Rangoon, about three hours away and make an emergency landing, hoping of course that the airfield had indeed been captured by the British. He agreed immediately and I gave him the necessary courses to get us there.

'We struggled along at about 2,000 feet to the west coast which we crossed at Tavoy Island and then turned north heading for Rangoon. The rest of the trip was a constant nightmare of continuous rainstorms and low cloud, with islands suddenly appearing through the clouds. We were all praying that the other three engines would keep going; any more trouble and we would be in the drink! I kept looking for signs that we were heading in the right direction, when below us, I noticed that the sea had started to turn brown. This was a great comfort because the brown colour was mud carried out to sea by the great Burmese river, the Irrawaddy. After another hour of flying we reached the coast of Burma and I had no problem in map reading to the Mingladon airfield which was north of Rangoon.

'It was nearly dusk and as we approached we could see fighters with RAF markings round the perimeter of the airfield, so thankfully we knew it was in British hands. We circled the airfield, contacted the control tower, explained who we were and asked for permission to land. 'Not likely!' was the reply. 'We have only been here a couple of days, the main runway is still full of bomb craters, the short runway has only been filled in to take Spitfires and Dakotas and then there is a drop of thirty feet at the end of the runway.' The officer of flying control said, 'You will never get that thing down in one piece.'

'Hard luck,' said our skipper, 'We've got to get down somehow.'

'The fact that I am able to tell you this story shows what a good pilot he was and that he did manage to bring the aircraft down successfully. We touched down just at the beginning of the runway and after one hundred yards the skipper slammed on the brakes. The Liberator shuddered and rocked and came to rest about ten yards from the opposite end of the runway. There was a cheer and a sigh of relief from everyone. (We learned afterwards that the RAF men on the ground had been placing bets on whether we would not get down alive). After we had landed we were told to remain on the runway until the Flying Control Officer had found a place for us to park the Liberator. There were no lights on the airfield and eventually a jeep came out to us and led us to a space on the grass by the flying control tower. As we climbed out of the aircraft we gave it an affectionate bang with our fists because we realised there was no way it would fly again. For many months after the war I met airmen who had been to Mingladon and reported that the 'King Kong Liberator' was still there, gradually rotting.

'After the aircraft had been parked we reported to the Flying Control Officer and messages were sent to our base in India that we were alive and unharmed. Accommodation was pretty chaotic, as the Japanese had been driven out only a couple of days before. However, we managed to get hold of a quantity of straw and we bedded down on a concrete floor in a hut and, in spite of the many 'creepy crawlies' we managed to get a good night's rest. The next day we talked to some of the fighter pilots based there and they told us a very strange story that retreating Japanese troops were discarding their uniform and dressing themselves as Burmese natives (their appearances were very similar). They were selling eggs and local produce, but hidden in their baskets were revolvers which they used on unsuspecting airmen with devastating effect. We thought that they might be joking, but to be on the safe side we remained well within the airfield boundaries.

'Supplying advancing troops and so on in this sort of country with its poor roads and monsoon rains is a major difficulty and to overcome this, many of the supplies were brought by air by the twin-engined Dakotas of the American Army Air Force. At this time, supplies were being flown from India and Northern Burma to Rangoon. After two days in Rangoon we managed to get a lift back to India in a Dakota with a returning American transport pilot and then completed our journey back to our base by rail. In spite of this long journey and the hours we had flown there was to be no respite for us. Two days later we were given another Liberator and were sent to bomb and machine gun retreating Japanese troops in southern Burma.

'A week later the captains and navigators of ten crews were called to a special meeting with the Wing Commander. He told us that we were being withdrawn from operations forthwith and that we would be given special training for operations which at this stage were highly secret. When I first heard this, my heart leapt with joy at the thought of no more flying over the Bay of Bengal and the Burmese jungles, but I soon became apprehensive on contemplating the vast area of South East Asia still occupied by the Japanese. It looked as if the war might last for years and I was sure that there were plenty of rotten jobs still lined up for us. We did about two and a half weeks of intensive special training. This consisted of long low-level flights (at about 1,000 feet) over different routes in Northern India. Whilst flying around these routes we had to find targets about the size of a small field marked out with the letter 'H' in white stone. Having found the target we came down to one hundred and fifty feet and dropped large containers by parachute. The purpose of this training was a well-kept secret, for no one had any idea what it was all about. In these circumstances, rumours flourished and a favourite one was that we were going to be dropping of spies in French Indo China (Viêtnam). What a daunting prospect that would be!'[8]

On 15 May 1945 200 Squadron at Jessore, equipped with Liberator VIs, had been re-numbered 8 Squadron and after moving to Ceylon a few days later, began making supply drops to guerrillas in Malaya and Sumatra together with 160 Squadron. One of the arrivals in Ceylon was Colin Berry, an air-gunner who had trained at Nassau in the Bahamas. In January 1945 he and his fellow crew members, a former Coastal Command crew, flew to Minneriya in Ceylon to join 200 Squadron, which at that time was acting in a Special Duties capacity supplying Force 136 in Malaya and Sumatra. Force 136 was the general cover name for a branch of the British Special Operations Executive (SOE) which was established to encourage and supply resistance movements in enemy-occupied territory and occasionally mount clandestine sabotage operations.[9] Berry recalls, 'To make room for more fuel, all the gunners, except the wireless-operator/air gunner, were dropped from the crew. During June 1945 an 8 Squadron Liberator established a world endurance record of 24 hours 10 minutes.'[10]

Warrant Officer Frederick W. 'Bill' Cooper was a flight engineer on 160 Squadron which in July 1945 became involved in special operations, which were solely the preserve of the Consolidated Liberator - the only aircraft with the lifting capacity and range. He describes a typical operation.

'Check fuel in bomb bay overland tanks; Check fuel transfer panel fully equipped with 'U' tubes Remove tail support ladder Close Bomb bay doors - roll down like roll-top desk; Check parking brake 'On' Check hydraulic booster pump 'On'; Check main fuel cocks 'On' Start up a APU (internal auxiliary power unit installed on this aircraft instead of using external accumulator trolley) Remove control locks Two pilots carried on these missions because of their great length - second pilot also a fully trained navigator. Crew also contained: navigator, flight engineer (self), two wireless operators (wireless operator mechanic (because of amount of equipment). The latter four had all additionally qualified as air gunners. There were no air gunners on the squadron as they would have been so much ballast to carry for the three hours or so we were within range of the enemy fighter aircraft.

'My immediate pre-flight duties were as follows: Start up engines Complete pre-flight checks: Check fuel pressures, oil pressures, oil temperatures, cylinder-head temperatures, vacuum pressures, hydraulic accumulators and check main hydraulic pressure gauge while pilot tested operation of flaps.

'In addition to the minelaying and photographic reconnaissance missions, I had been to Telok Anson (2), (chart) Kuala Lips (2), Alor Star and Kula Selangor in support of force 136, with one mission abandoned after fourteen hours due to bad weather. In recognition of the operations we flew our skipper was awarded the DSO and the DFC. Our navigator was also awarded the DFC. I'm proud to say that the whole crew was authorized to wear the Burma Star in recognition of the support these operations gave the Fourteenth Army in that theatre of war.

'On at least one occasion the Ghurkas were fired on as they made their short decent from 600 feet. After the 'drop' the ground party would melt away into the jungle, taking stores, parachutes and any 'bodies' who had been dropped in. Back on the ground parachutes would have to be quickly recovered - even from the tree tops if we had misjudged the drop - in order that they might not be seen by the Japanese aircraft.'

Tom Winup enrolled in the RAF Volunteer Reserve in December 1941 in London but his service was deferred until July 1942. He trained in Torquay at No.5 Initial Training Wing before going to Canada to attend No.4 Bombing and Gunnery School at Fingal, Ontario and No.1 Air Observer School in Toronto in the summer of 1943. He was awarded his air bomber's brevet in February 1944. Having had a lifetime's fascination with India, he was delighted when the RAF posted him to 1673 Heavy Conversion Unit at Kolar, India. In November 1944 it was formed into 358 Squadron (Special Duties) - dropping agents and supplies into enemy-occupied territory for Special Operations Executive's (SOE) resistance groups. He was later posted to 159 Squadron. He served with 231 Group, South East Asia Command, flying B-24 Liberators. His regular aircraft was a Liberator (EW287/R) called Rogues' Retreat whose nose art featured a scantily clad, buxom girl standing invitingly by an open door with a red light above it! Shortly before the end of war in the Far East Tom took a bombing leaders' course and returned to 358 Squadron as Bombing Leader. He was based at Digri, Jessore and Salbani (Bengal), Kunming (China) and Pegu (Burma).[11]

'If it hadn't been for a whim of fate (or something) I wouldn't be here now It was while at HCU on Kolar in southern India, 150 miles west of Madras, that we were formed into crews. We didn't have a choice: staff officers just put our names down. I was put with an Australian pilot, Flight Sergeant Porter, who struck me as a decent, dependable sort. I liked him from the word go and felt happy to fly with him. But then it was all changed and I was put down to fly with an Irish pilot,'Paddy' Drummond, who had a reputation for being drunk most of the time when not flying. I was hardly reassured and not at all keen. However, he proved to be a very good pilot.

'As it turned out, Porter's crew crashed doing circuits and bumps. Had the change not been made I wouldn't be here to tell the tale... The second reason occurred when, as part of our special duties (more of which later) three of us were given the task of a daylight drop on the coast of French Indo-China at a village called Moncay. The weather was awful - we never saw the ground for eight hours because of cloud - but we had to get there. As we approached the area to do the drop of supplies to the French by parachute, all our powers of navigation and the pilots flying skills were needed.

'Begin descent. Fifteen minutes to ETA,' said our navigator. We dropped through the cloud hoping we were more or less in the right place.

'Any idea where we are?' asked our skipper hopefully. 'Over land? Over sea? Hazard a guess, navigator!'

'No idea,' came the not-very-reassuring reply. At 100 feet we broke cloud.

'Over the sea, skip,' said the navigator confidently noting the water below us.

'It's not what's below us I'm worried about,' replied the skipper, 'it's what's around us.'

'On all sides of us, towering towards the sky with their tops shrouded in cloud were dozens of small volcanic islands like skittles in a skittle alley. They were not marked on our maps and we'd no idea they were there. Somehow we had threaded our way between them. It was sheer good fortune (and the whim of fate again perhaps) that we had not collided with one of them.

'Having established how I come to be here at all, I'll go back a little. My squadron, 358, was formed from 1673 HCU in southern India in November 1944. We were trained as a bomber squadron to do daylight formation bombing and despatched to bomb Fort Mandalay in Burma. (As you can imagine, there was much singing of *On the Road to Mandalay!*) The fort's location prevented heavy artillery from reaching it, hence the need for bombing. We had also undertaken a jungle survival course - that was worse than beings on ops but everyone survived - some better than others!

'As it turned out it was our one and only bombing raid, for after that, we were retrained for special duties and moved to an isolated base about eighty miles east of Calcutta called Jessore (now in Bangladesh). We took over houses in the town (about six miles from the airfield) for our accommodation and almost became part of the local community. We played endless football matches against local teams which, as they got knocked out in the preliminary rounds, simply transferred their best players to the next village team to play us until, in the final we were up against the best in the area. We lost.

'SOE's Special Duties for my squadron and the sister squadron (357) included dropping agents - Eurasians, British and Americans - by parachute into French Indo-China, Thailand and Burma. We didn't know who they were or anything about them. The only time we saw them was when we picked them up before the drop and that was usually at night. We also dropped supplies packed in canisters.

'Distances out there were so great and trips took many hours in the air, sometimes up to twenty-four. This involved stripping the aircraft down to a minimum and using overflow fuel tanks. Our casualties were actually higher than on regular bomber squadrons as we had no radar aids - it was all done by dead reckoning navigation - and some of that was based on travellers' records made in 1,870! Hardly the most up-to-date information.

'Consequently, there were many times when we hadn't a clue where we were - all those little islands didn't help either. Neither did the weather for the cloud base was often only just above the sea - or so it seemed. We'd often fly really low to try and find a landmark of some sort and could see peasants with cone-shaped hats running around. Sometimes we were so low that the map was no help - we were too close.

'One time we spotted a river with an odd-shaped bend that helped pinpoint our position and from there we could head for the dropping zone - a football field. Right in the middle of the circle was a French officer - riding breeches, boots, the lot - we had to pull up to 200 feet, almost back into the clouds in order to drop the canisters, otherwise they'd have been damaged and probably hit him too! We made three runs like this - avoiding islands, groping our way through cloud, finding the football pitch and dropping our canisters. Each time we could see the Japanese but, fortunately, they didn't cause us any trouble. That night in the mess one of the other two pilots on the same drop wrote, 'We broke cloud at sea level and climbed to five feet!'

'There had been three aircraft on those drops. They were hazardous runs, to say the least. The two officer pilots were awarded the Croix de Guerre but my skipper, Paddy Drummond, wasn't. He was 'only' a warrant officer...

'I was on a bombing leaders' course at Amarda Road camp in the Indian state of Orissa. Six of us were to fly in close formation on a fighter affiliation exercise with American Thunderbolts. A New Zealander who had served in my squadron (358) had a reputation for being the worst pilot in the world for keeping in formation. He had just been commissioned and sent to the unit as a staff pilot. My first thought was, 'Right, I'm not flying with you, chum!' However, I didn't have much choice and I was Number 4 with my aircraft's nose right under the leading aircraft which had our New Zealand friend as co-pilot. (He had, however, redeemed himself before he came to us by having plenty of guts and being awarded the DFC as a warrant officer - even so, his reputation stuck.)

'The weather was bad - it was the monsoon - but all was going well, even the New Zealander out in front was holding course. Suddenly, the aircraft to port hit the leader. With all four engines screaming the New Zealander's aircraft, minus its tail unit, went down into a paddy field whilst the other aircraft lost a wing and also crashed. Debris flew all over the place. I was waiting for something to hit us. Would we too follow him into the paddy field? However, a smart diving curve got us out of the way and, apart from superficial strikes by debris, we were unscathed. All the crew of the lead aircraft, including the New Zealander, were killed. In total fourteen men were lost in this incident.'

The official account of the accident from the Ministry of Defence stated that: 'At approximately 0945 hours the formation, which had been encountering medium to bad weather, approached a heavy bank of cloud. The leader, Squadron Leader Heynert, commenced to lose height in an attempt to fly underneath this, but reached the cloud before he was quite low enough and the formation entered the cloud. Number 6 by this time was some little way behind the formation. On entering the cloud visibility was reduced to nil and numbers 2 and 5 in the formation altered course starboard and number 4 altered course port. On coming out of the cloud aircraft number one (EW225 Flying Officer Ettlinger) and aircraft number 3 (EW247) captained by Pilot Officer Herbert, were seen to be in close proximity and number 3 was then seen to pull up and collide with number one. The tail unit of number one was torn off and the aircraft crashed out of control and one wing (which one not established) of number 3 was torn off, causing the aircraft to crash. Once the crash occurred neither pilot had any chance to execute a reasonable forced landing, nor was there sufficient time for any member of the crew to make a parachute descent, the aircraft being at 1,000 feet and 2,000 feet at the time of the collision.

On 5 June 1945 99 Squadron attacked Japanese supply dumps and the railway at Suratthani (or Surasdhani) in the extreme south of Šiam. Ron Davies, the ball-turret gunner on 'G for George' was one of those who took off at 0600 hours. 'Owing to the great distance the bomb load was reduced to 3,000lb. The rest of the bomb-bay was filled with two 300 gallon overload tanks, which had to be pumped into the main wing tanks before the fuel could be used. There were two of us flying low at about 300 feet over the Bay of Bengal. (The Japs had a radar station at

Rangoon and we hoped to avoid being picked up.) The other aircraft was about half a mile away on our beam, but for some reason was flying rather low. We sent messages on the Aldis lamp telling him to climb a little, as although the pilot was experienced over Germany, he was unused to the tropical, bumpy conditions, which could be experienced over the bay. He banked rather steeply without climbing. He dropped the wing tip, touched the sea and the aircraft plunged straight under. With full tanks and bomb load it blew up instantly, the sea was on fire and though we circled the spot for ten minutes, no sign could be seen of any survivors or bodies. We then carried on to the target.'

Tom Henthorne was flying his last operation on 99 Squadron that day and it proved a fine finale: 'Large oil fires were started when we left; the whole area was blanketed in black smoke. On the way back to Dhubalia an airfield near the target area was strafed and hits were observed on a twin-engined aircraft.'

'Mac' Baxter's crew on 99 Squadron were briefed to bomb the railway bridge on the Bangkok-Singapore railway on the eastern side of the Malay Peninsula. Leslie Parsons recalls that it was to prove their worst flying experience in South East Asia. 'We took off in 'K' and straight away were in heavy rain and thick, low clouds. There was no chance of a loaded Liberator being able to climb over the top of Monsoon clouds so we flew at about 15,000 feet. Unfortunately, after about six hours' flying we flew straight into cumulonimbus clouds which were invisible to us. Cumulonimbus clouds with the anvil top rising to 25,000-30,000 feet have the most violent currents and have sufficient power to tear the wings from an aircraft. The first indication that we were in trouble came when the aircraft was thrown straight up at what seemed a colossal speed, while the pilot struggled to hold the nose down. The next sensation was an equally violent downward plunge followed by a feeling that we were going round and round within the cloud. Then we were suddenly thrown out of the cloud and we could see Malaya below. To our intense relief and astonishment the Liberator was still in one piece and we were able to descend and bomb the bridge. But the violence of cumulonimbus clouds had taken its toll and after two hours on our return journey the number two engine failed and had to be feathered. It was clear to us all that with the reduced performance and the appalling weather conditions we would never make the return trip to India. The aircraft would barely climb so we were forced whenever possible to fly just below the cloud base at between 500 and 1,000 feet.

'I told 'Mac' Baxter that we had no alternative but to head for Rangoon and pray that the airfield there was suitable for landing a

Liberator. Many times it was necessary to make diversions to avoid cloud, storms and islands suddenly appearing out of the rain. The entire crew was tense, flying for two to three hours at only 500 feet above the waves and knowing that the slightest trouble would send us into the sea. The tension only started to ease when we saw the sea beginning to turn brown about thirty miles from the Burmese coast. We realized this must be due to the sand and silt of the Irrawaddy Delta.

'We hit the Burmese coast just south of Rangoon about an hour before dark and made our way to Mingaladoon airfield a few miles north of the capital. We asked for permission to land and were told that the main runway, which could take a Liberator, was still pitted with bomb craters and only the short runway for fighters had been repaired. We had no option but to use the short runway. Thanks to 'Mac's' usual great skill we succeeded in landing within the limits (much to the surprise of those on the ground who took bets that we would go over drop at the end of the runway).

'On 20 June 1945 we were withdrawn from operations and assigned to special training, dropping containers on parachutes from low level (about 150 feet) on to a small area. The bombing range at Salbani in northern India was the main training area. Many rumours circulated concerning our impending operations; from dropping spies in Šiam, to low-level attacks on highly secret targets or dropping paratroops on the Andaman Islands.'

All these rumours proved unfounded. With the demise of the Japanese forces in Burma focus of attention had switched to operations in Malaya and Sumatra.

On 16 July 99 Squadron was briefed to fly to Kankesanturai airbase on the northern tip of Ceylon. Each Liberator was packed with ground crew and all essential equipment. Les Parsons' Liberator carried the kitchen staff and all their cooking utensils. 'We left Dhubulia and landed in Ceylon in the early afternoon and were told to report for a further briefing to our ultimate destination in the late afternoon. We still had no idea where we were going - it was such a well-kept secret. But when we entered the Briefing Room we saw the long strand on the map of the South Pacific indicating the track from Kankesanturai and travelling towards Australia, stopping about two thirds of the way in what seemed like 'open sea'.'

What appeared to be a tract of 'open sea' were in fact the Cocos or Keeling Islands, about 2,000 miles from Ceylon and 1,000 miles from Perth, Australia, or about ten degrees south of the Equator. The plan was for the Island group to be turned into a fortress for Operation 'Zipper', the intended invasion of Sumatra, Java and Malaya. On 23 June 1945 Geoffrey Ely, Wing Navigation Officer and a member on 99

Squadron, had made a special flight in a Liberator to the islands. The flight took nine and a half hours and the return ten. Ely briefed the rest of the Squadron and at 1900 hours on 16 July 1945 99 Squadron crews began taking off for the Cocos. They flew until dawn and all made the long trip safely. 99 Squadron shared the Cocos Islands base with the Liberators of 356 Squadron. Les Parsons recalls, 'Failure to find the islands would have resulted in a watery grave but it was a thrill to finally see the white wall of water breaking on the coral reef.'

The direction of these Liberator operations was under the control of Army intelligence and a specially appointed Army officer carried out the briefings. He told the expectant crews that they were to drop arms and ammunition to guerrillas in the hills of Malaya in the Kuala Lumpur district. The guerrillas, consisting of Chinese Malays and escaped British and Australia PoWs, were to assist in the eventual invasion of Malaya. Les Parsons remembers the supply dropping operations. 'I was involved in two operations; 'Tideway' and 'Funnel'. Both were long, unescorted trips across the Indian Ocean to Sumatra where we crossed over the mountain range on the west coast of the Island. We flew on across the low-lying part and over the Strait of Malacca to the Cameron highlands. Both the dropping zones had code-names and it was pretty difficult map reading. We were looking for a small clearing in the hills marked with a white letter 'H' aided by a small fire. We always flew in daylight to enable us to arrive at the DZ at around 1600 hours so that the guerrillas could get back to their camps in the hills during darkness before the Japs could catch them. (It gets dark around 1800 hours.)

'Having found the clearing we flew in at about 150 feet and dropped the containers. We always circled long enough to see the guerrillas rush from the trees, collect their containers and drag them away. We were low enough to wave to each other. We were then faced with the long return journey in darkness. The more difficult part being the climb over the huge cumulonimbus clouds which had been built up by equatorial heat on the mountains of western Sumatra.'

Before plans could get under way for the invasion of Malaysia the first atomic bomb to be used in warfare was dropped on 6 August on Hiroshima. Three days later another was dropped on Nagasaki. The actions saved thousands of Allied lives who would otherwise have been lost in the invasion of Japan and its captured territories. On the morning of 10 August 1945 Japan sued for peace.

Four Liberator squadrons flew their final operations of the war during the first fortnight of August 1945. 356 flew its last combat mission on 6 August when three Liberators bombed and strafed Japanese aircraft at Benkulen. Next day 99, 159 and 355 Squadrons completed their tour of operations. Five Liberators on 159 Squadron attacked two bridges on the Šiam-Burma railway. Four Liberators of 355 Squadron were also involved in the bombing of the railway, in the Bangkok area, after their primary target of shipping off the east coast of the Kra Isthmus had been aborted. The 'railway of death' had cost the lives of 24,000 Allied PoWs involved in its enforced construction. Meanwhile four Liberators on 99 Squadron blasted two Japanese airfields south-east of Benkoelen. Five days later, on 12 August, 99 Squadron flew its final operational mission of the war when three Liberators dropped supplies to guerrillas at DZ 'Funnell 113', in Malaya and a fourth aborted.[12]

With the end of the war in Burma the Liberators switched to dropping badly needed food and medical supplies to thousands of beleaguered Allied prisoners of war scattered throughout the Far East. Their Japanese and Korean captors had resorted to the lowest forms of bestiality and depravity during their long imprisonment. Many had been in captivity for almost four years and almost all were walking skeletons. The Japanese, in many cases, had not even needed to erect barbed wire to keep the prisoners captive. The jungle was a natural barrier and lack of food and disease sapped the PoWs' strength and will, making escape virtually impossible.

On 28 August both 99 and 356 Squadrons took part in Operation 'Birdcage' when crews officially began dropping leaflets to PoW camps in and around Singapore. Unofficially, crews dropped all the cigarettes and clothing they could obtain on the Cocos. The sight of Liberators flying low over their camps dropping their very welcome supplies brought overwhelming relief. But the drops were not without cost. During a drop at Sungei Ron PoW camp at Palembang in Sumatra by a 99 Squadron Liberator, an entire crew met their deaths when their aircraft crashed. The PoWs conducted a funeral with all the resources at their disposal and the crew were buried with full military honours. The effect on the PoWs was such that no one could look at a low-flying aircraft for days afterwards. Among those in the camp who saw the crash were five survivors from a 215 Squadron (RAF) Liberator crew shot down on 14 August 1945 in the Sunda Strait. By September 1945 the emaciated PoWs were being flown out almost daily to Singapore. That month the main body of the British relief force arrived by sea and the remaining PoWs were taken aboard.

In addition to transport duties the Liberators of 159 and 355 Squadrons participated in Operation 'Hunger', the ferrying or dropping of rice to the starving population of South Burma. Rice cultivation in the hill districts of Burma had suffered heavily during the Japanese occupation and what little was grown was sufficient only for the

Bombs dropped by a Liberator B.Mk.VI on 356 Squadron explode on lock gates on the Khlong Phasi Charoen Canal near Bangkok in Thailand on 18 April 1945.

RCAF Liberator nose-art in India.
Above right: *Canadian Cutie.* Bottom left:
Lady X. Bottom right: *Jungle Joyrider.*

Above: Three Liberator B.Mk. VIs of 356 Squadron RAF after bombing Japanese positions on Ramree Island (Yangbye Kywan) off the Burma coast prior to the seaborne assault by the 26th Indian Division. 'Operation Matador' was fought in January-February 1945 as part of the XV Indian Corps offensive on the Southern Front in the Burma Campaign to retake Ramree and Cheduba Island to establish airbases on the islands for the supply of the mainland campaign.

Below: Liberators on 159 Squadron low level over Burma.

Bombs dropped by RAF Liberators destroy a bridge at Bam Tam Kan on the Bangkok-Singapore railway on 4 May 1945.

333783

Above: A Liberator of 132 Wing RAF over Tarhet during a daylight attack on a bridge.

Left: Wing Commander Eric James Brindley Nicolson VC.

Propaganda leaflets cascade from the bomb bay of a 231 Group Liberator during a daylight attack on the railway station at Pak Nam Phau.

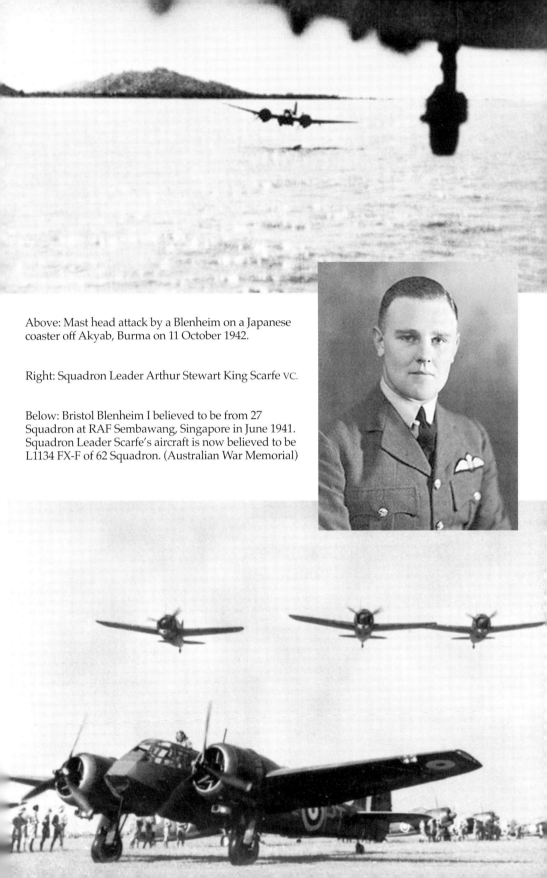

Above: Mast head attack by a Blenheim on a Japanese coaster off Akyab, Burma on 11 October 1942.

Right: Squadron Leader Arthur Stewart King Scarfe VC.

Below: Bristol Blenheim I believed to be from 27 Squadron at RAF Sembawang, Singapore in June 1941. Squadron Leader Scarfe's aircraft is now believed to be L1134 FX-F of 62 Squadron. (Australian War Memorial)

Above: The loss of 113 Squadron's V5589 was one of three Blenheims on 113 and 60 Squadrons shot down over the fiercely defended Japanese-held harbour of Akyab on the western coast of Burma on 9 September 1942. It is captured by the rear-facing camera on Wing Commander Walter's aircraft. Sergeant John Reid RAAF successfully ditched his aircraft in the sea, to be taken PoW together with his crew. Both ships attacked were sunk, including the supply ship *Niyo Maru*.

Below: Bombs explode on Ywataung-Myitkyina railway line near the Irrawaddy River in Burma, during a raid by Blenheims of 167 Wing RAF operating from airfields in India. At left can be seen teak logs, probably conveyed by Japanese trucks and off-loaded to await floating down the Irrawaddy in the monsoon season.

Left: Blenheim attack on the lower Chindwin River.

Below: RAF Liberators bomb bridges on Burma-Siam railway 1945.

Top: Liberator B.VI KH161 on 356 Squadron en route to bomb Armapura near Mandalay.

Below: Mitsubishi G-4M-50 Navy Type 1 Attack Bombers, otherwise known as the 'Hamaki' (cigar), in formation.

Above: Major inspection of a Liberator's Twin Wasp engine by ground crew personnel on 358 Squadron at Jessore in 1945.

Below: PBY4-1 *Mark's Farts,* Commander Harry Sears' PBY4-1 in VPB 104 otherwise known as 'The Buccaneers of Screaming 104'.

Top: A Kawanishi four-engined H8K2-L 'Emily' transport, a converted patrol flying-boat.

Centre: A smiling Lieutenant Paul F. Stevens, a 23-year old PPC (Patrol Plane Commander) and Squadron Executive of VPB 104, with good reason. On 17 March 1945 he shot down Vice-Admiral Seigo Yamagata, who was en route to Tokyo in a H8K2-L 'Emily' for an audience with the Emperor and to be promoted to full Admiral, and become the Under Secretary of the Imperial Japanese Navy. (Paul Stevens Collection).

Below: PB4Y-1 of the US Navy photographed in 1942.

Above: A Mitsubishi Zero A6M32s in formation.

Below: A Liberator is silhouetted on the ground during a raid on the wooden Road bridge between Pegu and Martaban in Burma, one of two attacked during a low level sortie by 231 Group.

Above: B-29-40-BW Superfortress 42-24579 Eddie Allen of the 45th Bomb Squadron, 40th Bomb Group, XX Bomber Command. Left to right, back row: Major Ira V. Matthews, pilot; 1st Lt Robert A. Winters, co-pilot; 1st Lt Herbert C. Hirschfeld, navigator; 2nd Lt Charles Behrle, bombardier; Flight Officer Louis F. Grace, engineer, S/Sgt John J. Mahli, crew chief; Sgt Claude L. Bolin, assistant crew chief. Left to right, front row: T/Sgt Fred H. Thompson, radio operator; S/Sgt S. V. Sienkiewicz; S/Sgt L. E. McBride; S/Sgt Samuel P. Winborne, top turret gunner and Powers. (USAF)

Below: 'War Over!

Ground crews on 356 Squadron RAF based at the Brown's West Island, Cocos Islands, celebrate in front of one of their Liberator Mark B.VIs on hearing the news of the surrender of Japan.

Top: Sunderland ML772 'D-Dog' which played a leading role in the Yangste Incident.

Centre: Flight Lieutenant Ken Letford DSO* DFC

Below: HMS *Amethyst*.

natives' immediate needs. In the Delta valleys the crops were plentiful but with the transport system in ruins there was little hope of transferring the rice other than by air. From September 1945 until early 1946 159 dropped one and a half million pounds of rice in 486 sorties.

On 15 November 1945 8, 99 and 356 Squadrons disbanded. Colin Berry recalls: 'Most of 8 Squadron's Liberators were flown back to various central units in India, among them 308 MU at Cawnpore in the Central Plains and just broken up. It seemed to us at the time to be a waste of perfectly good aircraft, some with less than fifty hours' flying time on the clock.'

In early 1946 159 and 355 Squadrons also disbanded. After their rice dropping missions the two squadrons shared an aerial survey assignment on behalf of the Government of Bengal and then on 30 April 1946 159 Squadron ceased to exist. One month later, on 31 May 1946, 355 Squadron also disbanded. Meanwhile, 160 Squadron continued food and mail deliveries to the Cocos Islands and other transport duties, until in June 1946 it returned to England and began re-equipping with Lancasters.

During combat operations from Burma, ground crews had performed miracles in often appalling conditions and with limited equipment and spare parts to keep the Liberators operational. These magnificent highly-adaptable bombers had served the RAF faithfully in the Far East; an airborne theatre of operations often forgotten by Press, public and historian alike.

Endnotes Chapter 13

1   James Blackburn DSO* DFC* (1916-1993) completed a record five tours of operations. Blackburn was born in 1916, in Acton, London, the son of Sir Arthur Dickinson Blackburn and was educated at Wellington College, Berkshire and The Queen's College, Oxford. Whilst at Oxford he joined the University Air Squadron and was commissioned in to the RAF Reserve of Officers in 1936. Blackburn served first as a Blenheim pilot on 57 Squadron and then on 70 Squadron as a flight lieutenant, later to be promoted to squadron leader and then wing commander. Blackburn was awarded the DFC in November 1941, followed by a Bar in September 1942. Blackburn was posted to North Africa in May 1942 to take command of 104 Squadron and remained in command of the squadron until August 1942. On 12 September 1942 Blackburn was travelling aboard the RMS *Laconia* when it was torpedoed 130 miles north-northeast of Ascension Island, by the German submarine U-156. The events that followed became known as the 'Laconia incident'. Blackburn survived the sinking of the *Laconia* and was taken prisoner; later to be imprisoned in Vichy controlled Morocco. In November 1942, Blackburn along with three other officers escaped and made their way to the American held lines in Morocco. In October 1943 Blackburn was awarded the DSO whilst in command of 148 Squadron. From March until July 1944 Blackburn commanded 227 Squadron. In December 1944, Blackburn was awarded a Bar to his DSO whilst commanding officer of 159 Squadron, working for Force 136, in recognition of his exemplary leadership during bombing and mine-laying missions. Blackburn was also awarded the American DFC by the

USAAF in recognition of the pioneering work that 159 Squadron carried out, extending the operational range of the Consolidated Liberator aircraft. Following his presentation with the medal, Blackburn held a party to celebrate at Firpos restaurant in Calcutta. Blackburn commanded 570 Squadron from 15 December 1945 until 8 January 1946 and then 196 Squadron until 16 March 1946.

2   Supply dropping missions for the 14th Army continued while Burma was cleared of the Japanese and in October the Squadron was moved to Malaya, Java and Hong Kong until the squadron was renumbered 48 Squadron on 15 February 1946.

3   Experiments with power settings to obtain minimum fuel burn-off for a given load were carried out on test flights. Eventually Blackburn established a combination of mixture, propeller speed and throttle settings which, plus a few degrees of flap, allowed the aircraft to mush along at 160 mph but produced a range of 3,000 miles. With the addition of forward bomb-bay fuel tanks the potential was as great as 4,000 miles. All this was achieved at around 8,000 feet with an aircraft originally developed to give optimum performance at 25,000 feet. *B-24 Liberator At War* by Roger Freeman (Ian Allan Ltd 1983).

4   356 Squadron went on to make their mark in the Asian skies and finished the war in the remote Cocos Islands only 1,200 miles from Australia. Dismore and his crew finished their tour of operations before the move to Cocos. They went back to their homes to enjoy a well-earned leave and alongside their campaign medals; three of them displayed awards for bravery and leadership. Frank Dismore was one. On his chest was displayed the distinctive ribbon of the Distinguished Flying Cross.Yogi by Frank Tisdale.

5   *B-24 Liberator At War* by Roger Freeman (Ian Allan Ltd 1983).

6   In 1947 at the war crimes trial of six of the Japanese personnel involved in the murders in Rangoon, Kanno, Okami and a corporal were convicted and hanged. Lieutenant Colonel Murayama was sentenced to death. It was established that Lieutenant Matsui had been killed in action during the Japanese retreat from Burma. On 28 September 1948 it was announced that Stanley James Woodbridge had been posthumously awarded the George Cross. The George Cross is the highest medal awarded to civilians or servicemen in a non-combat role for bravery second only to the Victoria Cross, for valour.

William Ellis Newton, VC was an Australian recipient of the Victoria Cross, the highest decoration for gallantry in the face of the enemy that can be awarded to a member of the British and Commonwealth armed forces. Born: June 8, 1919, St Kilda, Australia. Died: March 29, 1943, Salamaua, Papua New Guinea. Education: Melbourne Grammar School. Awards: Victoria Cross. Battles and wars: South West Pacific theatre of World War II, New Guinea campaign, Battle of the Bismarck Sea. Service/branches: Australian Army Reserve (1938–1940), Royal Australian Air Force (1940–1943).

7   Nicolson was born in Hampstead, London in 1917 and was educated at Tonbridge School. In 1935 he began working as an engineer and in 1936 he joined the RAF, joining 72 Squadron in 1937 and later moving to 249 Squadron in 1940. On 16 August 1940 near Southampton, Flight Lieutenant Nicolson's Hawker Hurricane was hit by four cannon shells fired by a Bf 110 , two of which wounded him whilst another set fire to the gravity tank. Injured in one eye and one foot and his engine damaged, he struggled to leave the blazing machine but he saw another 110 and managed to get back into his seat, press the firing button and continue firing until the 110 dived away to destruction, although as a result of staying in his burning aircraft he sustained serious burns to his hands, face, neck and legs. He bailed out and was able to open his parachute in time to land safely in a field. On his descent, he was fired on by members of the Home Guard, who ignored his cry of being a RAF pilot. Fully recovered by September 1941, Nicolson was posted to India in 1942. Between August 1943-August 1944 he was a Squadron Leader and CO of 27 Squadron, flying Bristol Beaufighters in Burma. During this time he was awarded the DFC. Nicolson was the only Battle of Britain pilot and the only pilot of Fighter Command to be awarded the Victoria Cross in WWII.

8   Adapted from *Over Hell & High Water: My Flying Experiences with Bomber Command & SE Asia Command during WW2* by Leslie Parsons (Woodfield Publishing, 2001).

9   Although the top command of Force 136 were British officers and civilians, most of those it trained and employed as agents were indigenous to the regions in which they operated. British, Americans or other Europeans could not operate clandestinely in cities or populated areas in Asia,

but once the resistance movements engaged in open rebellion, Allied armed forces personnel who knew the local languages and peoples became invaluable for liaison with conventional forces. In Burma in particular, SOE could draw on many former forestry managers and so on, who had become fluent in Burmese or other local languages before the war and who had been commissioned into the Army when the Japanese invaded Burma. By VJ Day Force 136 had infiltrated into Malaya 371 personnel, including 120 British officers; between 2,800 and 3,500 guerillas had been armed and no less that 50 W/T sets were operating. The personnel infiltrated included 56 British other ranks, 9 Canadian Chinese, 70 Asiatics and 134 Ghurkas (officers and other ranks).

10   160 Squadron's clandestine sorties over Malaya were of twenty hour's duration and they became almost commonplace. On the night of 20 July on 'Carpenter 30' Flight Lieutenant V. T. Davis and crew on BZ862/J landed at Minneriya, Ceylon after a flight lasting 22 hours 51 minutes. On the night of 29 July two Liberators flew to a dropping zone near Sedili Besar in Malaya to parachute supplies in the moonlight. Flying Officer L. W. Millard piloting BZ862/J was airborne for 23 hours 3 minutes while Flying Officer S. D. Turner piloting BZ824/W was airborne for 23 minutes' longer. Two nights later the same two aircraft were dispatched to a location near Kota Tinggi in south Malaya. Flight Lieutenant Magnus's aircraft completed the sortie after 23 hours 3 minutes. Flight Lieutenant Jack Muir and his six-man crew on BZ862/J beat this with an incredible flying time of 24 hours and ten minutes. Reaching the reception area none of the prearranged signal lights could be seen. Navigational checks were then carried out and these confirmed that the Liberator was at the correct location. Still with no signals from the ground and fuel reaching the level where only sufficient remained for the return trip, the 'load' (two British officers) was dropped near the Kota Tinggi-Johore Bahru road. Muir then spent 85 minutes' flying in the vicinity of the drop zone. BZ862/J landed at Minneriya at 0243 hours on 1 August having taken off at 0223 hours on 31 July and flown 3,735 statute miles. The aircraft had been airborne for which was the longest combat sortie flown by a Liberator and, it is believed, also the longest made by an Allied landplane during World War II.

11   Quoted in *Wings on the Whirlwind,* compiled and edited by Anne Grimshaw (North West Essex & East Hertfordshire Branch Aircrew Association 1998).

12   After the dropping of two atomic bombs on their home territory early in August, 1945, the Japanese formally surrendered. The Malayan People's Anti-Japanese Army (i.e. the Chinese communists) continued to attack the Japanese who, on occasions, defended themselves. It was a ticklish situation for the British liaison officers who now, formally, represented the victorious allies. They had to come between the Japanese and the Malayan communists. The pre-surrender plan had been for the allies to push down to Singapore from Burma, with the MPAJA holding the roads and joining up with amphibious force from India and Ceylon landed on the Morib beaches just north of Singapore, these beaches had been earlier photo-recced by my squadron. The landing on the Morib beaches was put into effect after the surrender of Japan in an effort to gain quick access to Singapore and its many British prisoners of war. In the event the Morib beaches were found to be made of quicksand!

Chapter 14

'The Erk'

It was 7 November 1941, I was with 214 Squadron and it was our twenty-fifth trip as a crew, our third trip to Berlin. It was 10/10 cloud most of the way. We thought we were over target and it was obviously defended, but we couldn't identify it, so we didn't know if we were doing the right thing. We had a load of incendiaries. We dropped them all and just as we were coming back we were hit with ack-ack.

Flight Lieutenant Lucian Ercolani

Wartime RAF bomber crew survivors are now thin on the ground and there are precious few reunions, but members of 99 Squadron still endeavour to meet every year. One of the most memorable occasions was in October, 1986, at RAF Mildenhall and was attended by a former commanding officer, ex-Wing Commander Lucian Ercolani. Know familiarly to his men as 'The Erk', he later became chairman and joint managing director of Ercol, the famous furniture manufacturers, of High Wycombe, Bucks. 'The Erk' won his first DSO when he flew on bombing raids over Europe. The squadron had an impressive history dating back to August 1917, when it operated with DH 9 bombers in France. In 1938 the squadron became the first to be equipped with Vickers Wellingtons and took part in many missions over Europe in the 1939-45 War from airfields at Mildenhall, Newmarket and Waterbeach. It was transferred to India in 1942 with 'The Erk' as CO to take part in the war against the Japanese and in mid~1944 it was re-equipped with four-engined Liberators, often flying arduous missions lasting up to 18 hours on shipping strikes and against land targets. Recalling those days at the reunion, Lucian Ercolani said: 'It was a squadron of exceptional spirit which always did more than one could reasonably expect. We managed to keep our identity. There was no distinction between maintenance personnel and flying crews and we also kept a balance of New Zealanders, Australians, Canadians and English among the fliers'. 'The Erk', who won a second DSO in India and the DFC for sinking an enemy submarine depot ship south of Bangkok, had to organise the conversion of the squadron from the two-engined fabric-covered, geodetic Wellingtons to the all-metal, big payload Liberators, a complicated and laborious job involving retraining crews and ground staff and extending runways. 'Statistically, bomber crews whose tour of duty was 30 missions survived only 20. I was one of the lucky ones,' he said.

Early in November 1941 Sir Richard Peirse, C-in-C RAF Bomber Command, decided to mount a major effort against Berlin. The operation went ahead on the night of 7/8 November despite a late weather forecast, which showed that there a large area of bad weather with storms, thick cloud, icing and hail would cover the North Sea routes to the German capital. 5 Group objected to the plan and they were allowed to attack Cologne instead but 169 bombers were sent to the Big City as ordered. Twenty-one aircraft including ten Wellingtons were lost. One of these was X3206 on 214 Squadron flown by Pilot Officer Lucian Ercolani, which ditched off Thorney Island, Sussex on the return. The son of an Italian furniture designer and manufacturer who had come to England in 1910, Lucian Brett Ercolani was born at High Wycombe on 9 August 1917 and educated at Oundle, where he excelled at sport. He left school in 1934 to work at his father's company, Ercol. When war broke out he joined the RAF and trained as a pilot in Canada, returning in May 1941 to join 214 Squadron. Ercolani had reached Berlin and he dropped his high explosive load successfully through a gap in the clouds but before the crew could release their incendiaries the gap closed as Lucien Ercolani recalled:

'It was our twenty-fifth trip as a crew, our third trip to Berlin. It was 10/10 cloud most of the way. We thought we were over target and it was obviously defended, but we couldn't identify it, so we didn't know if we were doing the right thing. We had a load of incendiaries. We dropped them all and just as we were coming back we were hit with ack-ack. What we didn't know was that one of the racks of incendiaries must have hung up inside the aircraft and when the ack-ack hit they were set off and of course they burn for a long time. So we were virtually alight with these things and they gradually burnt away all of the fabric. The belly of the plane was practically burnt out. The fabric round the mid-part of the fuselage was gone. The fabric on the starboard wing was all burnt away and both wings were badly holed and torn. The plane was nose heavy, although the trimming tabs were wound fully. My pals were marvellous, they put everything they could on the fires; when the extinguishers had run dry they threw the rest of our coffee over it and peed on it.

'There was smoke coming through into the cockpit and I opened the two lids over my head, which was the worst thing that I could have done, because that sucked all the acrid smoke past me. I got everybody to put their parachutes on and we were ready to jump out. I was about to tell them all to jump, but realised we were still flying. Where there's life there's hope and we kept on flying.

'We were burning all the time. We'd lost a lot of power, or rather we had a lot of increased drag; that was really the moment when we could have panicked and done all sorts of silly things. But we kept flying. It was quite difficult to hold the aircraft; all the centre section was badly gone. What made it worse was that it was difficult to find out where we'd actually got to.

'We were gradually losing height all the time. As we were approaching the coast I realised that petrol was being used up faster than normal; the question was whether to jump there, or take a chance of getting through. Everybody was very good about it. They were all getting ready to jump out and I had my parachute handy, but you want to hang on if you can. So we hung on. There was a hell of a wind blowing. We crossed the coast and we still hung on. Our wireless op. had got some sort of message through, but we didn't know where we were.

'Then, of course, we were over the water, a couple of hundred feet up. There was a gadget on the Wimpy where you pulled a knob and it put both engines on to both petrol tanks. Normally, one engine ran on one and the other engine on the other. The two engines didn't always use the same amount of petrol. So when you got right to the end, you pulled this plug and whatever petrol was left in either one, fed both engines. I did that and knew that we didn't have very long to go. We weren't much above the waves. We could see searchlights about the place and were hoping that we'd cross our coast, but we didn't. We had been flying back for three hours and still the plane was ablaze. Then the engines went and I said 'good luck' to everybody. When you know that you've come to the moment of truth there's almost a feeling of relief. I tried to make some sort of landing but the next thing I knew was that there was a terrific crash. 'Bang'! We came down nose first and as we went under I could hear the sound of things crumpling up and I saw the light of the moon shining down in the water. I felt like a spectator watching it all happen; it didn't seem to be happening to me at all. I tried desperately to get out, but the instrument panel had collapsed back on me, pinning me down. I definitely thought I'd had it and that I was finished. Then the plane floated up again out of the water. That freed me and I was able to pull myself out through the escape hatch in the top of the pilot's cockpit. The first thing I saw was the rear turret and the tail of the Wellington twisted right round, facing towards the front. I could see the dinghy and I could hear the rest of the crew calling to each other. I swam for the dinghy but, before we were all in, the aircraft sank.

'There was an extraordinary sense of quiet, a sense of relief. We were rather glad to be alive. But at the same time sad. I felt what a pity it was for those waiting at home, particularly my dear wife [Cynthia Douglas, whom he had married in 1941]. Then, of course, you begin to wonder where you are: do we just sit here; do we try to get back? If we're going to try and get back, what direction do we go in? Everybody was remarkably cheerful. In those days they had rum on the dinghies. We also had water flasks in the dinghy, but unfortunately the yellow stuff they had put in as a marker had got into the water. But the rum did us a bit of good. The flares didn't work. We could see searchlights and we thought that we were in the middle of the Channel. We had some funny little paddles; we felt that the right thing would be to try to aim towards England. We did everything we could to paddle that way. People were in remarkable spirits, we didn't actually have to do anything to keep spirits up. Everybody did it quite naturally. We just paddled and slept, paddled and slept.

'We had come down at about three o'clock in the morning. It was very cold. The weather wasn't too bad at first. The next day it got quite rough. The chaps were very good and we realised we were all in bloody trouble together. We couldn't blame each other for it or anything like that. We had a little miniature compass, an escape compass. We could see searchlights and we heard two or three aircraft, so again we tried to let our flares off, but none of them worked. I don't think any of us got to the stage of despair, or thought we weren't going to get out of it. That's the law of youth, of course, but I don't know how we thought we were going to get out of it. I suppose we weren't there long enough to get to the stage of desperation.

'On the third day I saw what I thought was a German submarine periscope, but in fact it must have been a lobster pot marker. It appeared to be moving very fast through the water, but that was just the tide sweeping past it. Then we saw land and I saw a bit of green and a football post and thought this is probably England. In fact it was the Isle of Wight. Then we gradually got closer, so we paddled harder with everything we had. We suddenly saw an Air Sea Rescue launch, but to our pride we got ourselves ashore, at Ventnor. By then some people had climbed down to help us in. I stood up to walk ashore, but fell down. My ankle had broken.

'I can't tell you what it was like to feel safe again. It was wonderful just to lie back in that ambulance and not have to worry about or think about anything. We were taken to the National Chest Hospital, where we were the only aircrew that they'd had and they made a tremendous fuss of us. They sent in whisky, everything. In my room there was a wardrobe full of all the booze you could want, including lots of champagne. In the mornings, we sent out for Guinness and played cards drinking black velvet. None of the crew was badly injured. I had my broken ankle and they thought that I was badly injured because I had blood all over my face, but in fact it was only a small cut.'

Flying Officer Ercolani was awarded an immediate DSO, a very rare accolade for so junior an officer, 'for 'outstanding courage, initiative and devotion to duty.'

In October 1942 Ercolani left for India, joining 99 Squadron near Calcutta. The squadron was one of two Wellington long-range bomber units used to attack enemy airfields and river, road and rail supply routes. Ercolani led many of these attacks over the ensuing months before the squadron switched to night bombing. Inadequate maps, appalling weather and poor aircraft serviceability due to lack of spares added to the hazards of flying during the 'Forgotten War'.

With the expansion of the strategic bomber force and the introduction of the long-range Liberator, in September 1943 Ercolani went to the newly-formed 355 Squadron. He flew many sorties deep into enemy territory, some involving a round trip of 2,000 miles, to destroy the supply networks used to reinforce and support the Burma battlefield. An important and frequent target was the Siam-Burma railway built by Allied PoWs. In September 1944 Ercolani returned as CO to 99 Squadron, where he won the respect and affection of his airmen, who affectionately dubbed him 'The Erk'. He led many of the most difficult raids himself, often taking his heavy four-engine bomber as low as 100 feet to drop his delay-fused bombs as his gunners strafed buildings or rolling stock. He attacked supply dumps and Japanese headquarters and throughout the early months of 1945 regularly led forces of up to 24 Liberators against targets in Siam, southern Burma and on the Kra Isthmus, often in the face of heavy anti-aircraft fire. He was the master bomber for an attack against the railway system at Bangkok and was mentioned in despatches. By the end of March 1945 the decisive battle for central Burma was won. He was awarded a Bar to his DSO. Ercolani was then put in command of 159 Squadron, part of the Path Finder Force, attacking targets in Malaya and flying a number of mining operations to distant ports, including Singapore - sorties of more than twenty hours duration. On 15 June he led a force of Liberators to attack a 10,000-ton tanker, the *Tohu Maru,* which had been located in the South China Sea. The mission involved a round trip of 2,500 miles. Flying in appalling weather, some of the Liberators were unable to find the target, while some were damaged by enemy fire. Ercolani attacked at low level and made three separate bombing runs, registering successful hits on the tanker, which caught fire. Subsequent reconnaissance reports confirmed that it had sunk; a devastating blow to the Japanese troops depending on its vital cargo of fuel. Ercolani was awarded an immediate DFC.

'There was an entirely different atmosphere flying in the Far East compared to the European show. The risk from enemy action was considerably less in the Far East, but, really, the anxiety and fear was probably worse. However badly one thought of the Germans, at least there was an element of European civilisation, as against our real fear of the Japanese and of coming down amongst them. I had a three-year spell out there and, apart from a six-month stint at Group Headquarters, I was fortunate to be on squadrons all the time. Our bases were always in the Eastern part of India, in Bengal, fifty-sixty miles from Calcutta. This meant that there was a lot of flying before we actually got to the business end, across the Bay of Bengal and, more often than not, flying over the Burmese mountains, to start with, mostly at night. Returning back in the mornings, though, could be a joy: the sun rising behind you, a glorious gold, lighting up the tops of the mountains, the valleys shrouded in mist, still in the dark. Although you had the worry of getting over them, they were very beautiful. The aircraft with less fuel and no bomb-load now, light to the touch, quite free and relaxed. It was quite an emotional feeling. I often thought I could hear the *Ave Maria* being sung.

'I joined 99 Squadron as a Flight Commander and, within a few days of arriving, was off over the other side. They still had the dear old Wimpys, but conditions were quite rustic. If you needed to change an engine, you had to push the aircraft under a tree and use a block and tackle from a branch. At that time, the Japanese were pushing right up through Burma and we were involved in bombing aerodromes and communications - anything that could help the Army. They actually got as far as Imphal and it was only the leadership and strong personality of General Slim which tipped the scales against their breaking into India.

'After some months, we heard that our Air Force was being built up with Liberators, that is, the American B-24, a four-engine job. They seemed very big to us in those days. They could carry probably four times as much as the dear old Wimpy and could be pushed to flights of nearly 3,000 miles. To start with they were intended to be crewed by twelve people, but we soon skimmed that down to six. I was posted as Flight Commander to 355 Squadron and was, for some time, Senior Officer to form up the squadron. When I arrived, there were only huts on the aerodrome, quite bare of equipment. Then people started arriving. We didn't even have enough knives and forks. We went round begging, borrowing or stealing equipment. Then the great day when, one by one, the Liberators came in. We did a quick conversion course and before long, to our great excitement, we were flying them.

'After a few trips over the other side, I was posted to Group Headquarters in Calcutta. I didn't think I was ever really cut out to be a Staff Officer and was only there for six months, but I learnt a lot. Then I was offered the great pride of the service, the command of a squadron and went back to my friends with 99 Squadron, where my experience with the Liberators was immensely valuable, as our first job was to convert 99 to the wonderful new Liberators. The scene over Burma had now begun to change. Although the Army was having a very rough time indeed in the Burma jungles, they first held and then began to push the Japanese back. We changed our role and switched mainly to daylight operations and learnt the art of flying these big aircraft in formation. It was a wonderful sight to be with your own squadron with twelve or sixteen aircraft all round you. Very small compared to Europe, but exciting for us. For some time, our targets were closely linked to a form of Army cooperation, clearing areas ahead of landings. We cleared the ground for the invasion of Ramree Island off the Burmese coast. We attacked aerodromes, supply depots and generally made life uncomfortable for the Japanese troops.

'It was then that we began to get involved with the infamous railway line linking Singapore right up through to Burma, built over the bodies of thousands and thousands of prisoners-of-war. It was a real 'hate' operation. Bridges and the trains themselves were the bomb targets. The Liberators were, of course, designed for medium- and high-level bombing, but as they were the only aircraft available which could do the considerable distances involved, we had to evolve new low-level techniques. We could hardly claim ever converting a Liberator into a fighter-bomber, but we must have come fairly close!

'Having flown 1,000-miles plus, to find our objective on the railway line, we would have to come right down on to the deck to try and knock out the engines. The terrible worry in our minds was that these trains and the lines, were crowded with our own people. It was a very deep emotional experience to see your own people on the ground, right down there in those terrible places, waving to us and encouraging us on. I cannot believe that some accidents did not happen, as many were very close to the engines, but their welcome was always the same. We felt awful when we had finished and pulled up to go home again, leaving them all behind.

'I was next offered the opportunity to move from 99 to 159 Squadron and to re-form the squadron into what might loosely be called the Pathfinder role. I was allowed the privilege of selecting the most experienced crews from those just being posted in and from the other squadrons. It could have caused a lot of bad feeling, but everyone was very generous and it seemed to work well.

'Our squadron was made up roughly in equal proportions of British, Australians, New Zealanders and Canadians. There was probably a higher proportion of the latter. This was far better than having British, Australian etc. squadrons. By mixing us all up together, you certainly had plenty of rivalries, but healthy ones to make things go even better. We all made many lifelong friends. Fine pilots amongst many other fine pilots.

'Strangely, whilst with Bomber Command, one used to do very little practice bombing, but bearing in mind our new role, we decided to work at it. Quite often we got down to 25 yards, but we used to post up the results in the Mess overnight and anybody who was outside fifty yards had to buy the drinks. This stood us in good stead when a large Japanese submarine depot ship ventured up the Gulf of Šiam. We found her just south of Bangkok, scored several direct hits, sinking her under a great cloud of smoke. As we hadn't used up our bomb load, we left her sinking and went after the escort vessels; but we missed them all, as they bobbed around like little 'water boatmen' beedes on a pond. Perhaps that taught us not to get too cocky!

'Similarly, we evolved a new method for low-level bombing to knock the bridges down. Bridges are, in fact, quite difficult to hit. Amongst many other successes, our squadron led the flight that knocked down the famous bridge over the River Kwai. Great annoyance was caused later amongst the crews by the film when it was said that the bridge was too far away for the Air Force to reach! The technique we worked out was to go as low as possible and fly slightly diagonally across the bridge and on each run to only use three bombs. Flying diagonally gave one just a little latitude fore and aft and also sideways. We used delayed-action bombs, certainly to avoid blowing ourselves up, but particularly so that they could really settle down before exploding, trying to get them as close as we could to the bridge supports themselves.

'The monsoon season used to be the season when everything stopped. Obviously we couldn't, so we had to find a way of getting through these frightening clouds. If you went in high, the up-currents had been known to break the wings off. We treated them with great respect. If we had to cross them in the middle of the Bay of Bengal and very often they were at their worst there, we found that our best way through was to go right down on to the deck, then try to work our way along the side of the cloud. At that level, beneath these enormous cumulus clouds and flying along their edges, it was rather like flying under the overhang of a railway station. I don't know quite how wide that overhang would be, but when we flew under the edges of these clouds, about 200 feet below would be the sea and about 200 feet above was the cloud. On one side a solid wall of rain and on the other you could look right out across the sea, a very strange feeling. We were very frightened of them.

'Out there we were rather a small Air Force and as a result knew almost everybody. We were allowed incredible independence; once given our detailed objectives, it was left to us how we set about it.

'Our squadrons were still units complete in themselves; they had not been 'rationalised' as in the UK with the squadron being flying crews only, with joint, combined, maintenance. We had the advantage of being a total unit along with all the chaps who kept our aircraft flying. There was a tremendous pride on the Squadron with everybody feeling that 'together' there was hardly anything that we couldn't accomplish.

'To have command of a squadron under these circumstances, with all those exciting opportunities at twenty-seven years of age, with probably 1,000 people to be responsible for, was a very great privilege.

'We had this freedom, had been wonderfully well taught to fly, but had had virtually no service training. We were presented with our job and got on with it. Where the lack of service training showed up was when we had the VE-Day celebrations and had to hold a parade. Although I was supposed to be the Commanding Officer, I hardly knew my left from my right. Fortunately for me, there were one or two people who did know what to do, so I just walked on and walked off.

'Although we had this VE-Day celebration, we thought, jolly good luck to them at home, but we still had a war on. Surprisingly enough, I never detected any jealousy or envy. The truth was that it had become difficult for us to appreciate that the war could ever end. Strangely too, throughout the entire war I never saw the enemy in a personal sense. I flew against the Japanese for three years and never saw one and I don't think I ever saw a German either. That, of course, was a joy and a blessing of the Air Force.

'On a day in late August 1945, we were briefed, bombed-up and ready for take-off, when, for no apparent reason, we were told to stand down. The same happened the next day. Then the news burst on us - 'the bomb' - it was all over. So our day arrived; VJ-Day. We certainly did have a celebration. We had one of our Liberators on the go, backwards and forwards to Calcutta, ferrying great quantities of beer and no doubt other bottles as well. On this occasion, the Australians felt that they should come into their own and show us how they could roast a whole ox over a bonfire. Beef? It was probably old Water Buffalo. That was my most vivid memory of VJ-Day - the unpleasant smoke and a piece of dripping red charcoaled buffalo.'

Ercolani left the RAF in March 1946 and rejoined his father at Ercol. He formally retired in the mid-1990s but remained closely involved with the company until his death on 13 February 2010.

Chapter 15

At War With The Japanese[1]

When war broke out they put up a big poster of a guy in a blue uniform with his flying helmet and his cleft chin and a Spitfire behind him, looking up at the sky: Wanted: young men of dash and initiative for aircrew duties in the RAF. I reckoned that I was just as good-looking as that bugger on the poster and I went in. I only asked what an aircrew consisted of and the next minute they had every bloody stitch of clothing off me and I'm standing on a wet towel to prove I haven't got flat feet. I was made an air-gunner and was posted to 21 Squadron at Watton which made low-level attacks on shipping. On our first morning in the Mess I was approached by a man from Northern Ireland who'd heard my accent. He said, 'Look, enjoy yourself, you've got two weeks'. Well, needless to say, I felt a certain amount of my Dutch courage begin to dissipate! My first raid, which was on the Frisian Islands, was a baptism of fire, because I didn't see a bloody thing. I was sitting on my tin hat because I wanted to get married later and they said that you could be decapitated at the wrong end. I'd been told that I had to belt away with my Browning guns at every target I could see. Well, I saw a ship above my head and I was belting away into the clear blue yonder! Daylight low-level ops on Two Group were far from healthy. A posting to Libya offered better chances of survival, but when Pearl Harbor took place and we were eastward bound, we flew into chaos. Landing at various places between Cairo and Singapore we found nothing but fear and uncertainty at every stop. As an operational squadron capable of attracting attention by our presence we were an embarrassment to people who had never heard a shot fired in anger. They didn't want us in Burma or in Malaya and at Singapore. They told us they couldn't handle us. Little wonder, for every time the air-raid siren sounded in Sembawang the entire station disappeared into the rubber.

Flight Sergeant David Russell

Despite apprehension amongst Allied intelligence about the intentions of the Japanese, nothing of any significance was accomplished regarding the aerial defences of the Malayan Peninsula, which were hopelessly inadequate. Amongst the RAF contingent in the country were four medium bomber squadrons of Blenheim Mk I (short-nose) aircraft, three stationed in Northern Malaya and one converting to the Mk IV. These were supported only by 21 Squadron RAAF, equipped with Brewster Buffalo single-engined fighters. They were no match for the modern fighters of that period. Two squadrons of obsolete Vickers Vildebeest torpedo-bombers formed the maritime strike component, with two RAAF squadrons of Lockheed Hudson aircraft in the support role of bombing or sea reconnaissance. The entry of the Japanese into the war with their strike at Pearl Harbor on 7 December 1941 coincided with attacks carried out against the Allied forces in Malaya. At this point the Blenheim squadrons were stationed at Sungei Petani (27 Squadron); Tengah (34); Alor Star (62); Kuantan (60 Squadron detachment from Burma of eight aircraft on training).

On 8 December it was reported that Japanese troops had landed on the beaches at Kota Bahru supported by the fire from their warships, whilst the main force was landing at Singora and Pattani in Šiam. All the Allied squadrons launched a dawn raid on the invaders at Kota Bahru, although some of their efforts were impeded by a blinding rainstorm over the target area. The Japanese had obviously learned a great deal in the use of aerial support and at 0700 that morning the aircraft of 27 Squadron were being refuelled at Sungei Petani when the aerodrome was bombed by Japanese aircraft. The crews who were with their aircraft were taken completely by surprise and found themselves engulfed in a storm of fragmentation and incendiary bombs. Within moments eight Blenheims had been destroyed, buildings set on fire, the airfield riddled with craters and many of the personnel either dead or injured. Not content, the raiders returned for an encore during the morning, inflicting further damage although, remarkably, the four remaining Blenheims were not seriously damaged. The next day the remnants of the squadron made their first retreat to RAF Butterworth, which had already received similar treatment from the Japanese Air Force. There were now the remnants of two squadrons (27 and 34) at Butterworth, the latter having lost six of their Blenheims in a raid on Singora airfield. There was to be no respite from raiding enemy bombers, who returned at 1700 to complete the destruction of Butterworth. On the 8th meanwhile, at Kuantan, the detachment of 60 Squadron had taken part in the dawn raid on Japanese shipping near Kota Baru, experiencing their first bombing raid in which they had lost two aircraft, one piloted by 28-year old Squadron Leader George Patrick Westropp-Bennett, the other by Pilot Officer William Bowden, whose crew were killed on L4913 which was shot down by anti-aircraft fire over the Gulf of Šiam while attacking the *Awagisan Maru*. Bowden was the first allied airman captured by the Japanese and was imprisoned at the Zentsūji PoW Camp where he remained until late June 1945. He was then transferred to Tokyo No. 12D Camp at Mitsushima where he was eventually freed in September 1945.

At Alor Star the Blenheims on 62 Squadron were being refuelled and re-armed after their return from the dawn raid on the 8th, when they too were attacked by some thirty Japanese bombers. The raid caused the usual death and destruction, only two Blenheims being left airworthy, though the ground-crews worked feverishly to patch up a few of the damaged aircraft. On the next day they also were directed to move to Butterworth. On their arrival the 62 Squadron crews were briefed, together with the survivors of 34 Squadron, to take-off at 1700 to bomb the enemy airfield at Singora. In Malaya near the Šiamese border all available aircraft had been ordered to make a daylight raid on Singora (where the Japanese Army was invading), in Šiam. The first Blenheim to become airborne was that piloted by 28-year old Squadron Leader Arthur Stewart King Scarfe. He had attended King's College School in Wimbledon and was a RAF Cranwell trained regular, joining the RAF in 1936 and being accepted for pilot training. On gaining his wings he was posted to 9 Squadron, operating the Handley Page Heyford. In 1937 Scarfe transferred to 62 Squadron, a light bomber unit which received the Bristol Blenheim in February 1938. Just prior to the outbreak of war in September 1939, the Squadron was detached to bases in northern Malaya. From July 1941 62 was based at Alor Star near the Thailand border and at the outbreak of hostilities in December 1941 the squadron came under heavy air attack.

Scarfe, as leader of the raid, had as his crew Flight Sergeant Freddie Calder, observer and Corporal WOp/AG Cyril Rich, gunner. They had hardly taken off when a formation of Japanese bombers swept in, dropping their bomb loads on the waiting aircraft destroying or disabling all the rest of the machines. It was quite evident that none of his colleagues were going to be able to join him and he would have been justified in going in to land but the sight of his comrades being killed or injured merely fuelled his anger and made him determined to carry out the mission alone, so they set course for the target keeping close to the ground. Their progress was impeded by Japanese fighters, with Rich using his gun to beat them off, then, on reaching the target they became the target of yet another group of enemy fighters. Despite this Scarfe made a steady run across the enemy airfield dropping his bombs amongst rows of Japanese aircraft, whilst Rich strafed the enemy with his single machine-gun. On turning for home they flew head on into twelve Japanese fighters, whose pilots were obviously thirsting for their blood. Clinging as close to the ground as possible, using all his skill as a pilot to evade attack, Scarfe flew on while Rich emptied a total of seventeen ammunition drums in a desperate engagement with the enemy. Despite attacks from roving fighters Scarfe completed his bombing run and was on his way back when his aircraft became riddled by cannon and machine-gun fire. Scarfe had no protecting armour plate and was severely wounded, his left arm being shattered whilst several bullets had opened up a large hole in his back, causing him to fall forward over the controls. Calder rushed to his aid, putting his arm around Scarfe's chest and calling for Rich to come to his assistance. The latter abandoned his turret, crawling over the bomb-bay to lend a hand. This truly courageous young pilot who, drifting in and out of consciousness, continued to fly the aircraft. Fortunately the enemy fighters had withdrawn, probably because they had run out of ammunition, so the Blenheim continued alone and unmolested.

Sighting their old base, Alor Star, Scarfe decided to land. With the assistance of both Calder and Rich, Scarfe brought his badly damaged Blenheim in to make a belly-landing, coming to a halt a mere 100 yards from the hospital that adjoined the aerodrome. About to become a father for the first time, his pregnant wife Sally, a nurse in the hospital, had just been evacuated south. He was still conscious on his arrival, though tragically he died two hours later on the operating table. Because of the chaotic nature of the Malayan campaign, the facts concerning Scarf's act of true heroism were not known until after the war when those involved were finally released from the custody of the Japanese. Sergeant Paddy Calder (later Squadron Leader) was awarded a DFM and Sergeant Cyril Rich (KIA in 1943) received a posthumous Mention in Despatches. On 21 June 1946 the *London Gazette* reported that Squadron Leader Scarfe had been posthumously awarded the Victoria Cross. His wife, attending an investiture at Buckingham Palace, accepted the award on his behalf on 30 July that year.[2]

On 9 December also, the last four Blenheims, their crews and two spare pilots of 60 Squadron arrived at the airstrip at Tengah, which was being vacated by 34 Squadron during the morning. The newly arrived aircrews were briefed to bomb targets in the Singora area, flying three out of a formation of six Blenheim Mk IVs on 34 Squadron. They were also given the heartening news that as they had insufficient fuel to fly back to Singapore they should land wherever they could. They took-off on schedule, bombing Japanese shipping in the Singora area, when they were pounced on by a horde of enemy fighters, who chased them over the Malayan border. Five of the Blenheims were shot down, crashing into the jungle. The only one to survive, which was piloted by Flight Lieutenant J. W. Appleton, managed to return, landing his badly battered aircraft at Butterworth. The four Blenheim squadrons had in a matter of three days been put out of business, the remnants retreating to Tengah airfield Singapore, together with RAAF units. On 23 December the few remaining Blenheims on 60 Squadron were handed over to 34 and 62 Squadrons, which were well under strength. These two units were then withdrawn to operate from Sumatra. On 24

December 1941 the remnant of 60 Squadron's ground crew and a few of its air crew, having lost all their aircraft in action, sailed from Singapore on the ss *Darvel* to Burma. They arrived in Rangoon on 1 January 1942 and were joined on 7 January 1942 by 113 Squadron and a couple of 45 Squadron's Blenheim IVs. 60 Squadron's spare aircrew were assigned to 113 Squadron as needed.

The Blenheims were not the only ones to suffer, the Buffalo and Hurricane fighters were being out-performed and outmanoeuvred. The obsolete Vickers Vildebeest torpedo-bombers in Malaya were being used outside their role, in daylight and in an environment that could only ensure heavy casualties, due to the decisions of an out-dated GHQ. These lumbering underpowered biplanes were intended for maritime strike at dusk or dawn and could just about stagger along at around 100 mph. Yet on 26 January twenty-four Vildebeests and Albacores on 36 and 100 Squadrons, followed by Hudsons from Sumatra, were detailed to attack in daylight a Japanese amphibious landing at Endau on the east coast of Malaya, which was supported by warships, an aircraft-carrier and the deadly Zero fighters. The 36 and 100 Squadron strike force was operated in two formations approximately four hours apart and supported by a minimal fighter force, which was already decimated. The Japanese had already discharged their troops and cargoes before the Allied aircraft had taken off, so the whole action was a tactical mistake and resulted in the loss of ten Vildebeests and two Albacores from this obsolete strike force, as well as fighters and Hudsons. Squadron Leader Allison on 36 Squadron, who took part in the second strike, said: '7 brought one Vildebeest (36 Squadron) back and there was one other got back. The whole thing was an absolute disaster and it should never have been ordered by anyone with any intelligence'.

On 8 February 1942 the Japanese invaded Singapore Island, the few remaining RAF fighters flying to Sumatra two days later. This was followed on 15 February with the inevitable surrender of Singapore, just over two months after the invasion of Malaya by the Japanese. The massive air support afforded to their ground troops by the Japanese, who had literally bombed the small Allied Air Force out of existence, would have done credit to the German Blitzkrieg. As in the conflicts in Norway and Greece, belated and pointless efforts were made to reinforce the beleaguered Allied Armed Forces in Malaya. In the case of the RAF, the nearest source of reinforcements was to be found in the Middle East. On 10 June 1940 RAF bomber squadrons in AHQ Egypt, under the direction of 202 Group RAF, totalled five squadrons of Bristol Blenheim IVs, one of Vickers Valentias at Helwan and one of Bristol Bombays at Heliopolis, a suburb outside Cairo, which could either be used as troop transports or medium bombers. No.250 Wing was comprised of 30 Squadron at Ismailia, 55 Squadron at Fuka and 113 Squadron at Ma'aten Bagush. No.253 Wing with Advanced HQ Ma'aten Bagush comprised 45 Squadron at Fuka and 211 Squadron at Daba. At the beginning of January 1942, 45, 84, 113 and 211 Squadrons, who had been supporting an extremely successful advance in the desert by the 8th Army, were withdrawn. Whether they were glad to leave is not recorded but in the words of a popular Army ditty at the time, it certainly seemed that Cairo was no picnic for the common 'erk':

Land of heat and sweaty socks
Sin and sand and tons of pox,
streets of sorrow, streets of fame
streets for which we have no name,
streets of filth and stinking dogs,
Harlets, thieves and pestering wogs,
clouds of choking dust that blinds
And drives poor blokes clean off their minds,
aching hearts and aching feet,
Gyppo guts and Camel meat.
The Arab's heaven - the Soldiers hell.

But the Blenheim squadrons were about to swap one hell hole for another. On their arrival at Heliopolis the personnel of were informed they were being posted to Malaya. In the event, only 84 and 211 Squadrons arrived in the battle zone before the Allies final surrender in Java on 8 March 1942; 45 and 113 Squadrons got no further than Burma, where they provided support along with 60 Squadron for the Allied retreat into India.

Coinciding with the decision to transfer 84 Squadron to Malaya, Wing Commander Boyce was replaced as CO by Wing Commander John Raymond Jeudwine. Considering that the latter had a specialist post at a radar station in Egypt and had hardly any experience of Blenheims, it was, it seems to me, to be a strange decision. One capability which Jeudwine possessed, which was to be an advantage during the latter part of the war in the Dutch East Indies, was experience of sailing, which he had acquired before the war whilst attached to the Royal Navy.

In the case of 84 and 211 Squadrons, they were each equipped with 24 aircraft, extra aircrew and approximately 500 airmen. On being briefed for their long flight they were informed that their destination was RAF Butterworth in Malaya which, as it had already fallen to the Japanese, shows a lack of good intelligence. The plan was for the aircraft to fly out in groups of six each day, with a fitter and rigger travelling as passengers and servicing the aircraft en-route. The remainder of the personnel would follow by sea. The first aircraft to set off on this epic journey left on 14 January, with stops at Habbaniya on the west bank of the Euphrates about 55 miles west of Baghdad, Bahrain Island, Sharjah, a British Overseas Airways Corporation station in the Persian Gulf, offering excellent accommodation, Karachi, Bombay, Hyderabad, Calcutta and then across the Bay of Bengal to Akyab. The next port of call was an airstrip in the Burmese jungle at Toungoo, 300 miles north of Rangoon, where they paused.

Jeudwine flew to Rangoon for instructions as to their destination. On his return he informed his airmen that their destination was now no longer the airfield at Butterworth, but an airstrip at Lhoknga in Sumatra, from which they were to fly to Singapore. Their route was to take them over the Andaman and Nicobar Islands, another lengthy flight requiring accurate navigation as they would have little fuel to spare.

Of the Blenheims of 84 and 211 Squadrons which left Egypt few of them arrived in Sumatra, some being lost en-route, others held up by mechanical problems and others crashing. The Blenheims landed at Medan on 23 January, having completed a journey of 6,000 miles in only eleven days, a remarkable achievement. Some of the crews had already flown their Blenheims out to the Middle East, so they could rightly claim to have flown halfway around the world. There were no facilities and little food on the airstrip, accommodation being provided in Palembang, where the airmen had to buy their own food. Life was further complicated in that the journey to and from Palembang necessitated crossing on a ferry, which only operated in daylight. From an operational aspect P2 had no early warning system or search radar unit, there was no HF or VHF radio, the airfield was crowded with evacuated aircraft and the airfield itself had insufficient protective pens, with a water-sodden short runway.

Flight Sergeant David Russell recalled: The Dutch at Medan couldn't give us any bombs. So we flew to Palembang Airport (known as PI), about 600 miles away in the south of Sumatra and there they said they could adapt some bombs and give us at least something to work with in the meantime. Jeudwine was getting all sorts of garbled orders from Singapore. Finally we were given orders to fly up to take on fuel at Medan and do operations on Thailand, Malaya and Burma, looking for ships on the way. There was no radio contact because there were no radio stations. We sent out an aircraft now and then to look for targets. It was as bad as that. We had no ops room to work from. At no time did Jeudwine ever have more than six aircraft that he could use for operational purposes. So we'd fly up to Medan; refuel, find a target, bomb it and then back three hundred miles to Palembang. We had to scrounge for food and fight for a bed and I was getting terribly tired and very fed up. We bombed Kuantan and then a ship when we didn't even know if it was Dutch or not. And the oil wells in Sumatra after we evacuated it.

'We were setting off from Palembang one day on an operation against an invasion fleet coming into Sumatra when we saw this squadron of aircraft coming in the opposite direction. They looked like Lockheed Hudsons, but they were Japanese. I looked behind and I saw parachutes going down into the airstrip 45 miles away called P2. Some of our friends were in P2. If they dropped parachutes at P1, too, we were going to come back to an infested aerodrome. We must have had a dozen aircraft at our service that day, which was great, but we bombed at too low a height and the aircraft were walloped all over the place after the bombs dropped. We came back up the river strafing their barges, which were absolutely down to the gunnels with soldiers. Of course the awful worry was not knowing if they'd already taken P1.'

At P2 airfield the Blenheim crews shared the airfield with two RAAF squadrons equipped with Lockheed Hudsons and one Hurricane squadron. Crews flew both day and night operations against the advancing Japanese, although life was complicated in that each 'op' meant flying first to Medan to refuel, a round trip of eight hours, before flying the operation for which they had been briefed. 'When we got back [to Palembang] it was completely evacuated' recalled David Russell. 'There were no Japs there. Only a few RAF personnel had stayed. We found their billets empty, their clothing all over the place. The place was a shambles. It was like a ghost-town.'

On 16 February, the RAAF squadrons having already left, the Blenheim contingent was directed to move to Java as the Japanese had already landed at Palembang. Packing five ground crew into each of the surviving Blenheims, they flew to the civil airport at Batavia where they were re-routed to Kalijati, eighty miles to the east and forty miles from the coast. Conditions were little better than at P2, personnel being billeted some twelve miles away at Soebank. The Japanese did their best to make life uncomfortable for them, coming over and bombing the airfield on several occasions. Despite their difficulties the aircrew carried out a series of operations against the enemy, losing both aircrew and aircraft on the ground and in the air, until the numbers of Blenheims remaining was not even the complement of one squadron. During the night of Saturday 28 February the remaining aircraft of the two squadrons had been engaged on night operations. At daybreak, they realised that the unit of the Dutch Army detailed to defend the airfield had pulled out. It was decided that without further delay the six remaining Blenheims should be flown to Bandoeng, carrying as many personnel as possible, the unserviceable aircraft being destroyed. It was at this juncture that Japanese lorried troops and a tank appeared at the other side of the airfield, firing their guns in a most unfriendly fashion, killing or wounding large numbers of RAF personnel, so it was a case of every man for himself to get away from the enemy. The remaining personnel of the squadron found their way over the fifty miles of rough country to Bandoeng, each of them having his own story to tell of the journey and their encounters with the enemy.

'In the meantime, unbeknown to us' continues David Russell, 'the HMT *Yoma*, a British passenger liner built in Scotland in 1928, was on its way full of squadron ground crew and spares. Up until 1940 *Yoma* had run a regular route between Glasgow and Rangoon in Burma via Liverpool, Palma, Marseille and Egypt, until, in January 1941 *Yoma* was converted into a troop ship. On 18 February carrying 1,628 troops she sailed from the Firth of Clyde with Convoy WS 6B to Freetown and on 8 April 1941 she left Freetown with Convoy WS 6 to Cape Town. After rounding the Cape of Good Hope she spent the next two years in the Indian Ocean, moving troops mostly between Mombasa, Aden, Bombay, Colombo and Bandar Abbas in Iran. In January 1942 when Japan invaded the Dutch East Indies and in February *Yoma* took troops from Colombo to Batavia, arriving with Convoy JS 1 and returning with Convoy SJ 5. '*Yoma* came later to Sumatra and the boys were ordered off to defend the island against the Japanese invaders. Eventually the *Yoma* picked them up again and took them to the northern coast of Java and just put them off on the island where they all became prisoners, never having fought. There were thousands and thousands of guys coming in from Singapore, Malaya and Burma. Java was the only place left and it was living with troops of all kinds, trying to get out. The squadron organised raids back into Sumatra. We bombed P2 and P1 and we bombed the oil wells. We'd been at Kalidjati in northern Java maybe two weeks when word came through that the Japanese invasion fleet was already off the north coast - fifteen minutes from our drome.[3]

'I did three operational flights that night on the fleet. We saw them dimly by the moon, but I don't think we hit anything. When we landed at dawn we got to the dispersal point and the aerodrome was pretty well empty. Nobody came to meet us. Then three tanks came out: the Japs had already landed. They'd come in unhindered by the Dutch, through the bush and were right on the aerodrome's perimeter. They began firing all over the place. We put a flare into the aircraft to set it alight, but the thing didn't catch! By then the Japs had opened up and we had to run like hell. To do them justice our boys had stayed behind at the safe side of the drome to evacuate us when we landed. We were told we were to go to Bandoeng in the centre of Java. Well, that was the most humiliating experience of my service career - I saw my aircraft sitting there waiting for the Japs to take it, knowing that I hadn't helped to do any damage to anybody and that the whole thing had been just a token presence. The squadron had been sacrificed for the sake of somebody's face somewhere in the background.

'I think one of the most telling moments was when an Air Marshal came to Sumatra saying there'd been far too much defeatism and we were going to fight to the last man. Sumatra had to be held and we needed to smarten ourselves up, we needed to shave. Within two days the Air Marshal gave orders for us to evacuate Sumatra. That's how we fought to the last man! We knew damn well that Java was going to fall. We were billeted at the time in a huge colonial bungalow belonging to a rubber planter. He saw the writing on the wall and presented the keys of the place, including the one to the cellar, to myself and Douglas MacKillop. We owned the estate for one day only, spent sampling every bottle in the cellar. Douglas was later drowned when the prison ship he was in was torpedoed on the way to Borneo.

'We joined a convoy of trucks, an old bus and a couple of motorbikes and then we met a Dutchman who had six brand new Chevrolet cars. He gave them to us tanked up. Doug Argent took one of the Chevrolets and piled four fellows into it - with Doug and me in the front. Just outside the village on the way to Bandoeng we came across a single Englishwoman wearing a print dress, a pair of white shoes, carrying a fox terrier dog and a little handbag, her sole belongings. We stopped the car and gave her a lift.[4]

'Bandoeng was absolutely crawling with servicemen of all ranks and descriptions - Dutch Navy, Home Guard, Aussies and Chinese - all wondering what the hell the future was going to be. We were there three days during which the Japanese simply bombed the place to hell. We were on an aerodrome and we were trying to defend it with Lee Enfields and pea-shooters. The Air Marshal then said, 'you'll get some ammunition and you'll go into the jungle and fight as guerrilla fighters.' Eventually [on the morning of Wednesday 4 March] we were told that that order had been rescinded and aircrew and senior officers were to proceed to the port of Tjilatjap [on the south coast of the island; a journey of 100 miles] where they would be evacuated on a ship that was en route from Australia. [They commandeered two lorries and an assortment of cars, setting off on arriving at their destination at 1 am the following morning]. It must have taken us nine or ten hours to get down to the south coast and into Tjilatjap. We no sooner arrived than a score of Jap 'Bettys' bombed the place to hell. It was Sumatra all over again. There had been three or four big bombings and there were debris and dead animals in the river and dead bodies. There were ships that had been sunk and were still burning. It was a very extensive port with a couple of oil wells, big oil holders. The CO said for our last effort against the Japanese we'd burn the bloody place. I had the night of my life, because we set fire to everything. We got pissed on Scotch whisky, I was absolutely paralytic. There were fifteen brand new American cars and we just took the handbrakes off and pushed them all into the river.

'There must have been forty-five of us left. Johnny Jeudwine got us on parade and said, 'Look, I'm afraid it's every man for himself. Now, that's an expression I'd never heard spoken. Of course I'd read it in adventure stories. 'Christ, if it's every man for himself, I haven't got a bloody chance!' I said. Jeudwine replied, 'I want you to forage. If you find a boat, try to go to Australia'. Australia was at least two thousand miles away! But we hunted around and got two lifeboats. Everybody piled into them. There was a sail. We filled them with fresh water tins and tins of biscuits, tins of Pabst beer, anything that could be kept. Somebody got this little flat-bottomed river barge and three officers got into it. [65 airmen climbed on board the motor-boat and the two lifeboats]. They were going to get rope, tie the two lifeboats on and tow them out of the estuary and out to sea. By sheer magic we would go south-east from Java and maybe, after two months, reach Australia. We had pretty poor maps but we had a compass. I was in the second boat and I was up to my knees in water. The thing was leaking like a sieve. We got away down the estuary with this wee boat looking like the *African Queen* ahead pulling us. It was giving off fumes, the crew were out cold and the boat was veering off course. We had to pull the rope back to get the three guys off it and then we just cast it adrift and it just went putt-putt-putting away on its own.'

Within an hour the engine on the motor-boat died and no amount of persuasion would bring it back to life. It was now the turn of the crew of one of the lifeboats to take to the oars and tow the other two boats away from the port, when it was decided to land on a small and secluded beach. Unfortunately, in coming into land the motor-boat and one of the lifeboats were holed and sank, though the crews got ashore, before salvaging all the provisions from the wrecks. They thought they had beached on an island but, as they were to discover, it was on the mainland separated from Tjilitjap by some marshy ground.

'We had come to the mouth of the estuary where there was a little island' continues David Russell. 'As we put in towards the island, my boat hit a coral reef and the arse came out and we all had to go overboard. I had my kit with me and managed to swim to the shore. The CO put an anchor over the side of his boat, which was safely in ten feet of water. We put all the stores on the shore and he lined us up, about forty-five of us and said it was obvious we couldn't all go. Twelve was the absolute limit and with that number he hoped to get to Australia. The rest must stay on the island and find a spring. There was a banana plantation. There was a lighthouse. If he hit Australia, he would get a flying-boat and come back to pick everyone up, signalling a letter 'P' on an Aldis lamp.

'My navigator Geoff and I both got our kit. After all, we'd been flying with the CO from the start. But Wing Commander Jeudwine took us down the beach a little and told us he wasn't taking us. We had no knowledge of sailing and a lot of the Australians did. He was going to take only Australians and Squadron Leader A. K. Passmore and his crew. Passmore was English, but had done a lot of sailing. We were heartbroken. The CO then swam out to get on the boat and I shook hands with him. I was crying my eyes out, treading water. He wished me luck.'

The rest of Jeduwine's party comprised Pilot Officer S. G. Turner, Flying Officer C. P. L. Streatfield, who alone knew the elements of sailing and seven Australian sergeants. Turner could handle a sextant and was chosen as navigator, using a school atlas they had found in Tjilitjap. The journey was to be made in the *Scorpion*, the remaining seaworthy lifeboat, under a sail they had made. Flight Lieutenant George Milson, one of the Blenheim pilots, had the dubious honour of taking charge of the beach party with Flying Officer Keble-White, Pilot Officers Millar and MacDonald with 48 aircrew and two drivers. The plan was for Jeudwine on reaching Australia to arrange for them to be picked up by submarine. With this in mind Milson was to arrange a 24 hour watch, given a recognition signal and told to leave a cross of stones on the beach if they left voluntarily. In his view, Milson felt in Jeudwine there was a real possibility he might be able to arrange their rescue.

At 1700 on Saturday 7 March, the day before the Dutch Army on the island surrendered to the Japanese, having shared out their rations, Jeudwine and his crew set sail on their epic journey, watched by their colleagues. One wonders what thoughts must have gone through the minds of the castaways, who can have had little hope of being rescued. Jeudwine and ten others boarded the *Scorpion*. On the evening of 7 March they put to sea, bound for Australia which the navigator calculated would take sixteen days. It took forty-seven. Through all that time they never lost heart, though as day after day passed in blazing sun or torrential rain, the chances of reaching land grew smaller and smaller. They played games, held competitions, but found 'that the mental exercise made us very hungry and that talking and arguing brought on thirst'. Saturday night at sea was kept religiously, a ration of liquor being issued, which was found on closer investigation to be a patent cough cure. Their worst experience was the visit paid to them by a young whale, about twice the size of the *Scorpion,* who came to rest lying in a curve with its tail under the boat. 'Eventually it made off and when we had regained the power of movement, we passed round a bottle of Australian '3 Star' Brandy ... after which we did not care if we saw elephants, pink or otherwise, flying over us in tight formation'. At long last, they sighted land near Frazer Islet, were found by a Catalina flying boat of the United States Navy and taken to Perth. An American submarine sent at once to Java found no sign of their comrades. Of the thousands of RAF and RAAF officers and airmen who fell into Japanese hands in Malaya, Sumatra, Java and later Burma, 3,462 only were found alive, after due retribution had fallen from the skies above Hiroshima upon the sons of Nippon.[5]

After watching Jeudwine and his crew sail away, the 'beach party' had settled down to wait in conditions which were quite encouraging. The beach was well-screened by thick foliage with a fresh-water stream flowing into the sea nearby. They had accumulated a reasonable supply of food with the bonus of cans of beer, minerals and even spirits. A look-out was kept religiously in the faint hope they might be rescued and so they spent their time eating, sleeping, swimming and talking. Four Australians and a few Englishmen, including David Russell, attempted to set sail in a lifeboat more seaworthy than the boat that had been lost and about thirty feet long. It had a sail, but the mast was very badly cracked at the bottom. After five days in the boat the men were bailing all day. After ten days on a flat sea, when they were about three hundred yards off Java, the boat encountered huge swells and eventually they were thrown on to the beach in total darkness and lay there exhausted until the next morning. They reached a small village, but everyone fled when they saw them. As they sat recuperating under the palm trees the headman returned with Japanese soldiers with him. (David Russell was sure he got five bucks a head for them). They were taken to Jogjakarta and put into a prison camp where there were six hundred Dutch. Later they were marched into Bandoeng to a much larger camp where they were reunited with the remaining men who had been six weeks on the beach. Eventually they ran out of food and one of them had syphilis so they had surrendered. 'We later discovered' concludes David Russell 'that the CO had reached Australia in forty-six days and had flown back, as he had promised.'[6]

Russell and the other PoWs captivity was to last for 3½ years and which they would never forget. They all suffered varying degrees of degradation, suffering and hardship, which not all of them survived before the Japanese finally surrendered.[7]

The Japanese meanwhile, having completed their occupation of Malaya, Sumatra and Java, now turned their attention to the conquest of Burma and India. Prior to the war starting, 60 (B) Squadron ground personnel at Mingaladon (near Rangoon, Burma), having few Blenheims left after the departure of the armament camp detachment, had assembled a number of Brewster Buffalo fighters from their packing cases. With the arrival of 67 (F) Squadron from Singapore without aircraft, these aircraft were taken over and the other Buffalo fighters assembled and made battle-worthy, the squadron having operated this type of aircraft previously. As regards the Blenheim squadrons who covered the retreat of the Allied forces in Burma, these eventually included 11, 34, 42, 45, 60 and 113, although initially, 60 Squadron was the only bomber unit in Burma and that at reduced strength when the war commenced. On 23 December 1941 the Japanese Air Force attacked Mingaladon, survivors said the sky looked full of aircraft, two Buffaloes were shot down and two others on the ground wrecked, although 67 Squadron and American Volunteer Group (AVG) P-40 fighters claimed ten enemy aircraft shot down. This was followed on the 25th with the enemy arriving in force at 5,000 feet and in their attack destroyed the airmen's cookhouse and their Christmas dinner, the hangar, the transport and equipment sections. The destruction of the Christmas dinner was considered by the airmen as sacrilege.

On 7 January 1942, 113 Squadron commanded by Wing Commander Stidolph arrived at Mingaladon from the Middle East. Immediately on their arrival, the AOC Burma, Air Vice-Marshal Donald Faskern Stevenson CB CBE OBE DSO MC* ordered them to attack Bangkok. Thus, within hours of their arrival in Burma, on 8 January five Blenheims took-off led by Flight Lieutenant Peter Duggan-Smith to bomb Bangkok docks, one Blenheim failed to return. This was the beginning of a campaign that was mainly comprised of low-level bombing and strafing, which resulted in the destruction of some sixty Japanese aircraft on the ground. The decimated 60 Squadron having only a few serviceable Blenheims left and with their surviving personnel returned from Malaya, operated alongside and with 113 Squadron. General Claire Chennault had allocated a number of the American Volunteer Group's (Flying Tigers) Curtiss P-40 fighters to help out the newly arrived 135 and 136 Squadrons of Hurricanes at Mingaladon and on a number of raids by the Blenheims these units provided a fighter escort. However, Japanese fighters escorted bomber attacks on both Rangoon and Mingaladon set fire to the former and made operating from the airfield almost impossible. This in the end and with the Japanese ground forces approaching Rangoon, resulted in the evacuation from Mingaladon airfield, serviceable aircraft being flown away and the others destroyed. The Hurricanes continued their operations from a dirt airstrip at Zigon, followed by a forced move to 'Park Lane' airstrip and finally to Magwe airfield, from where the Blenheims were operating. It was at Magwe where 'Burwing' was formed from the remnants of 45, 60 and 113 Squadrons and the 'Flying Tigers' P-40s. Simultaneously with this, 'Akwing' was formed at Akyab and comprised the remnants of 135 Squadron of Hurricanes and 139 Squadron of Lockheed Hudsons. They had just arrived from England, being merged with 62 Squadron. 139 Squadron was reformed at RAF Horsham St. Faith on 8th June, 1942.

Both Wings carried out offensive operations against the enemy whilst the fighters attempted to drive off attacks of Japanese fighter escorted bombers. Whilst the Japanese suffered losses, the smaller Allied forces were losing aircraft and crews in the air and on the ground to a well-equipped enemy of superior power and were fighting with diminishing resources and means to counter the unannounced Japanese raids, no radar units or air raid warning system being available. However, one successful attack by nine 45 Squadron Blenheims escorted by ten 17 Squadron Hurricanes (the total strike force) was carried out against Mingaladon airfield on 21 March. The Hurricanes provided top cover over the target as well as sending a strafing section in, with the Blenheims getting in an effective bombing raid complete with a strafing attack, without losing a single aircraft. This was but a rare instance of success, for the continual enemy bombing and strafing took their toll of aircraft and crews. Few replacement aircraft were provided, surplus ground crew and aircrew were flown or shipped out, although some rear-party ground crew members made a perilous journey by road to Myitkyina, where they were airlifted back to India. The Japanese ground forces took Mandalay on 3 April and Myitkyina on 7 May, the Allied retreat out of Burma was more or less complete by 20 May 1942, with the ground forces, those who had survived, regrouping within India. The Burmese terrain, with hills and rivers running roughly north to south, was to provide for the Japanese a logistical nightmare in the battles ahead, as it had for the Allied forces on their retreat. Meanwhile, both 'Akwing' and 'Burwing', with only a few aircraft left, had withdrawn into India. Amongst the aircraft being used for the evacuation were both old and modem, including an early 1930s Vickers Valentia troop-carriers.

During March 1942, 60 Squadron were reformed at Lahore, moving to Asansol in Bengal in May, from where they were soon in action. Meanwhile, 113 Squadron, which had arrived in Burma from the Middle East in January and suffered losses during operations, was also reformed at Asansol; whilst 11 Squadron arrived from the Middle East in March was based at Colombo, Ceylon. 45 Squadron, who should have followed the ill-fated 84 and 211 Squadrons to Java, operated successfully during the retreat from Burma and joined the offensive against the Japanese from India. Another unit which had been decimated after the invasion of Malaya, 34 Squadron, was reformed at Allahabad in India April 1942.

The Blenheim squadrons were constantly in action, operating in very difficult circumstances, as there was a shortage of spares and aircraft arriving from the Middle East were often old 'tired' ones. Yet because of lack of more modern aircraft, the Blenheims continued operating in support of the Allied Armies in South East Asia for another 15 months, by which time they were well overdue for replacement. Some squadrons operated the last version of the Blenheim, the Mk.V (Bisley). This version was originally considered for army-ground support in Europe, but was only operated in the Middle and Far East as a bomber. It was more powerful, well armoured and with a fully rotating mid-upper Bristol turret, but due to all of this flew no faster than its earlier brother, the Blenheim Mk IV. In August 1943, 11, 34, 45 and 113 Squadrons flew their last operations on Blenheims, followed by 42 Squadron the following month. All five squadrons were re-equipped with Hurricane fighter-bombers, leaving the observers and WOp/AGs to seek alternative employment.

Endnotes Chapter 15

1   Adapted from *Churchill's Light Brigade; The Bristol Blenheim Bomber Crews in Action* by Flight Lieutenant James W. Moore DFC; *BBC Peoples War Website* and *Forgotten Voices Of The Second World War: in the Words of the Men and Women Who Were There* by Max Arthur (Random House 2012).
2   His Victoria Cross is displayed at the RAF Museum London.
3   *Yoma's* final Indian Ocean voyage was with Convoy PA-33 from Bandar Abbas to Aden in April 1943. She was sunk with great loss of life in the Mediterranean on 17 June 1943 by the German submarine U-81 commanded by Oberleutnant zur See Johann-Otto Krieg. Captain Patterson, 29 crew members, three DEMS gunners and 451 military personnel were killed.
4   Incidentally Doug survived the war to become the producer of *Steptoe and Till Death Us Do Part.*
5   *Royal Air Force 1939-45 vol 2 The Fight Avails* by Denis Richards and Hilary St. G. Saunders HMSO 1975.
6   Group Captain Jeudwine, who was awarded the DFC and the DSO whilst leading 619 Squadron during the European bomber offensive was awarded the OBE for the escape from the Japanese. (His escape and the story of his courage and endurance in reaching safety are recorded in the book Scorpions Sting by Don Neate and published by Air-Britain and Price of Peace by Colin Cummings). On 19 October 1945 Group Captain John Raymond Jeudwine DSO OBE DFC, aged 32, was killed flying Typhoon IB JR390 of the Station Flight, RAF Little Staughton. He had over 2,200 flying hours but almost no experience at all on the Typhoon and had been airborne for about six minutes when he attempted a slow roll to the left at a height of 3,000 feet. The aircraft entered a spin to the right and probably stalled during an attempted recovery from the inverted position. It crashed into the ground but there is no evidence that the aircraft suffered a structural failure or that the pilot attempted to abandon it
7   See *BBC Peoples War site and Voices.*

Chapter 16

Escape From Šiam

'Two fighters over on the starboard skipper.'

Fair-haired Flight Sergeant Cyril 'Curly' Copley, 'P for Peter's 23-years-old Yorkshire rear-gunner, stiffened at the bomb-aimer's sudden warning over the intercom. He tightened his grip on the triggers of his two .5s as he sat hunched in the rear turret of his 358 Squadron Liberator at half-past six on the morning of 29 May 1945. The Liberator, on a top-secret mission from its base at Jessore, Calcutta, was within half an hour of dropping three American officers to join Thai underground forces deep in the interior of Japanese-occupied Thailand (Šiam). As he peered out of the turret, straining his eyes in search of the hostile fighters, he noticed there was not a scrap of cloud within reach into which they could nip to seek refuge. And then, scanning the sunlit sky 6,000 feet above the dense green jungle, Copley saw two more fighters. Altogether, there were nine Japs and they were formating in three vies directly ahead of the Lib. 'Curly' tensed as the voice of his Canadian skipper, Flying Officer Harry 'Smithy' Smith, crackled in his earphones: 'Watch them, gunners. They're turning in to attack.'

The Liberator jinked from side to side as Smith weaved to avoid the impending head-on onslaught. Suddenly, Copley heard a colossal clanging noise behind him like hail rattling on a tin roof. Jap cannon-shells were ripping into the top of the Lib's fuselage as the first enemy fighter made its attack. The acrid smell of burning cordite filled 'Curly's nostrils. As the Jap broke away down to port, Copley glimpsed the dirty-brown fighter as clearly as in a recognition book. An Oscar! Swivelling his turret, he checked range and deflection.

A second later, another Oscar flashed past. The Liberator juddered awkwardly as the second pilot, hit head-on by a cannon-shell, slumped across his control column, making the aircraft difficult to control. The navigator, too, was soon shot up. Copley swung his turret and squirted with his guns as Jap after Jap disappeared far below.

A few seconds afterwards, in a flash, Copley saw the elevator trimming-tab just beside him fly off and go floating down. This shook him, for he realised how close the enemy shells were coming. But still he bore a charmed life, for none hit him.

Out of the corner of his eye, Copley saw white smoke pouring back. He heard the engines spluttering and knew they were hit and on fire. Steadily, in attack after merciless attack, the nine Oscars hit one after another of the Lib's engines until, finally, all four were practically put out of action. The Liberator was losing height rapidly.

Fortunately, the intercom, which had been transmitting only scraps of noise for some minutes, now had a spasm of life. And then Copley heard the shattering message from the skipper:

'Prepare for crash-landing.'

Escape From Siam by Paul Clifton. Liberators on 358 Squadron at Jessore were normally engaged on clandestine operations over Burma, Šiam, Indo-China and Northern Malaya. This entailed night flying, during the moonlight period of each month, descending to 700 feet - usually into steep valleys - to drop agents and supplies behind the Japanese lines. 357 and 358 Squadrons carried out Special Duty activities throughout South East Asia Command for British SAS, American OSS and the French SIS transporting agents and supplies into Drop Zones in Burma, Malaya, Šiam, French Indo China and the Dutch East Indies.

Canadian Flying Officer Harry V. 'Smithy' Smith had just celebrated his 21st birthday and VE Day (Victory in Europe) was a distant three weeks in the past. It was clear and cloudless on the morning of 29 May 1945 when he prepared for his 25th clandestine operation of the campaign. 'We were however working harder than ever as the allied winter offensive of 1944/45 pushed the Japanese south out of Burma' he recalled. 'We flew American B-24 Liberator bombers, which had the required range and carrying capacity. Takeoffs were in the afternoons to give the maximum number of hours under the cover of night while over enemy territory. This often provided spectacular sunsets outbound and colourful sunrises many hours later on the return flight. The blackness of night also enabled us to penetrate the monsoon weather fronts by flying between the lightning flashes emitting from the ever-present cumulonimbus clouds. The missions were solo, unescorted sorties that penetrated deep into enemy territory. The shortest mission was to Burma and the eight-hour duration was considered only a circuit and bump. A day earlier we completed our longest mission, which was to Singapore where four Australians were disrupting the Japanese from a hideout in the mountains. The mission covered 3,000 miles and took 23 hours and fifty minutes. It was flown at 500 feet above sea level except for the actual drop at the DZ. The payload was only four containers as three of the four bomb bays were required for fuel cells. The next day we were being briefed for what was to be our most dangerous and costly sortie. The mission orders were being read: 'Smith, you will be dropping three OSS (Office of Strategic Services) agents [Major Johnny Gildee, Staff Sergeant E. J. 'Mac' McCarthy and Corporal 'Nap' Naporalski] and fourteen containers into a DZ near a village called Klong-Pai [meaning 'Bamboo Canal'] in the province of Nakon-Sawan [the name literally means 'Heavenly City'], near the town of Khorat, Šiam. There will be an OSS observer [Lieutenant Reid S. Moore] along to witness the drop. Your takeoff time is 00:00 hours to place you over the DZ (Drop Zone) at dawn. Your aircraft is 'P for Peter'. The IO (intelligence officer) will brief you on enemy activities. Good luck.'

'Well isn't that just peachy keen. This means we will be returning in broad daylight from 600 miles behind enemy lines with only the tail and mid upper turret. The front turret, ball turret, beam guns and armour plating had all been removed long ago to make room for heavier payloads. In addition, it was to be the first trip under the new policy of making the drops at dawn or dusk. Oh well, there are always plenty of clouds to take cover in. Sure! Following the briefing we drew our parachutes, weapons and rations from stores and checked out the B-24. Everybody would be fully armed. This was to be the last mission of my tour and I was looking forward to more pleasant pursuits. In fact, a plan was already in place to meet up with my best friend Jim Gibson who had re-mustered to bomb-aimer and recently arrived at 356 Squadron from Boundary Bay. We had been together all through school and joined up together in May 1942. The reunion was set for July in Darjeeling. As it turned out we did meet in July '45 but not as planned. We had a long flight of over fifteen hours ahead but I was too keyed up to rest. I finished reading a Mickey Spillane novel *You Only Die Once* and after dinner sat through the station movie *For Whom the Bell Tolls*. What could be more prophetic?'

Flight Sergeant William 'Whacker' Pugh, the second WOp/AG, recalled that it was, 'Quite a peaceful day, sweated almost continuously. We were briefed about a very special job that night to carry four American OSS underground agents, three to be dropped at the DZ, the other to observe. Take-off was scheduled for midnight. We all went for supper, not much as usual, but no point in complaining. The Gharries picked us up about 2230 hours and off we went to dispersal. We were flying in 'P' that night, not a bad kite, done a tour for 159 Squadron and had new engines, straight from the Maintenance Unit. 'Timber' and I climbed in and did our check over, set-up the Auxiliary Power Unit (APU), everything in order, parachutes, rations all in position, then went for a smoke on the other side of the dispersal. When the Americans arrived, Flight Sergeant 'Taffy' Parsons the dispatcher and Jim 'Ramsay' Roe the 'Screen' Dispatcher - helped them do a dry run by putting on and adjusting their parachutes and equipment. The gear these fellows carried was amazing! The second-pilot, 21-year old Flight Sergeant 'Bob' Poole, kept saying to me, 'I hope these guys don't get jammed in the hatch with all that gear on!' Believe me it was a job fixing them up, however it all had to come off again until we were thirty minutes or so from the DZ.

At 2230 hours Smithy, Bob and Taffy were running up the engines. 'Okay, pile in boys,' signalled Smithy. It was more pleasant taking off at night, no sweating, just cool and refreshing. At the end of the runway we could see the moon coming up; the weather looked pretty bad down south. We called up Control for permission to take-off; nobody else out the same time as us, so there was no delay. No sooner had the Control R/T said, 'you may' than Smithy let go of the brakes and we lurched down the runway, with those four great engines roaring as if they wanted to break away from us. We were taking off into the wooded area of the airfield and, with an all up weight of 64,000lbs. (This was the maximum weight limit although many flights were overweight by as much as 9,000lbs). Nearly everyone was a bit wary of takeoffs in this direction at night. We were well airborne and on the Intercom I heard Flight Sergeant Peter 'Lofty' Brenchley our navigator and Flight Sergeant Jack Draper our bomb aimer (who also assisted with navigation on these long flights), report from their position as did Cyril 'Curly' Copley who was now in his rear turret. 'Lofty' called up on the intercom and confirmed with Smithy that we were on course for 'George'. Everybody settled down. It was quite bumpy and raining heavily as well. Out over the Bay of Bengal, Smithy decided to come down to 500 feet in order to miss the heavy clouds above and ahead of us. The radio was crackling like heck and I could barely hear Control Broadcasts. Everybody seemed unusually quiet that night, maybe because we were all feeling a bit tired. The poor weather and being knocked about in the sky did not make any of us feel like singing although we usually did. At about 0415 hours we crossed the coast and altered course for Nakhon Sawan Province, Šiam.

Harry Smith picks up the story: At 0630 with the coastal mountains far behind, we began a descent to reach 500 feet at the DZ in Šiam. This was when, one by one, things started to go wrong. The sun was rising earlier than expected and for the first time in 1½ years the sky was completely clear; wall-to-wall CAVU (ceiling and visibility unlimited). No hiding place today! Just then the intercom came alive when Jack Draper called 'enemy fighters at 2 o'clock.' Nine 'Oscar' fighters were closing in fast. Three set up a racetrack for head-on attacks; three did the same on the starboard quarter and three strafed from below and above. Mostly they stayed away from the tail turret. I began violent evasive manoeuvres and dived for the deck. The frontal attacks were devastating. We were systematically being shot to pieces. 'Lofty' Brenchley was killed in one of the first attacks. Bill Pinckney, mid-upper gunner fired steady bursts at the fighters coming in head-on until he too was hit. Soon the flight deck was in a shambles with the cannon shells and bullets slamming about everywhere. The noise was deafening. I couldn't raise the bomb aimer on the intercom so I gave Bob Poole the order to jettison the containers. The jettison toggle is located between the pilot's seats and just as Bob began to pull the toggle up he was mortally hit full in the chest which caused him to straighten and pull the toggle right through without the pause needed to let the bomb bay doors to open. Five containers dropped free but the rest were hung up inside the bomb bay.

'The fighters kept up their attacks destroying the starboard elevator, radios, generator panel, engine controls, instruments and what was left of the engines. The last of our airspeed was bleeding off as I gave the 'Crash Landing' order. We had rehearsed this drill many times and I prayed the crew in the aft section would hear it and act quickly. We were too low to parachute even if we had wanted to. The only hope of survival was to try the treetop landing technique used by Canadian Bush pilots.'

Unplugging his intercom, 'Curly' Copley climbed out of the turret and scrambled down into his crash-landing station beside the waist-gun positions. Here he found an absolute melee of six struggling bods. Some of them had not been on intercom and so had failed to hear the crash-landing message. Several were clipping on 'chutes, or already had them in position on their chests. They had the rear escape-hatch open and were preparing to jump. As Copley glanced out of the hatch he saw the solid green of the jungle only a few hundred feet below. 'We're crash-landing,' he screamed madly, to stop those about to jump from committing certain suicide. At the last minute Harry Smith lowered the flaps to reduce the airspeed and dropped the undercarriage to absorb some of the energy of the impact.

'When the sound of the trees began scraping along the belly of the aircraft I braced both feet against the instrument panel and hauled back on the control column with all my might. Even with the co-pilot's inert body draped over the controls, the strength born of necessity helped me put the B-24 into a full stall. There was a colossal rendering of metal as the plane crashed through the trees. The wings, with their load of fuel sheared off right away: good riddance I thought. The fuselage careened on hitting more trees before coming to rest deep in the forest. The impact knocked the wind out of me and when I recovered I was folded up around the control column. There was a small hole in the side of the fuselage, which I soon made large enough to crawl out and was quickly followed by 'Whacker' Pugh. His foot caught in some jagged metal and he ended hanging upside down. A bullet through his hand made it quite useless but with my newfound strength I just picked him up and lowered him to the ground. I made my way to where the aft section of the B-24 had come to rest. Most of the bomb bay had been destroyed when the wings sheared off. What was left was in flames with ammunition from the containers that had hung up exploding in all directions. More chaos was added as the fighters kept strafing the crash site.'

Flung back by the impact, Copley blacked out. When he came round, a few seconds later, he found himself in a large detached section of the fuselage. The smell of burning fuel and dope was overwhelming. Gazing dazedly round, he suddenly saw that his section was blazing. He prepared to get out quickly. But, pulling himself up, he discovered that one of his feet was trapped. The flames were licking nearer. He wrenched his leg hard and the foot came out, leaving the shoe wedged in the fuselage. He pushed his way through a gap in the wreckage and limped out. Standing among the jungle shrubs, he stared at chunks of wreckage scattered in all directions. Orange flames and black smoke spiralled up from the blazing metal. Mingling with the oily fumes was the nauseating smell of bodies burning. Surely, Copley thought, no one else could have got out alive. A wave of anger flooded through Curly's mind as he stood there, alone. This had been the final op of his tour. He had at last got the boat in sight after four years overseas. Yet, now, here he was down in the middle of the Thai jungle, about a thousand miles from the nearest Allied territory, with more than 100,000 Japanese troops around him in a country that was at war with the Allies - and there appeared to be no hope whatever of getting back. What was worse, he seemed to be the only survivor. This would have to happen to him!

Just as he was thinking 'Poor old Smithy,' to his astonishment his skipper walked round the front portion of the crackling kite. Flying Officer Smith looked as grey as ash. Blood was streaming down his face from a ghastly gash in his scalp which hung limply down in a jagged four-inch flap. But he was alive. Curly heaved an enormous sigh of relief that he had not been left on his own in these alien surroundings.

'To my great relief' continues Smith, 'I found the OSS agents and the rest of the crew in the wreckage of the aft section of the aircraft where they were struggling to escape with the wounded. Just then 'Curly' Copley approached from the remains of the tail section. We made two trips into the wreck to bring all the survivors out. The list of injuries was daunting. Corporal Naparolski had a gaping hole in his abdomen and would not survive the day. 'Lofty' Brenchley was lying fifteen to twenty yards from the aircraft, lifeless. Bob Poole was dead in the cockpit. The mid-upper gunner, 21-year old Flight Sergeant Bill Pinkney was in the telescoped crackling front section. Bomb-aimer, 23-year old Flight Sergeant Jack Draper was trapped in the bomb bay, where he had been crushed to death when the kite had hit. Gildee had a broken collarbone. McCarthy had a fractured back and other injuries. Moore had such serious burns to his left thigh that he could hardly move but he was able to hobble about. Bill 'Taffy' Parsons had a bullet through his foot but was mobile.'

In all nine had survived the action. With rounds of ammunition exploding in every direction, Copley and Smith dragged the others out. Then one of the WOps, Flight Sergeant Ray 'Timber' Woods, appeared round the far side of the burning fuselage. Blood dripped down his face and he could hardly speak because of a piece of shrapnel blocking his nose. With him came 'Whacker' Pugh. A bullet straight through the centre of one of his hands had made the hand useless. While 'Curly' Copley ached and had a few scratches along his back, he and Flight Sergeant Ramsey Roe, the screen dispatcher, were the only ones who were not seriously injured. Having rescued everyone it was possible to get out, 'Curly' Copley took stock. '

It was small consolation to realize that we were probably the first to ever live through a crash landing in a B-24 says Harry Smith. 'We began taking stock and tending to injuries. I had just started to cut some small trees to make a litter when voices were heard. They may belong to Japanese soldiers so it was decided to leave the site and find a place to hide. McCarthy would have to be carried but we couldn't carry Naparolski as well and because of his grim condition I decided to send the group away under Major Gildee, as he was the senior and most experienced man on the ground. I elected to stay behind with Naparolski and give the rest a chance to escape. Not an easy decision but who ever said war was easy. I gave Gildee my Smith & Wesson revolver, a compass and a map showing our present location and told him to head south, as there were 300,000 Japanese troops north of us who were on the run from Burma.

'After the group left I tried to comfort Naparolski but he was in a desperate condition and died without waking. I checked the crewmembers who had perished and destroyed maps etc. I had lost a lot of blood from a head wound and rested against a tree for a while trying not to think of the consequences if the voices were from Japanese soldiers. The treatment of captured aircrew by the Japanese was brutal and final. A crew on 159 Squadron, which crashed in Burma in 1945, was systematically tortured and then beheaded. The three Japanese officers and three NCOs were later tried and executed for this atrocity.

There were other similar reports. I had kept a Sten gun just in case.

Next morning 'Curly' Copley had a horrible shock when he awoke. Staring bleary-eyed out of his bamboo hut, he was startled to see a party of mounted men, in uniform, galloping round the village. 'The Japs are here!' 'Curly' yelled, rousing the others. Immediate panic broke out: though, in their pitiably injured condition, there was little they could have done to defend themselves. The leading horseman trotted up to their hut and stared in. He had protruding yellow teeth, slanting eyes and Oriental-style uniform. He looked like a true son of Nippon. But then, to everyone's surprise, the leader warned them, in gestures and pidgin English, that a Japanese patrol was on its way in and that the crashed airmen must leave the village immediately. The horseman, it turned out, was a Thai police lieutenant who had come to help them.

Harry Smith came fully alert when he heard voices 'but happily they belonged to natives and not military uniforms. They were local natives from a nearby village who had found the main party and had been sent back for 'Nap' and I. So far so good. I stopped for a rest during the walk to the village and woke when I felt a tugging on my arm. It was a native who took a fancy to my wristwatch. The last I saw he was making off with it on a white horse. Well I thought; he's welcome. I was given a bowl of hot rice broth, which helped revive me. A mirror was produced and I soon realised the extent of my head wound. I got the flap of scalp more or less in place and wrapped it with a bandage. By evening we had all been reunited at a village, which was just like something out of National Geographic. The small huts were bamboo and thatch structures supported off the ground on spindly legs. We were very happy to have this shelter. Next morning we were startled awake when a group rode up on horseback. The leader was a Thai police lieutenant who had come to help us. He warned that a Japanese patrol was coming and we had to leave the village immediately. We went by bullock cart to a hiding place by a nearby stream. The last 'K' ration was produced and we shared four 'Camel' cigarettes and chuckled at the incredible message inside the book of matches, which read: *Jolly Good Luck To You Wherever You Are From Dromedary Foods, Chicago, Ill. USA.* We travelled for two days with bullock carts carrying the wounded and eventually came to a river where a boat was waiting to take us south to Bangkok. The first night on the river we stopped at a house located on an island where a Chinese couple fed us a hot meal, rice and something. Using two chopsticks, the wife rolled some cigarettes that looked as big as cigars. The tobacco was rolled up in a large leaf and tasted just fine.

'I don't know what the ingredients were but it hit the spot and we slept like logs despite the hoards of mosquitoes. Next morning Lieutenant Reid Moore related a dream he had where, he said, we were taken to a BOAC building, fed ice cream, weighed our baggage then boarded a flying boat for home. All this after only one smoke!! The next day we arrived at the house of Captain Rian Pacheetool, police captain for the province of Nakhon-Sawan.'

Eventually they came to a stretch of water. As he sat staring out across the river, 'Curly' Copley wondered what was to become of them. They hadn't a clue where they were going and they didn't know why the police were helping them. He tackled the police captain. But the officer merely grinned reassuringly and said: 'Not worry. You all right.' The evaders were even more puzzled, but resigned themselves to leaving their fate in the hands of the Thai police. After some food and first aid the party crouched in some bushes near a railway track. They watched breathlessly as the police captain crept cautiously up the embankment. He was checking if the coast was clear. Then they saw him beckon. The first evader slipped silently across the track. At length it was 'Curly' Copley's turn to go across. Noiselessly, he slung one arm around wounded 'Mac' McCarthy, while Ramsey Roe supported Mac from the other side. Crouching low to remain unseen, Copley and Roe dragged the helpless 'Mac' up the embankment. McCarthy never once uttered a sound although he must have been in serious pain. 'Curly' looked anxiously up and down the track as he nipped across the gleaming metals. Armed Japanese guards, he knew, were patrolling within a few hundred yards. But he saw no one. Then, his heart still pounding wildly, he hopped down to the river bank on the other side, the whole time dragging Mac with him.

The next two days were spent on an old motor launch crouched down most of the time to avoid being seen by Japanese patrol boats. Sometimes the heat became so unbearable that the rush mats hiding them from prying eyes had to be rolled up. Frequently, the police captain yelled a sudden warning as a Japanese craft came near and they had to bob down their heads, hoping they would not be seen. The slightest mishap would have given them away. They arrived in Bangkok and were left on the boat tied up to a jetty for two hours. A huge crowd of Orientals stared at them from the quayside and it was obvious from the evaders' colouring that they were Europeans. Worse, they knew that in Bangkok 15,000 Japanese soldiers manned the local garrison. They seemed to be everywhere. One yellow-skinned man kept eyeing them continuously. He was an evil-looking fellow who wore a military-style green uniform. He appeared the epitome of a Jap soldier. He stared at them for a whole hour, giving the boys the jitters. But he did nothing. Eventually, to the evaders' enormous relief, an ancient bus rolled up. The airmen piled on board, then drove through the main streets of Jap-occupied Bangkok, It was broad daylight and, as the rush mats at the side of the bus flapped in the breeze, Copley saw scores of Jap soldiers, wearing their characteristic long peaked caps and puttees up to the knees, walking the street. They were so close that Copley could almost have put out his hand and touched them and several stared at the men in the conical rain hats seen in the Orient for uncomfortably long periods.

The evaders soon arrived at Thai Police Headquarters where, that night, they went to bed in a long, cell-like dormitory. Though their beds were solid boards, covered only with straw mats, they fell sound asleep within a matter of minutes.

'Before sleep' continues Harry Smith 'we were led outside to a rain filled mud hole for a much-needed bath. I was reminded of the water holes seen on many prairie farms. Even though we were standing ankle deep in mud, it was a welcome dip, at least until I lost what was apparently the last bar of soap in the entire army. One guard was very upset. Earlier a RAF bombing raid had knocked out the electric and water services so maybe he didn't think too kindly of British airmen. I learned months later that 356 Squadron had made the raid on Bangkok and my best friend (and bomb-aimer) Jim Gibson carried the movie camera in his aircraft. Fortunately no one was injured.'

Suddenly, in the early hours of the morning, 'Curly' Copley felt a hand shaking him. Waking up with a start, he blinked bewilderedly at the yellow beam of a torch shining into his face. He tried to move his lips, but a firm hand was clamped over his mouth to stop him speaking. And then, from out of the shadows, he heard his skipper whisper in his ear: 'Come with me.' Completely mystified, Curly slipped off his bed and padded over to three dark figures standing outside the beam of light in a corner. One of the three 'Curly' recognised as Major Gildee, but he had never seen the other two men before. And then he was staggered to hear 'Smithy', after introducing him as his rear-gunner, add: 'Meet Dick Greenlee and Howard Palmer.' To Copley's utter astonishment, one of the strangers then reached over from the shadows and, in a strong American accent, said: 'Hallo 'Curly'. Have a drink.' A moment later, the stranger thrust a bottle of Johnnie Walker into Copley's hands and offered him a packet of 'Camels'. The sudden shock of this surprising encounter shook Curly to the core. A minute ago, all he had to hope for, at the very best, was internment by the Thais for the rest of the war even if he managed to escape falling into the hands of the Japs. Now, he found himself unexpectedly among friends who could obviously help him and freedom was practically within his grasp. This sudden change of fortune was almost more than 'Curly' could believe. It was then that Copley learned, in quick whispered explanations from Smithy, the whole astonishing set-up. Major Dick and Captain Howard were American Office of Strategic Services (OSS) secret agents. Operating from a secret headquarters in the heart of Japanese-occupied Bangkok, they were working hand-in-glove with the Free Thais. These underground forces included members of the Thai police, which explained why the police had been so helpful to the evaders. Understandably, the shooting-down of the 'Lib' had given the OSS men in Bangkok a colossal headache. Immediately, the Thai Chief of Police had sent out a police patrol to pick up the pranged crew. The patrol had been ordered to prevent, at all costs, the airmen falling into Japanese hands. A patrol had also been dispatched by the Japanese. The Jap patrol, had, in fact, searched the first village half an hour after the evaders had left - but they had later been ambushed by the Thai police and all the bodies buried. Astoundingly, the Regent of Thailand himself was head of the Free Thai underground movement. Thailand was, of course, technically at war with the Allies. Yet, while the Regent officially assisted his Japanese 'allies' in their struggle against Britain and America, in fact he was passing top-secret military intelligence to the Allies and was preparing the Thai underground forces for a projected possible revolt to drive out the Japs. His motive for double-crossing the Japanese was that he feared a stab in the back from them.

'Our presence in the country placed the whole underground movement in serious jeopardy' continues Harry Smith. 'Although the Japanese occupied Šiam, all of their army, navy, air force and police made up the Free Thai underground with the Regent of Šiam in command. The General of the Army was second in command. We had been instructed that if we were ever shot down in Šiam to surrender to the Šiam forces who would protect us from the Japanese. Well, this certainly applied in our case. A similar underground had been operating in French Indo China until it was discovered by the Japanese with disastrous results. The police patrol that found us had been sent out with orders to prevent, at all costs, our capture by the Japanese. A Jap patrol had in fact searched the village half an hour after we left. The patrol was later ambushed by the Thai police and the bodies buried. A plan had been hastily devised to smuggle the OSS agents out of the country. The OSS agents were being spirited away to keep their presence secret from the Japanese. They also wanted me as Captain of the aircraft out of the reach of the Japanese. There was room for one more British airman and 'Curly' Copley was chosen because of his long service overseas.

The rest of the crew would be safe in a Thai internment camp. The OSS officers would keep tabs on the rest of the crew in the Thai internment camp and get them out at the earliest opportunity.

'With the skipper gone and the navigator and bomb aimer both dead' continues Harry Smith, 'the air gunners, WOps and dispatchers would tell the Japanese interrogators that all they knew about their mission were routine duties. The idea was that with five graves at the crash site and with four interned crewmembers, the Japanese could be persuaded to believe that the complete nine-man crew had been accounted for. I woke 'Timber' Woods and told him of the plan and instructed him to tell the Japs that the Lib had been on a meteorological flight. The OSS officers would keep tabs on them and get them out as soon as possible. The five of us were taken by auto to the OSS headquarters located in the palace of the Regent of Šiam. The Regents' elegant dining room table served as an operating table for the two Thai doctors who worked for hours repairing our injuries. One had received his training in England and the other in New York. We were obviously in very good hands however there was not much in the way of first aid or medical equipment. The laceration in my scalp was stitched together using a curved shoemakers' needle and a pair of electrical lineman's pliers. A car battery tester was used to flush out the wound. I found out quickly just how tough the scalp really is and I remember wishing I had one of the cigarettes the Chinese lady had made. Major Gildee was a huge man more than six feet tall and over 250lbs. It took the combined strength of four of us to set his broken collarbone. However during the night his arm came loose from our makeshift bandage and the break needed to be reset. The decision was then made to risk a trip to a hospital and have plaster casts put on Gildee's and Mac's fractures. Gildee related later how a Jap patrol had come while they had left the car and before reaching the hospital doors. He said he was so scared that he hid behind a tiny nurse. We had a chuckle at that image.

'The food at the palace was remarkable. It was prepared at a five star hotel about four miles away and brought on foot by servants using shoulder yokes. We even had ice cream once! After a few days the Regent, whose code name was 'Ruth', announced that he had arranged a few days of R & R for everyone. A few months back an OSS agent stationed in Bangkok for several months had gone off his rocker and there were tremendous difficulties getting him out of the country. After some half dozen rendezvous with Catalina flying boats and submarines in the Bay of Šiam, he was finally evacuated to India. The Regent didn't want a repeat of this harrowing incident. He believed that the reason for the agent's difficulty was the confinement and stress of the job and the lack of female companionship. He was probably right but his idea of R & R was incredible. He had apparently bought a house and stocked it with food, wine and of course female companions. He also cordoned off the area with soldiers for a mile on all four sides. However Greenlee and Palmer considered the plan too dangerous. Anyway, it was clearly 'above and beyond the call of duty.'

'The Regent's last plea was 'but Dick, even I can't afford these women'. The matter was resolved as some Chinese had moved in across the street and began spying on the palace. The poverty in the country made it easy to find people willing to spy. A speedboat was kept moored by the river's edge at the back of the property and some vehicles were kept inside the palace grounds in case a hurried escape became necessary. There was also a company of soldiers next door. Anyway, the decision was made to move out and we began another leg of the journey to freedom.'

At about midnight on their sixth day in the secret headquarters, Copley and Smith, together with several other escapers who had joined them, piled into a battered old bus to begin their journey home. 'An Australian who had escaped from a prisoner of war camp on the Jap railway came with us' says Harry Smith. 'He was just skin and bones and crouched in a corner all the time without ever speaking. The plan was to proceed to a rendezvous about 150 miles north of Bangkok. We hadn't travelled very far however when half way up a hill in heart of the city the bus began backfiring.'

The Thai police driver kept getting out, tinkering under the bonnet and yelling loudly to the police escort in Thai. Then he would get in, let in the clutch and further tremendous bangs would echo through the still night air. Sitting in the back, with a Tommy-gun gripped between his knees, surrounded by tough Thai policemen also heavily armed. 'Curly' Copley knew they were fully prepared to fight their way out if surprised by the Japanese. Copley expected a Jap patrol to challenge them at any minute. They were in a main street of Bangkok in the early hours of the morning and there was a curfew in force. It wasn't very long before a Jap patrol arrived. The clicking of breach blocks inside the bus announced that they all intended to fight if necessary. The straw curtains on the windows were held closed while the driver explained to the patrol that he was transporting prisoners to jail. All the time he kept the starter engaged and the bus slowly crested the hill and coasted down the other side. They turned into an old racetrack and hid in the abandoned horse stalls. Luckily the Japanese had decided to let them pass. The Thai police driver and escort showed incredible ingenuity, courage and control in saving the situation. A runner was sent back and soon two British-type cars arrived to take them back to the Palace. There was no problem fitting their bulk into these small cars.

'The next night' continues Harry Smith 'we left Bangkok with a tow truck and a spare bus following along and travelled several hours north to a small airfield in the village of Ban-Pe. Lieutenant Moore, Major Gildee and I were passengers in an antique Fairchild piloted by no less than the head of the entire Thai Air Force. The mag drop on run up was a whopping 400 rpm but we took off anyway. There was a tense moment in route until we crested a hill along the flight path. 'Curly' was in a Taylorcraft that became lost and had to make an emergency landing.'

Suddenly, after Copley's Taylorcraft had been airborne for a while, the Thai pilot made hopeless signs at the fuel gauge, which indicated empty; gestured frantically at his map; and looked desperately down at the jungle. He was lost! A few minutes later, a small airstrip came into view and the young pilot indicated that he was going to land.

'Japanee?' someone asked.

'Thai-Japanee,' replied the pilot. The airfield below was under joint Thai and Japanese control. Almost certainly the Japs would not permit a strange aircraft to land without investigating. It looked as if the game was up!

The Taylorcraft landed and the pilot yelled to a mechanic for fuel. Then, to his dismay, Copley saw the mechanic returning with a 45-gallon drum of petrol, together with a hand-pump. Refuelling would obviously take ages - and a Japanese patrol was likely to roll up at any minute. Suddenly, a small twin engined Beechcraft 11A landed. Its pilot, an elderly, grizzled Thai, taxied over and called out with a reassuring grin: 'My friend lost. You come with me.'

They all hopped out into the Beech and within twenty minutes, they landed at the airstrip which they had originally been seeking.

Next day, 14 June a DC-3 from 357 Squadron piloted by Flight Lieutenant Larry Lewis arrived to fly the Liberator crew back to India. One of seven children, Laurence 'Larry' Godfrey Lewis was born in Bristol on 25 October 1918 and educated at Bristol Grammar School. He won a Peloquin Scholarship but had to leave school at 15 to help support his family. Lewis had earned the DFM as an air gunner before training as a pilot. Lewis took off in his Dakota and flew at very low level to a remote airstrip at Pukio in Šiam. He found the short runway adequate but the aircraft became bogged down at the end of the landing run. Within an hour, however, it had been recovered with the aid of Šiamese workers and Lewis took off with seven passengers, including some of the crew of the crashed Liberator. The citation to his DFC concluded, 'he successfully completed a mission well into enemy territory, in daylight. The results obtained are an excellent tribute to his outstanding ability.'

'A replacement OSS group was on board' continues Harry Smith 'as well as a few cases of American beer in cans and cigarettes. This was my first taste of the famous Budweiser beer and I order it today just to relish the memory of that first taste. The DC-3 had suffered a tear in the

Flying Officer Harry V. 'Smithy' Smith's crew: Back Row: Flight Sergeant 'Bob' Poole; Les Ladds; Flight Sergeant Peter 'Lofty' Brenchly; Flight Sergeant Jack Draper; Flight Sergeant Ray 'Timber' Woods. Front Row: Flight Sergeant Cyril 'Curly' Copley; Flight Sergeant 'Bill' Pinkney; Flight Sergeant 'Taffy' Parsons; Flight Sergeant 'Whacker' Pugh; 'Smithy' Smith.

fabric of one elevator during the landing in the rough field and there was a moment of panic until a piece of cloth and some glue were produced. The beer and smokes were heaven sent and our spirits rose. Within the hour we were airborne and headed for home. A refuelling stop was made at Rangoon, which had just been captured, from the Japanese. Seven hours later we landed at the Alipore airport in Calcutta. It was difficult to believe that the entire episode had taken only three weeks.

'Curly' and I and the Aussie spent two weeks at Escape and Evasion HQ in Calcutta. A period of hiding was necessary for the safety the Šiamese villagers and others who helped in the escape and until the crew were secure in the internment camp. We made a clandestine visit to the Calcutta General Hospital for checkups and returned to the squadron at the end of June 1945. The rest of the crew were brought out about two months later for a grand celebration.

Flying Officer Harry Smith was subsequently awarded a DFC for the magnificent way in which he crash-landed the Liberator on dead-stick in spite of his serious injuries. The four crewmembers who died have been buried at the Kanchanaburi War Cemetery in Thailand. This is a picturesque, beautifully kept and very large cemetery located by the Khwai Noi River. It also contains the remains of the many allied prisoners of war that perished while building the infamous Japanese railway.

Chapter 17

The Buccaneers of 'Screaming 104'

Around dusk on Wednesday 14 March 1945 a Kawanishi four-engined H8K2-L 'Emily' transport, a converted patrol flying-boat, arrived at the Second Southern Expeditionary Fleet HQ in Surabaya Naval Anchorage on Java from Ambon (Amboina), an island near New Guinea. On board the secret flight was 54-year-old Chujo (Vice-Admiral) Seigo Yamagata, Commander of the Fourth Southern Expeditionary Fleet, eleven crew and twenty-two passengers, comprising six officers, eleven non-commissioned officers and five civilians. Their final destination was the Yokosuka Naval base in Japan. The Vice-Admiral had recently been relieved of his command following the Japanese defeat in the region. American forces had liberated Manila on 3 February and Corregidor on 27 February. By 1 March Clark Field on Luzon in the Philippines was filled with US Army Air Corps and Navy aircraft. At sea, Admiral 'Bull' Halsey's 3rd Fleet, Spruance's 5th Fleet and Kincaid's 7th Fleet were sweeping all before them. From 16 February to 1 March 1945 Admiral Marc Mitscher's Task Force 58 had accounted for 648 Japanese aircraft destroyed and over 300,000 tons of Japanese shipping sunk. Yamagata and his staff knew there were no fighters left that could be spared to escort the 'Emily' to their destination. The Vice-Admiral had been nominated for promotion to Kaigun Tasisho (full Admiral) and an appointment to become the next Under-Secretary of the Imperial Japanese Navy. Yamagata was looking forward to a fleeting family reunion with his wife Aiko and their daughter Akiko in Sakurayama, Zushi before his audience with Emperor Hirohito in the Imperial Palace in Tokyo.

American and Allied air and fleet units were even then patrolling the East China Sea and the Vice-Admiral and his staff were very worried about the large numbers of B-24s in the area. However, the 'Emily' was at that time still one of the fastest and most outstanding patrol seaplanes in the world and the Vice-Admiral hoped that they could outrun any American aircraft. His H8K2-L was a 'Fat Cat', with two decks and some of the guns and armour removed to cut down on weight and make room for the officials and their baggage. Only the bow and tail guns, armed with one and two 20mm cannon respectively and two 7.7mm machine-guns, had been retained. It would have to make several refuelling stops en route. At each stop Yamagata's staff would gather intelligence information about American times and routes of possible patrols and choose the least dangerous time to fly. The departure time would therefore vary each time.

On the evening of the fourteenth, the main pilot, Johiso (Chief Flight Petty Officer) Yoshikazu Yasuda and twenty-four-year-old Nobuyuki Taniguchi, a Chief Flight Petty Officer in the crew, who had been classmates from the reserve pilot trainee programme and both of whom came from Kyoto, had drinks together. Yasuda confided in Taniguchi that his superiors recognized his excellent flying skills as a pilot and he was honoured to be chosen as the pilot to transfer Yamagata back to Japan.

On the morning of 15 March the 'Emily' took off from Surabaya. The first leg of the journey to Japan was an 875-mile flight to Singapore. After an overnight stop in the former British colony to enable the crew to rest and allow refuelling of the aircraft, the 'Emily' took off again next morning and headed for Saigon. Yamagata and his staff spent the night in Saigon and on the sixteenth the 'Emily' flew out towards Hong Kong intending to reach Shanghai. However, bad weather or an engine malfunction caused the 'Emily' to return to Sanya (Ya Xian) in Hainan Dao. Yasuda landed on the water and hit a reef, damaging the underside of the hull. Water was bailed out of the 'Emily' and it was refuelled all night long. Next day, Yamagata had first decided to resume the journey to Japan in a conventional aircraft, but one was not available so he decided to use the flying-boat as soon as it was repaired. On the morning of the seventeenth the party boarded the 'Emily' again. Yamagata wished to stop at Taipei in Formosa where there was a seaplane facility. The waves there are usually high but they subside from time to time. If the waves were not too high, they would land there. If it was not possible, they would fly to Kyushu.

The 'Emily' departed at around 1000 hours. They saw Formosa and flew along the coast. Soon they found Tan Shui. While they were circling two or three times to decide what to do, the communication officer on board delivered a radio message to Yamagata. An air-raid alarm was sounding in Formosa and the Japanese were being attacked from an aircraft carrier. The Vice-Admiral thought for a while and then asked the captain how much fuel remained. He replied that there was enough for one hour and twenty minutes flying time. Yamagata calculated the distance and ordered Yasuda to fly to Shanghai. Immediately, the pilot turned westwards and headed towards Shanghai at 160 mph at 13,200 feet. Yamagata thanked the crew for its good work and told his staff to distribute some snacks. The weather was getting worse. Clouds were hanging low and the captain ordered Yasuda to reduce the seaplane's altitude. Yasuda quickly finished eating and took over control of the aircraft and relieved the co-pilot, since they were entering a danger zone. The 'Emily' descended and the crew saw the Chinese mainland. Yamagata and his staff smiled with relief. Had they known that their plans for this 'secret' flight had been intercepted by US Navy cryptologists before leaving Java and decrypted, they would have been less than relieved. Thanks to the unceasing work of Radio Intercept Unit, known as the 'On-The-Roof-Gang', due to their having been trained in a classified area, US Naval Intelligence knew the Vice-Admiral's schedule and plans had already been set in motion to shoot *down Yamagata's plane.*

Early in the war the US Navy had recognized the need for a very long-range patrol aircraft and the Liberator was the answer, because its 3,000-mile range was just what the Navy needed to extend its range beyond that of the amphibious aircraft then in service. However, the Army Air Corps had no intention of letting the Navy muscle in on their land-based bomber offensive and aircraft for anti-submarine operations were operated by the USAAF. Nevertheless, early in 1942 the Navy and Army chiefs reached a compromise: the AAF wanted a fourth production facility to turn out more B-29s, so the Navy agreed to give up production of the PBB-1 Sea Ranger seaplane at the Boeing Navy plant at Renton so that Superfortresses could be built there. In return the Army ensured that, starting on 7 July, some B-24s and B-25s and Venturas could now go to the Navy.

The first B-24 squadron in the Navy was VB-101 and it evolved from VP-51, the Navy patrol squadron flying PBY Catalinas from Ford Island, Pearl Harbor in January 1942. This squadron, commanded by Lieutenant Commander William A. Moffett, moved to Barber's Point Naval Air Station on Oahu, Hawaii in October 1942 and there received fourteen PB4Y1-D Liberators. Training was cut short because of high losses in the south Pacific and in January 1943, VB-101 was ordered to Guadalcanal via Palmayra, Canton, Nandi and Espirito Santo. At about the same time, VP-102 and a marine photo squadron also flew out to the forward area in the Pacific. (In the spring of 1943 they were joined by Navy Photo Squadron VD-1.) On 12 February, off the coast of Bouganville, nine Liberators from VB-101 escorted by P-38s, F6-Fs and F-4U Corsairs bombed and sank a large Japanese transport and destroyer from 22,000 feet. Later referred to as the 'St. Valentine's Day Massacre', two Liberators and four escorting fighters were shot down when the formation was attacked by around sixty enemy fighters. VB-101 would continue to make patrol and bombing missions for seven-and-a-half months, at which time the squadron was relieved by VP-104, which had been commissioned at Naval Air Station, Kaneohe Bay, Hawaii on 10 April 1943 with Lieutenant Commander Harry E. Sears as commanding officer. Formation of the squadron resulted from splitting VP-21 in two, thereby immediately creating a unit experienced in flying PBY-5 aircraft. By mid-July all the air crews were proficient in all operational procedures and a month later the squadron was dispatched to Carney Field, Guadalcanal to form the first Navy long-range search group with VP-102. In March 1944 VPB-116 began flying ECM missions from Eniwetok Atoll against Japanese radars on Truk.

Meanwhile VP-104 and VP-102, now under the command of

Lieutenant Commander Gordon Fowler, continued operations against the enemy in the Pacific. In addition to their primary role of daily search and tracing of enemy task force units, a large number of formation strikes were made against the land targets and one strike against a Japanese destroyer fleet. Individual strikes were made when the opportunity arose. Burton Albrecht and his crew made a lone strike on a convoy of nine armed cargo ships, sinking three and fending off fourteen fighters. He claimed three kills. He also avenged van Voorhis's death with an attack on Kapingamarangi, sinking six 'Zero' floatplanes from among the dozen or so high and dry on the beach.

On 6 February 1944 VPB-104 moved to Munda Field, New Georgia where it continued operations until the end of March 1944 when it was relieved by VPB-115. VPB-104 had flown well over a thousand sorties, destroying or damaging thirty aircraft and fifty-one enemy surface vessels for the loss of only seven Liberators. VPB-104 returned Stateside for leave and reformation and was subsequently awarded a Presidential Unit Citation. On 15 May 1944, VPB-104 was reformed at Naval Air Station, Kearney, Mesa, California. Training was carried out until late June 1944, with Lieutenant Henry S. Noon as acting commanding officer. In the summer of 1944 the 'Buccaneers of Screaming 104' came under the command of Lieutenant Commander Whitney Wright.

On 30 October 1944 after months of intensive training and familiarization flights, VPB-104 began its move to the Pacific war zone, at Morotai in the Netherlands East Indies, arriving there on 3 November after bucking bad weather fronts en route, to relieve VPB-115, which had originally relieved the Buccaneers. VPB-104 and VPB-101, also equipped with PB4Y-1s and VPB-146, equipped with PV-1 Harpoons, now formed the Navy search group attached to the US Seventh Fleet. Morotai was anything but peaceful and crews were 'welcomed' on the first night by a large Japanese air raid. By the end of the month this had been followed by a further forty five attacks. Day and night artillery and mortar fire could be heard near the Japanese lines close by. Skirmishes and infiltrations made for little sound sleep and crews kept their side-arms close by at all times. There are other diversions too, like the appearance of large, lithesome pythons around the tents and 'Long Tom' trees which were brought down on living quarters by strong winds.

But Whit Wright soon had his men organized and preparations were made to get eighteen flight crews and fifteen PB4Ys ready for combat. On 6 November, Whitney Wright made the first flight from Morotai and successfully intercepted a 150-ton lugger. He achieved three direct hits with 250lb bombs and the 90 feet long craft sank immediately. Another lugger loaded with oil-drums was also sighted and repeated fire from Wright's gunners soon had it alight from end to end. It burned fiercely until it sank. But on 11 November Lieutenant Maurice Hill was attacked by two Kawasaki 'Tonys' (Ki-61 Hien 'flying swallow') while on regular patrol and his PB4Y-1 hit the water and broke up. Only four of the eleven-man crew survived, although they were rescued by friendly natives.

After less than two months' operations from Morotai the Buccaneers prepared to follow the advance north to Leyte, where 'Screaming 104' came under the new command of Fleet Wing Ten. Lieutenant Paul F. Stevens, who was born in Joplin, MO and in 1939 attended Joplin Junior College where he studied aviation, was a 23-year old PPC (Patrol Plane Commander) and Squadron Executive who had flown PBY Catalina missions at night against the 'Tokyo Express' and against airfields in the Rabaul area 1942-43.

'Operating the PB4Y-1 - a B-24J painted blue - for armed reconnaissance missions in the South Pacific during World War Two provided the flight crews with the full range of emotions - excitement, exhilaration, boredom, poor living conditions and on occasions, stark terror. As a matter of fact, living in tents, sleeping under a mosquito net and existing on dried rations were enough to make most of the patrol plane commanders (PPCs) downright mean.'

On 9 December, fourteen crews flew to Tacloban on Leyte, which was to be their new home and they were joined by the remaining four crews later that month. Although everyone was relieved to leave Morotai, Tacloban was not without its problems, as Paul Stevens explains:

'Tacloban was the only Allied air strip in operation in the area and consisted of a single strip built of lashed steel Marston matting laid on loose sand. Aircraft were parked wing-tip to wing-tip on each side of the runway. This allowed only about thirty feet of wing-tip clearance for take-off and landing and the dimly lit flare pots provided little line-up guidance. Takeoff was critical. The B-24/PB4Y-1 Liberator was one of the all-time great combat aircraft - with outstanding performance in all areas. It could take punishment and still get the crew home. It had a high degree of reliability, due in large part to the Pratt and Whitney R-1830 engines. However, the unwary or careless could experience some nasty characteristics. We did operate the airplane well above its maximum emergency war overload to achieve the range and carry the bomb-load for our missions. The crews on Tacloban were operating the PB4Y at 68,000lb gross weight. Because of the overload condition, every take-off from Tacloban presented a challenge. To add to our giggles, immediately after lift-off we were only about ten feet above the black waters of Leyte Gulf. Nor did our fun end with the lift-off, gear-up and flaps-up, because a climb to about 8,000 feet was then required to clear the mountains of the central Philippines. Power was set at 45 inches MAP and 2,500rpm and our cylinder-head temperatures usually exceeded the maximum of

232° - temperatures of 240° to 260° were common. It was a continual play of opening cowl flap to control temperatures and avoiding spoiling lift with too great an opening.'

The area of search from Leyte included two sectors extending to Cap San Jacques and Camranh Bay, French Indo-China, another sector to Balabau Strait and down the west coast of Borneo. Other sectors covered the area from Hainan Strait up the coast of China to Foochow and eastward to include Okinawa and Daito Jima. During the first few days at their new base a number of VPB-104 crews made repeated attacks on Japanese shipping and aircraft. On 2 December Lieutenant Ray Ettinger sighted a convoy of six ships north of Balikpapan, Borneo. He went in about four miles off the convoy and was fired upon, first by one of the ships and then by three Ki-43 Hayabusa ('Peregrine Falcon') 'Oscar's; these opened fire at 600 yards, making a co-ordinated attack from 3, 5 and 9 o'clock. They closed to 200 yards, but the PB4Y's return fire forced them to climb 1,500 feet above it. The 'Oscars' then dropped four phosphorous bombs dead ahead of Ettinger, but they exploded 200 feet distant at about 8 o'clock. For thirty minutes the 'Oscars' made high side- and tail-runs before the PB4Y was able to lose them in cloud.

On 10 December Lieutenant Henry S. Noon's PB4Y-1 was attacked by eight 'Zekes' ('Zeros') and two 'Tonys', which dropped a total of eight phosphorous bombs, some bursting very close to Noon's aircraft. He managed to reach safety after a running fight involving head-on attacks and passes from every position of the clock, lasting for about an hour. One 'Zeke' was definitely destroyed, bursting into flames as it hit the water and two more limped away from the scene trailing smoke after being hit in the engines and wing-roots. When ships could not be found, the PB4Y-1 crews sought targets inland. On 12 December Lieutenant Joseph D. Shea's crew bombed and strafed numerous targets in and around Brunei Town, Borneo. First he attacked an airstrip under construction and then a motor convoy loaded with ships. Proceeding over the harbour, Shea made three bombing and strafing runs on shipping, setting a 1,500-ton 'Sugar Charlie' on fire and damaging other ships and luggers. Return fire put many holes in the PB4Y, holing a fuel line from the main wing-cell and filling the aircraft with fumes. Five crew-members were overcome by the fumes and the bomb-bay door was opened to secure some fresh air. Tragically, William E. Abbott passed out while transferring fuel by holding the connection together by hand; he became unconscious and fell through the bomb-bay door at an altitude of 1,500 feet over Borneo. All the other crew-members later recovered after treatment at base. Recalls Paul Stevens:

'Freely translated, armed reconnaissance missions boiled down to two things: one, it was a must that you covered your assigned search sector;

and two, having accomplished that, then a PPC could do just about anything he had the guts to do. VB/VPB-104 was therefore running an impressive kill record. Utilizing mast-head bombing attacks against Japanese shipping and other targets of opportunity, scoring against enemy aircraft to an amazing degree, the squadron was to receive a second Presidential Unit Citation for this combat cruise. Morale was very high - and even occasionally, a two-bottle ration of Iron City beer became available.

'An armed reconnaissance on 5 February 1945 provided emotions for this PPC and crew beyond that normally experienced. Rolling out of my cot at 0200 and striving for an early takeoff, 1 was delighted with my assigned search sector - virgin territory! Departing our home base at Leyte in the central Philippines, my patrol was to proceed south-westwards through the South China Sea, then east to the coast of Borneo and then hack to Tacloban. As per usual this was a 1,000 nautical mile leg outbound, a 100 nautical mile cross-leg and on back to home base. But what a great joy - the fast carrier task force had not swept this area, nor had the USAAF bombers hit here. There was no question about it! I would make a kill, or kills, this day.

'To achieve the range for the assigned patrols, careful planning and close attention to cruise control was a must. A target speed of 135 to 140 KIAs [knots indicated airspeed] was difficult to maintain initially with maximum continuous cruise. Often, the first hour or so of the patrol was flown with auto-rich and 35 inches MAP [Manifold Absolute Pressure] and 2,300rpm; the airplane was truly behind the power-required curve during this period. Also, at this time much of the wing panel could be seen from the cockpit over the engine nacelles; later, as the aircraft weight was reduced due to fuel burn, the nacelles blocked this view.

'Once clear of the mountains and when daylight had arrived, I let down to about 1,500 feet; this would provide defence against enemy fighters and at the same time provide a good search pattern by our ASP-15 radar. At this stage of the war there were still plenty of 'Zekes' to create a real hazard if caught high. Though the might of the Japanese had been 'broken' by this time, a great many of the enemy fighter pilots did not know this and had plenty of fight in them. Then, too, those fighter airplanes with the stars and bars sometimes generated an even greater hazard to our single airplane patrols.

'Arriving at the end of my search sector, I made the turn eastward toward the coast of Borneo. My plan was to approach the coast at Bintulu airfield. Almost immediately we gained a radar contact. Since the contact appeared to be quite small and always conserving fuel, I just sauntered on, believing a small, wooden 'sugar dog' vessel awaited us just beyond a few scattered showers. These small ships were easy kills for us and collectively, they transported a great deal of tonnage for the enemy.

'Surprise! Just clearing a shower, the *Terrisuki*, [an *Akizuki*-class destroyer of the Imperial Japanese Navy] greeted us with bursts from his heavy AA batteries. We had learned to respect this class of destroyer: they were tough customers and could shoot very well. Fortunately, being just beyond effective gun range and combined with a diving turn, his firing was inaccurate. Had I taken the initial radar contact seriously and approached at wave height with max power, we could have made a mast-head bombing attack and possibly scored a kill - or the Jap destroyer gun crews could have painted another American flag on their gun-mount. Whatever, add one notch to my frustration level.

'About fifty miles from Bintulu we set max power and descended to 50 feet altitude. This gave us a blinding 205 KIAs and as the sea state was slick calm, we were generating a wake upon the water by our down-wash. While this approach was evading radar detection, it also limited our forward visibility. Even so, as we identified the coast line, it became apparent that we had hit our landfall of Bintulu right on. The opening of the harbour was sighted, as well as a good-sized warehouse on the dock. Our bomb-load for the day was ten 100lb GP bombs with 4-5 second delayed fuses and the warehouse qualified for at least half of that. Immediately after release and by laying my head in the bubble side-window, I saw that warehouse blow up with a force well beyond that generated by our bombs. Most enjoyable and even more so due to the lack of return gunfire. This indicated that we had achieved complete surprise.

'Now we were coming upon the airfield. Two 'Oscars' (the Japanese Army's 'Zero'), two trucks and a number of people were obviously servicing the fighters and were unaware of our presence. 1 heard sounds similar to shrapnel hitting our airplane, but seeing mud splashes upon the windshield, I realized that the forward-firing .50 guns were kicking up mud from the dirt runway and we were flying into it. My thought was to avoid the rain on the way home so as to keep the mud splashes as evidence. Previous such occurrences had been met with considerable scepticism as to my claims of very low strafing attacks. We were hitting the fighters, as the tracer bullets were flashing as they hit along the fuselages of the 'Oscars' and I saw three men fall as they were hit. But pulling up and looking back I was disappointed that neither airplane was burning. There could be no claim for a kill if the airplanes did not burn. Obvious hits did not count.

'Pulling hard to come around for another firing run, I could now see the left tyre of one of the fighters burning, but no other apparent damage. Now, into the second strafing run, I pressed in even lower and closer. Yes, many tracer flashes, but again the airplanes were not burning. This was ridiculous! We had hit them repeatedly, but still there was no fire. A third run was made, with the same disappointing results - I was furious. Also, I had broken the cardinal rule when attacking well-defended targets: make one firing/bombing run and keep right on going! We were lucky; there had been no return gunfire. But I had been very foolish and over-eager. Add several more notches to my level of frustration.

'Some degree of sanity had been regained. We departed Bintulu and proceeded north-westerly toward Brunei. This was a hit spot. The Japanese had been receiving oil from the Brunei oilfields for some period ot time. Their fleet had used Brunei Bay as an anchorage and major units sortied from here for the Battle of Leyte Gulf. I flew several miles inland and at 500 feet or so to avoid radar detection. We swept the South China Sea with our radar to cover our search sector. As we passed the oil-fields and were approaching Miri airfield, a ' Val' [Japanese dive bomber) was seen turning into a final run for landing. I had a dangerous mind-set: we would make this kill! But we must do it quickly, for to follow the 'Val' over the airfield would have been suicidal, since Miri served as the airfield tor Brunei and was heavily defended.

'We added power and closed quickly. Opening fire at a close range, both the bow and top gun turrets were shooting very well. We must have been hitting, but I could see no results. Continuing to close I could now see tracer hits, but no fires, no evidence of real damage to the 'Val'. Very close now, I started to fly under him. We were now at about 300-400 feet above the ground. Suddenly he pushed over, or stalled - he was coming down on top of us - we were going to collide!

'I could see every detail of that 'Val' - the neat rivet rows, the bomb hanging between his landing gear: there was no question, he was coming right into our cockpit. We'd had it! There was little we could do. My life did not flash in front of me; my thought was, T wonder what the guys back at the squadron will think when I don't get back tonight.'

'The 'Val' passed over the cockpit unbelievably close. I felt a jolt and shudder as he struck the right vertical stabilizer. The top turret gunner, who had been firing at him and had swung his guns around aft to see him hit the tail, said with amazement, 'Well, that son-of-a-bitch is still flying!' However, the collision momentarily straightened the 'Val' upright, he immediately rolled inverted and crashed and there was a large explosion. Our airplane was descending. At 200-300 feet I instinctively pulled hard, but the elevator was jammed. My co-pilot had a strong sense of survival, however and he joined to pull, which we did with all our combined strength. The elevator broke free, but our pull-out was much too low; the empennage was twisted and distorted, the rudder remaining jammed. But we were still flying!

'We were a long way from Tacloban and would be very vulnerable should we encounter enemy fighters, so we decided to try for San Jose airfield on Mindoro Island, which was some newly acquired real estate. Needless to say, our course for Mindoro would be carefully planned to stay well clear of Japanese airfields.

'San Jose was a very busy airport and we landed and taxied without directions to a hard stand; there was no attention given us or our aircraft whatsoever. Lee Webber, our bombardier and a first-class metal smith, climbed onto the horizontal stabilizer and began to hack away at the damaged tail. Soon the shattered metal pieces were cut away and the rudder was freed; we took on 1,400 gallons of fuel and departed for Tacloban. The one-and-a-half hour flight was relatively uneventful. The entire empennage was replaced with a salvaged USAAF model, so my PBY4-1 was now unique: it was the only blue B-24 with a bare aluminium tail dressed with the 13th Air Force black markings!

'In some instances, adverse occasions may be for the best. In this case, I became convinced that I was not totally invincible. I had done it to myself and an over-eagerness for a kill had backfired quite badly. While we continued to make kills and covered our sectors aggressively, you can believe that more sober judgements prevailed.'

At Clark Field US Navy crews - the 'Buccaneers of Screaming 104' - were tumbled from their tents late on Saturday morning, 17 March. VPB 104, flying PB4Y-ls, VPB-119, equipped with PB4Y-2s and VPB 146, equipped with PV-1 Harpoons, formed the Navy Search Group attached to the US 7th Fleet. Lieutenant Paul F. Stevens takes up the story:

'The morning of 17 March was different from the usual activities for Armed Reconnaissance Missions. Usually, we arose at 0200 hours, but this morning I rolled out of my cot and left the tent about 0700 hours. After breakfast, our briefing at Wing HQ was routine and brief. It consisted mainly of search sector assignments, issuing code books and weather reports. Since we were to search cui sectors, regardless of the weather, the weather briefing received little attention. However, of considerable importance and very much out of the ordinary, was our primary mission of the day. This was to intercept and shoot down an 'Emily' reportedly carrying high-ranking Japanese officials. It would be a tremendous feat to accomplish this intercept. All crews flying this day were elated with the prospect. My own feelings were somewhat dampened by two factors. One, our search sectors where the 'Emily' was most likely to be found were assigned to crews from another squadron, VB-119. This irritated me very much as our squadron's crews of VB-104 and my own crew in particular were far more combat-experienced than those of VB-119. We were approaching the end of our combat tour, whereas VB-119 was still in the early stages of their tour. However, the VB-119 crews were flying the PB4Y-2 Privateer, the single-tail development from the PB4Y-1 (or B-24). The Privateer was faster and more heavily armed than our older aircraft. My second feeling of detraction was my growing apprehension concerning the return portion of the flight, which would be con-ducted during hours of darkness, adding to the operational hazards of flying in the forward areas.

'Departure from Clark Field was made at 0915 hours. Our patrol was up the eastern side of Formosa (now Taiwan), between Formosa and Sakishima Gunto into the East China Sea, then southwards along the China Coast searching for Japanese shipping, aircraft and any targets of opportunity. After passing Formosa and when descending through some clouds, for one of those rare times in the South Pacific, we collected a little ice on the airplane. We proceeded in towards the China coast just above the water. We felt this was our best offensive, as well as defensive tactic when deep in enemy territory. We could then both fight off Japanese fighters and achieve the element of surprise when attacking Japanese shipping. However, there was a fog bank lying on the water and I could go into the coastline only so far. I was then concerned about running into a hill or mountain along the coast, as my forward visibility was virtually nil. We then turned south-westwards and proceeded down the Chinese coast.

'This portion of the patrol was flown about 100 feet above the water and about three to five miles offshore. We were enjoying a relatively strong tail wind, when about 150 miles south-west of Hangchow Bay I sighted a Japanese freighter leaving a harbour. Further out to sea a Japanese destroyer was obviously conducting an anti-submarine search. I judged him to be far enough away to be just outside effective gun range. I immediately applied full power and started running in on the freighter. The Japanese destroyer then opened fire on us, but was ineffective. As we closed on the Japanese freighter, my top and bow turrets, manned by Allen Anania and David Gleason, opened fire. When firing forward, the muzzles of the top turret, twin .50 calibres, were just behind the pilot's head. Believe me the muzzle blasts from these fifties nearly drove one out of the cockpit! The noise was deafening. Running in closer against the Japanese freighter, our gunners generated a beautiful sight. The bow and top turrets appeared to be hitting with every tracer. And, more importantly, we caught him by surprise and there was no return fire. With the engines set at forty-five inches of manifold pressure and 2,500 rpm and assisted by the tail wind, our attack speed was about 235 knots.

'The bomb load this day was ten 100lb bombs. These bombs were equipped with a five-second delay fuse. This permitted us to make a masthead bombing attack and then get clear before the bombs exploded. With a load of ten 100lb bombs we were thus equipped to attack large shipping, dropping the entire string of bombs and assuring hits, as well as attacking small shipping and dropping one bomb at a time in order to sink as many ships as possible. In attacks of this type, the bombardier released the bombs utilising the 'seaman's eye' method. That is, simply, a visual judgement of when to release. At masthead level and dropping a string of bombs, by an experienced bombardier, it was virtually impossible to miss. If we had surprise on our side, which we strived for, a bombing run of this nature with the B-24 pitted against a Japanese merchant ship was really not all that hazardous. However, if the element of surprise was not on our side, such a masthead attack could be fatal for the attacking aircraft.

'Just after the bombs had been released and a pull-up made, by laying my head up in the bubble side-window, I could see the explosions of the ship, though several bombs had overshot. With the destroyer still out of gun range, I circled back, flew up-wind and came in for a high-speed strafing pass to ensure that we obtained a good photograph. The ship was burning and had made a 180 degree turn. As we passed by the ship, I observed crew men jumping over the side. (The following day one of our planes patrolling this area found conclusive evidence that this ship had been sunk and we were credited with this kill. It was identified as the 3,000 ton 'Fox Tare Baker', AGS-2 *Koshu*).

'Shortly after pulling up from this second strafing and photo run, we sighted two Aichi E13A 'Jake's. They were slightly above and on an opposite course from us, in a formation, right echelon. They apparently did not see us and, staying low on the water, we turned and pulled up to join in as number three man in their formation. As was my practice, when assured that we had surprise, our aircraft would be flown to a position behind and slightly to the right of the enemy aircraft. Our gunners were not permitted to fire until we were at point-blank range. As we slid into the number three slot we were very nearly lapping wings. I was impressed with the sleekness and as with most Japanese aircraft, the very smooth finish. [At Morotai in October 1944, while en route to join 'Screaming 104', Stevens and his crew had spent four days sanding and waxing down their PB4Y-1 with two gallons of floor wax to add 5-10 knots to their speed]. I noted that this aircraft was equipped with radar. It had the 'clothes line' antenna wiring all around the fuselage and wings. The rear seat man was seated aft and performed the classic 'double take'. As we joined in, he first glanced over at us, turned his head back then quickly turned back to look at us again. He made no attempt to use his 20mm gun. At that time we opened fire and very quickly the 'Jake' started down. Following him down, we observed him crashing into the water.

'So far it had been a good day and as we pulled up from shooting down the first 'Jake' my thought was to take on the other 'Jake'. However, the pilot of that aircraft used his head and flew directly to the Japanese destroyer and began circling overhead. Japanese destroyers were greatly respected by us. Their gunnery was excellent and we rarely caught them by surprise. We, therefore, turned southward and resumed patrol. The 'Jake' remained in a safe haven over the destroyer.

'Twenty to thirty minutes after the attack on the 'Jake', while travelling southwards along the China coast and continuing just off the water, I looked up and about five to eight miles ahead and approximately 3,000 to 4,000 feet above, I spotted the aircraft we had been sent out to find - the Japanese 'Emily'! It was a very slicked up airplane and a pretty sight. There was no question but that we had found what we had come for. Immediately upon sighting, I put on full power and told my crew to stand by to attack. My first thought was to pull directly head-on into the aircraft for no-deflection shooting. This is what I should have done. However, I discarded that idea and decided to climb in on a beam attack and, hoping to stay with the aircraft, to ensure bringing it down. With full power on we began a climbing approach and, as yet, they had not seen us.'

Aboard the 'Emily' Nobuyuki Taniguchi was keeping watch next to Yasuda and he spotted the Liberator. I immediately informed Yasuda and the captain, who reported this to Yamagata. The Vice-Admiral asked how far we were from Shanghai. The captain answered, 'Twenty minutes'. Yamagata entrusted the captain with the task of taking evasive action to avoid attack.'

Stevens continues: 'A zoom-climbing 180 degree turn was made into the aircraft at point-blank range. The 'Emily' put on power, increasing speed but attempted no evasive manoeuvres. We opened fire and both the top and bow turrets were shooting well. There were numerous tracer flashes on the deep fuselage indicating hits.' Nobuyuki Taniguchi says: 'The shooting by the enemy plane was fierce and I saw bullets coming through the fuselage. The chief engineer, a Taisa (captain) in the Fourth Southern Expeditionary Fleet, died instantly from a round that went through his chest. He died with bubbles of blood coming out of his mouth. The Vice-Admiral sat in his seat, holding his sword with both hands. He asked me how many bullets remained for the 20mm gun. I answered that there were ninety bullets remaining and 400 bullets for the 7.7mm gun. He encouraged me to do my best. The young gunner was having a problem changing a magazine. This was his first aerial warfare. I took over from him and started to shoot. When the enemy plane came within 330 feet I fired heavily. After a while, the Vice-Admiral asked about the remaining number of bullets. The Vice-Admiral patted me on the shoulder and was pleased with my performance. At one point during the attack the distance between the two planes was only 100 to 150 metres and I could clearly see an American pilot's face.'

The PB4Y was not hit. Stevens, though, regretted his method of attack. 'I did not direct my gunners to shoot out an engine. Had we shot out an engine, it would have slowed him sufficiently to ensure a kill. With the zoom climb and turn into the 'Emily', a loss of air speed resulted and temporarily stalled our aircraft. The altitude difference was more than we could make and still maintain our flying speed. After recovering from our stall, the 'Emily' was seen flying northbound, slowly descending, but apparently still in flying condition. We pursued the 'Emily' but were only gaining slowly. Ensign John McKinley, my co-pilot, then asked me how far I intended to chase him. I was alleged to have replied 'All the way to Tokyo if necessary!' His query reminded me that we were at the end of our patrol sector, had already engaged in combat and used a good deal of full power 'fuel-eating' settings. I continued the chase for approximately fifteen to twenty minutes when I sighted tidal mud flats off the China Coast south of Haimen and Tai-chou wan (bay). It now became a question of whether to break off the attack and head home, or continue the chase and face the certainty of running out of fuel and ditching at night. With a very sick feeling and great reluctance, I broke off the chase and set course for Clark Field.'

The joy on board the 'Emily' was short-lived. Nobuyuki Taniguchi recalls: 'The pilot informed us that we had only enough fuel left for five minutes' flying time.' During the encounter with Stevens' PB4Y, the 'Emily' had executed several full power speeds and turns southwards to escape its pursuer. This, aided by a brisk thirty-knot north-east wind on the surface (and upwards of forty to forty-five knots at the higher altitude) pushed them further south than they realized. By the time the 'Emily' regained its northern track and following the fire-fight with Stevens' PB4Y, they had consumed an exorbitant amount of fuel. Thus, the 'Emily' could not reach Shanghai, another 240 statute miles north of Haimen. Taniguchi recalls: 'We tried to determine our location and a possible landing site. We saw what we believed was the Huangpu River [actually the upper north-west reaches of the Chien Tong River, north of Wenchow] and decided to land there. After landing on the water we feathered two engines to save fuel. We taxied on the water using the two engines, looking for a good site to dock the flying-boat. We realized it would be near a village on the right bank of the river, facing the ocean. All the engines were shut down.'

As Stevens turned homeward, much of the joy in shooting down one of the 'Jakes' and sinking a Japanese freighter became dulled. He then believed he had missed the chance of a lifetime. 'Our homeward trip was uneventful, except for the apprehension of insufficient fuel and a very dark night. Finding the airstrip at night with no navigational aids was an additional concern. And, of course, the tropical weather was always a factor. Thanks to a very strong tailwind, we arrived back at Clark Field at 2239 hours with 350 gallons of fuel remaining - about one hour and thirty minutes' more flying time, a reasonable reserve.

'Two days later, while having lunch in our mess hall, I noticed our Wing Commander, Captain Carroll B. Jones USN with his staff at the head table having a rather gleeful conversation among themselves. They were laughing and patting one another on the back. I soon sensed that I was the topic of conversation, as they kept glancing my way. They finally waved me over to their table. I could hardly believe the words, when they said: 'You got him, yes, you got him!' Needless to say, I was thrilled with the news. I returned to my table and informed my two co-pilots, even though the nature of the mission was still classified and was to be closely restricted.'

Nobuyuki Taniguchi relates the events after landing: 'No additional personnel were killed or injured as a result of the forced landing. It was dusk and the high tide was rapidly running out and soon the flying-boat ended up sitting on the mud-flat beach. Hatsuji Nakano the Taisa Gunicho or Captain and Senior Medical Officer of the Fourth Southern Expeditionary Fleet HQ was aboard. He had served as the director of a hospital near Shanghai during the China Incident. He spoke Chinese. He asked a Chinese fisherman where we were. The doctor told the crew that it was near Linhai, based on the fisherman's answer. High officials on board said there was a possibility that Japanese Army Units were stationed in this area. Some people were going to be sent out as scouts. Two of the Vice-Admiral's staff and two crew members left to ask the Chinese location of the nearest Japanese unit. Just as the men jumped off the main wing to start their search, about 200 Chinese soldiers appeared on the bank about 990 feet ahead. They opened fire immediately and our search teams could not move from that point. They threw themselves to the ground and returned the fire.'

Although the Japanese held military control over Shanghai and some major Chinese cities, there existed a well-organised network of Sino-American espionage agents and saboteurs. Unfortunately for the complement of the 'Emily', they had force-landed in SACO's (Sino-American Co-operative Organization) Camp No.8 sector and near the Guerrilla Raiders Group at Haimen in Chekian (Zhejiang) Province. The first guerrilla columns on the scene belonged to the Haimen Raiders Group which had been alerted by SACO's coastal watchers, which had reported the 'Emily' heading inland.

Nobuyuki Taniguchi continues: 'We saw more Chinese guerrillas on several junks on the river. They were approaching and taking us under fire at the same time. We were now being attacked on all sides. I removed the 20mm machine-gun from the stern turret and placed it at the door of the plane to respond to the enemy fire. We fired about 200 rounds sporadically to make it appear we had plenty of firepower.

'A staff member announced that a suicide squad was being organised and everybody, except those manning machine-guns, should gather. Everyone, except the Vice-Admiral, five of his staff members and three gunners, jumped onto the ground from the wing carrying guns and Japanese swords. The man who organised the suicide squad (I believe it was Commander Sado Ashiwara) was shot in the head as soon as he climbed out of the plane. He died instantly and fell to the ground. Half of the people died on the wing. Only a few made it to the ground. I was firing the machine-gun and did not know what happened to them. I was told later that four of them hid in a village, but were found by Chinese guerrillas. They put up a struggle with guns but all of them were shot to death. I kept shooting until we ran out of ammunition. I then moved to the 7.7mm gun, but it was broken. I did not see the crew anywhere. As I walked through the passenger section of the plane my left arm was hit and injured in three places by bullets from small-arms fire from one of the junks. I fell and remember the Vice-Admiral holding me, saying 'Be strong', but I lost consciousness.

'When I came around, I heard people down in the lower level talking. [The flying-boat had two decks and the lower section was where the fuel tank/baggage storage area was located.] I was still alive. I tore my scarf in half, tied it around my wounds and went to the deck below. The Vice-Admiral then called for the crew and as I was nearby I answered 'yes'. He said: 'This is the end; destroy all classified documents and material and then burn the flying-boat!' A Taii (lieutenant) from the Ambon Seaplane Corps was looking for a container for fuel to start a fire to burn the flying-boat. I brought him a container. The Vice-Admiral asked me to send a radio message before starting the fire. I operated the transmitter and sent the message in plain language. It was sent to Surabaya, Sàigòn, Sanya (Ya Xian, the southernmost city on Hainan Island), Shanghai and Taiwan and it read: 'We engaged in battle with an enemy plane and made an emergency landing due to the fuel shortage. The location is the shore of Huangpu River, near Linhai. We will make an attack as a marauding unit. Long live the Emperor: 1630 hours.' I shut off the power to the transmitter without waiting for an acknowledgement from those bases. I confirmed to the Vice-Admiral that the message had been sent and then threw the crystal and code-book into the ocean.

'I then rushed to the fuel room, removed my scarf and soaked it in gasoline, lit it with my lighter and threw it under the fuel tank and left the area. Fire soon started to burn the front portion of the flying-boat. The main wing then began to burn. At that moment there was a huge ball of fire and it even engulfed me. In astonishment I rolled on the deck two or three times and finally extinguished my flaming clothes.

'As I climbed the stairs to the second deck where the other people were, I suddenly felt the pain from my wounds and fainted near the entrance. When I again regained consciousness, the left wing was almost completely burned and heavy; thick smoke filled the inside of the flying-boat. Breathing was getting difficult. I sensed someone was there and raised my head. I saw the Vice-Admiral holding his Japanese sword in his right hand and sitting with his legs crossed.

'In front of the Vice-Admiral were three or four staff members. The Vice-Admiral was composed and said gently: 'All of you have assisted me well so that I could serve the Emperor and our country. I deeply appreciate your support. You are still very young and have a future. Escape this situation and serve the Emperor. Thank you!' The four officers listened silently with bowed heads. The Vice-Admiral then pulled his sword from the pinkish-brown sheath and without hesitation performed seppuku [a form of Japanese ritual suicide by disembowelment originally reserved for samurai].'

Taniguchi and four others, including Captain Nakano, the doctor, were captured and held as PoWs in China. Taniguchi was sent to Kunming and interrogated by the Americans. On the way to Chongqing, where I was detained in jail as a PoW, I was interrogated by a Chinese who was fluent in Japanese. He showed me a few photographs. One photo showed about twenty bodies on the bank beside the destroyed flying-boat. He asked me which one was the Admiral. I answered that the Admiral's remains were not there, since of course he must have been burned in the aircraft after committing seppuku. Vice-Admiral Seigo Yamagata was the only one aboard the aircraft who committed seppuku.'

The day following the 'Emily' landing, 18 March at 1000 hours, two Japanese gunboats and a 4,000-ton transport came from the south and attempted to recover the plane and passengers. Barges were lowered from the transport and sailed up the river. The Chinese mustered about 2,000 troops and gave them considerable small-arms opposition from shore. Four Japanese planes joined in the search but neither the ships nor the planes were able to find the seaplane as it had been sunk and covered with earth and straw by the Chinese. In the evening an American plane came on the scene and the Japs withdrew. The transport was sunk by an American plane near Do Chen Island at about 1700 hours that evening.

Stevens was awarded the Silver Star for his successful patrol and mission. His citation read, in part: 'By employing continued vigilance, he sighted another hostile aircraft which he destroyed, thereby depriving the enemy of the services of a group of its highest ranking officers and officials.' Stevens was awarded the Navy Cross, two Silver Stars, the

Presidential Citation and other awards for many combat actions against the Japanese forces. Post-war, his duties included command of squadrons, an air wing and an auxiliary ship. In 1963 - as Captain Paul Stevens, the CO of the USS *Procyon*, a Naval Auxiliary Refrigerator Ship - he hosted a luncheon for a group of Japanese businessmen during a port visit at the Yokosuka Naval base, Japan. During the course of the luncheon conversation, one of the Japanese guests stated that he had been a Navy Captain in the Imperial Japanese Navy. Further conversation revealed that he had served as the Engineering Officer on Vice-Admiral Yamagata's staff in Java and, on 15 March 1945, had been assigned to remain behind to close down the base operations. Stevens related his role in shooting down the Admiral's plane. The Japanese then confirmed the details that Stevens had essentially learned from the SACO unit's briefings.[1]

Endnotes Chapter 17

1   Captain Paul Stevens, USN (Ret), age 93, made his last take-off in Nashville, TN on 27 August 2014. He joined the Navy in January 1941 in Pensacola, FL and received his wings on 31 July 1941. His first assignment was to VP-21 in Pearl Harbor, HI, from 9/41 to 3/42. From April 1942 to November 1943 he was in VP-101 in Australia and New Guinea where he flew 64 combat missions. From 12/43 to 5/44, he was in operational training in PB4Y-1's at NAAS Camp Kearney, CA and then joined VPB-104 in Kanehoe, HI and flew 50 combat missions from Morotai, Tacloban and Clark Field in the Philippines. He dive bombed with a PBY at night off Rabaul to score hits on a Japanese Cruiser and Destroyer. He also shot down six Japanese aircraft confirmed (got one by ramming), destroyed six Japanese aircraft on the ground confirmed (these were much harder according to Paul) and destroyed one Maru transport with 2,000 Japanese troops aboard. Several Naval aviators 'vacationing' on the Bondoc Peninsula, Philippines, witnessed this attack. Paul was also credited with downing Vice Admiral Yamagata and his entire staff, March 17, 1945. He also scored hits on the Japanese Heavy Cruiser *Ashigara* off Mindoro Island, Philippines, 26 December 1944 during an individual attack in a PB4Y-1. His combat awards include the Navy Cross, 2 Silver Stars, 2 Distinguished Flying Crosses, 2 Air Medals and the Presidential Unit Citation.

Chapter 18

The *Eddie Allen*
Jim O'Keefe and Captain Ira Matthews

All of us who flew the fire-storm raids knew that we created a hell on earth for the people in the Japanese cities and after many years it is still not an easy thing to look back and reflect upon. But we also have chilling memories of a ruthless, brutal enemy: Pearl Harbor, the Bataan Death March, the thousands of British soldiers who died building the Kwai railroad, the bombing of Chungking, the execution of captured B-29 crews, the gunning of comrades descending in parachutes. And we know now that Japanese physicists had begun work on atomic weapons in late 1941.
1st Lieutenant James J. O'Keefe USAAF

Up forward at the bombardier's station of the B-29, things looked pretty tidy and efficient. When turned on, the Norden bombsight whirred away, ready to make all the intricate calculations and corrections for ground speed, altitude and drift. Peering through the electronic gunsight, which directed the fire of six .50-calibre machine-guns, I could see the cross-hair reticule glowing brightly and I knew that the little electrons raced about making their own prodigious calculations of an enemy fighter's closing speed and wingspan.

So now, with confidence in our plane and equipment, we awaited the unveiling of the map in the Hsin-Ching briefing room which would reveal the target for 7 December 1944.

It was cold in northeast China. For the first time we slept in our down, sleeping bags, a novelty in 1944. Upon awakening in the unheated barracks, we slipped immediately into lined parkas, our uniform for the day. Looking down on the assembled crews, the briefing officer must have been reminded of a gathering of medieval monks, their faces obscured by hoods and clouds of vapour from their breath. Certainly there were a few silent prayers being said also.

The target was an aircraft factory in Mukden, Manchuria. From a mysterious source we received a weather report - below freezing temperatures at ground level and a cloudless sky. Balanced against the advantage of a clear view of the target was the threat of frostbite, a serious crippler of aircrews of the 8th Air Force on their winter missions over Europe. Forty-eight hours earlier we had been enjoying the pleasant winter weather of India - suntan pants and shirts - the shirts were discarded for the afternoon ballgames. Now in the early morning we waddled to the planes. Long underwear, woollen shirts and sweaters, parkas, fleece-lined flying boots, heavy gloves.

At about 9 am, over a small island in the Gulf of Po, the 40th Bomb Group began to assemble into formation. Major Weschler wheeled us into the No. 4 position of the lead element, which put us directly behind but below the lead plane. The formation began a slow climb to bombing altitude - 20,000 feet. A few minutes later we crossed the Manchurian coast, noting the iced-up bays and coves and the sprinkling of snow on the low hills. As predicted, the sky was clear and from our altitude we could see for a hundred miles - but we could also be seen.

The fighter defences of Mukden were formidable. Because of distance, the Japanese air bases here were safe from strikes by General Chennault's 14th Air Force. Their planes then stood ready on the line, fresh and unscarred, the engines tuned by unhurried mechanics, the guns cleaned and oiled. Seeing little action, their pilots probably chafed and moped about from day to day and dreamed of what would happen to any American planes foolhardy enough to invade the Manchurian skies. We anticipated, correctly, that they would lack the caution and wariness of their embattled colleagues further south and would probably hurl their planes at our formations in reckless and uncoordinated attacks. Undoubtedly our adversaries saw themselves as warriors imbued with the true banzai spirit. Ours was a different view; we thought they were all a little crazy! On this morning we were glad for our unlimited visibility, for we would be able to see all of our attackers no matter from which direction they came at us and we could not be ambushed by planes suddenly darting out of the clouds.

Signs of battle appeared before us. A B-29 from the preceding formation had gone down, the burning wreckage marked only too clearly by the rising cloud of ugly, black smoke. It was not an easy victory for our enemy. Several smaller streams of flame and smoke - their fighters - spiralled down to crash around the downed bomber.

I swung the gunsight into position as the 40th Group prepared to run the gauntlet of fighters and flak. We were still miles from Mukden. Rail lines leading to the city glistened far below us. All at once, a few miles ahead, a section of tracks disappeared in a cloud of exploding bombs. Inexplicably, an entire formation had released their bombs miles from the target. There was no time to puzzle further over this action, as fighters were now swinging into position to begin their runs on us.

As they bored in, those of us up front saw, to our horror, a film of ice forming on the inside of our windows. I shoved the gunsight to one side and brushed frantically at the ice with my gloved hands! It was a useless effort and our view of the outside world and its perils quickly glazed over. From the navigator's spot, Clark Thomas saw the problem, thought quickly and seconds later came forward and thrust into my hands his set of plastic starfinders. Using them as scrapers, I cleared a panel for Major Weschler and then one for myself and then back to the Major's panel as the ice quickly reformed. Shelly Green, the co-pilot, peering through the glaze, called to my attention the opening switch, then passed the bomb toggle switch on its cord top to Clark. He would drop our bombs when the leader's bombs went away; I would carry on as ice-scraper.

I could not gain on the ice. My arms, enveloped in layers of clothing, became heavy. A lifelong concern with physical fitness now paid off ... thank God for the thousands of push-ups ... the straining muscles ... the heaving lungs ... the gallons of sweat....

I was aware of fighters hurtling by. Now and then I got off a frantic burst, but I doubt if I fired more than twenty rounds that day. Sturdy though my arms were, I began to tire and the ice gained on me. But knowing we were close to the critical bomb release point, I gave another mighty effort, cleared the top panel and looked directly up into the bomb-bays of the lead plane. There above us hung twelve 500lb general purpose bombs. Had there been time, I could have amused our crew by reading to them the obscene messages to the enemy scrawled in chalk on the underside of some bombs. I didn't bother with the intercom, I simply pointed upward. A split second later Major Weschler throttled back and, several seconds later, the twelve bombs left the lead plane on their way to the aircraft factory, clearing our nose by what was probably a few feet, but to my wide, blue eyes seemed to be no more than a few inches.

The turn for home swung the nose directly into the sun and the formation began to descend to a lower, somewhat warmer elevation. Within a few minutes the temperature climbed from -50 degrees F to a balmy -30 degrees F and the ice began to disappear from the windows. We pulled away from the flak zone and presently the fighters left. I slumped in my seat, suddenly aware of moist patches of sweat under my arms, ominous little patches should the cold penetrate the layers of clothes and freeze them. I took off my flak vest and felt with gratefulness the sun of my face and parka. It is perhaps a strain on the verb 'to bask' if you are 'basking in the sun' at -30 degrees F, but, however, as I absorbed the solar energy, the problem of the sweat patches soon disappeared.

After a while, I gathered up the shreds and mangled remains of the plastic starfinders. They would be of no further value for navigation; on them, the North Star was probably found somewhere over the Argentine. We now looked forward to landing back at Hsinching, where we would offer some suggestions to be forwarded to the factory which turned out our plane.

Ours was one of the older B-29s. We learned at the critique that most of the older models that went to Mukden that day had undergone the same ordeal. The nose of the lead plane of the formation (which had dropped its bombs so many miles short of the target) had become so iced over that the bombardier, desperately searching for the target through the glazed windows, had mistaken rail yards for the factory.

Why, amidst the many intensive planning sessions which had resulted in America's most advanced bomber, had no one ever brought up the problem of solid condensation at low temperatures? Surely this had been a problem years' earlier, one that had been dealt with by our 8th Air Force, the Royal Air Force and the German Air Force. The solution was a simple one. Two weeks later, when we returned to Mukden, all of the 40th Group planes had defroster tubes and ducts installed in their noses. We had a few problems that day but icing was not one of them.'

On that same Mukden raid, a good friend of Jim O'Keefe's, Captain Ira Matthews, from the 45th Bomb Squadron of the 40th Bomb Group, had been piloting the *Eddie Allen*, which bombed targets in seven countries before getting badly damaged over Tokyo on 25 May 1945 and sent to salvage. The aircraft had been named after the Boeing chief test pilot who made the first flight of the experimental XB-29. Allen died shortly after in the crash of the second prototype.

The following article, which involves a certain terrifying trip for Captain Ira Matthews and crew aboard this plane, is a joint literary effort by both Jim O'Keefe and Matthews.

'One by one the hazards expected on the seven-hour flight to the target in Manchuria were ticked off by the briefing officer. An early morning take-off would be followed by several hours of night flying in the company of other bombers, with none of them showing running lights. At daybreak we would cross into Japanese-occupied China, where we could expect vigorous resistance from enemy fighters. On the bombing run at 19,000 feet, the cold would be extreme and the direction and velocity of the wind could only be guessed. A final admonishment from the briefing officer, 'Men, be sure to wear your GI shoes, laced to the tops, in the event you are forced to bail out and have to walk to safety.'

'After making the usual feeble jokes about hailing a rickshaw following a bailout, the crews compared notes. Yes, it had been a thorough briefing; no, we had been told nothing new or extraordinary.

'The date, 7 December 1944; the place, an advanced Air Force base near Chengtu, in western China. We were members of the 40th Bombardment Group flying a handful of the first B-29s to go into action in World War II. In its six months of overseas operations the 40th had flown missions to targets ranging from Sumatra, below the equator, to icy Manchuria. We had encountered a formidable number of meteorological hazards - cyclones (hurricanes), cold fronts, warm fronts, tornadoes, updrafts, downdrafts, winds of incredible velocity, heat, icing, dust, plus vagrant birds. The experience gained was precious insurance.

'Tested and battle-hardened, the crews on this December morning were eager to get on with the mission, cope with whatever came up and get it over with. In the early morning darkness planes began to rumble down the feebly-lit runway.

'Shortly before dawn, B-29 #579, the *Eddie Allen*, neared Sian, in the Yellow River Valley. Close at hand was the northernmost airfield held by General Chennault's 14th Air Force. It was comforting knowledge that, in the event we were intercepted, friendly fighters could come to our aid.

'At 14,000 feet the skies were clear and the air was smooth. Major Ira Matthews had the *Eddie Allen* on automatic pilot. The members of the veteran crew searched the sky for other planes, friendly or enemy. So far the flight had been uneventful.

'Without warning the plane swerved sharply left, the nose pitched downward and the autopilot disconnected. Major Matthews and the co-pilot, Captain Alvin Hills, struggled to level the wings and raise the nose. Severe vibrations wracked the plane and it pitched and rolled as if caught in a violent thunderstorm. An emergency interphone check found all crew members in position and strapped in. The gunners scanned the wings and tail and reported that all surfaces appeared normal. Vibration and turbulence increased. Major Matthews considered alerting the crew for bailout, then reconsidered when he realized that no one could crawl to an escape hatch; vibration had reached a point where all movement was impossible. The flight instruments merged into a shimmering blur.

'The frightening motion ceased abruptly. An interphone check found all crew members shaken but uninjured. Safety belts were unbuckled and scattered equipment was cautiously retrieved. Another scan of wing and tail surfaces showed nothing abnormal. How long had the turbulence lasted? The navigator, with admirable coolness, had timed it. His log entry read, 'Five minutes of stark terror.'

'The *Eddie Allen* completed the mission. At debriefing, the crew members were as anxious to report the wild, completely unexpected turbulence as they were to report bombing results and the heavy fighter attacks over Manchuria. An Intelligence officer, politely sceptical, listened and recorded, then compared notes with other interrogators. No other crew reported the turbulence, although navigators' logs showed a number of planes near the Eddie Allen's position at that time.

'The *Eddie Allen* was carefully checked by the ground crew. There was no evidence of structural damage. On the return flight to the 40th Group's home base in India, the flight crew put the plane through a number of flight checks while over the dangerous mountainous stretch known as the HUMP, an unlikely area for testing. The plane passed all tests and the crew, sensing that to talk further about their unique experience would draw derisive comments and hints of 'battle fatigue,' resolved to say no more about it.

'A possible explanation for the turbulence came several days later when survivors of a catastrophic earthquake in the Yellow River area streamed into Sian. The extent of the tragedy in terms of loss of life was never learned, nor was the quake's magnitude measured. An indubitable fact is that the quake occurred early on the morning of 7 December.

'Some members of the 40th Group were trained in physics and meteorology. We don't recall that any of them offered an explanation of this atmospheric phenomenon. They had, in fact, no time to give to leisurely speculation about an isolated, unlikely-to-ever-occur-again incident. December 1944 was a grim, desperately busy month for the 40th Group.

'But sometime in the 1950s a DC-7, flying at 20,000 feet near Arequipa, Peru, encountered severe clear air turbulence. The plane was badly damaged and several passengers were severely injured. After an emergency landing, the pilot learned he had flown over the site of a great Andean earthquake.

'We know of no other incidents of this nature and we know of no studies of these two. So for those of us who flew over northern China on a cold December morning long, long ago, the questions remain: Was the heaving of the earth's surface under the passing B-29 responsible for the savage turbulence that rocked the *Eddie Allen* and terrified its crew? And if so, what were the physics of the interaction between surface and atmosphere?'[1]

Endnotes Chapter 18

1   Quoted in *Maximum Effort: The Big Bombing Raids* by Bernie Wyatt.

Chapter 19

Yangtze Incident

At Langar on 3 September 1943 Wynford Vaughan Thomas, an accredited War Correspondent and a BBC Home Service commentator and Reginald Pidsley a sound engineer (who as a civilian was made an Acting Sergeant (unpaid) on 207 Squadron for two days in case they were shot down and captured) who would record his impressions on a one sided wax '78' aluminium disc that he had cut lying prone in the belly of the Lancaster four miles high over Berlin, stood by to fly with Flight Lieutenant Ken Letford and his crew on 207 Squadron. Because of the high casualty rates among Halifax and Stirling aircraft in recent raids on the 'Big City', the raid was made up entirely of 316 Lancasters. Letford's Lancaster returned safely and Vaughan Thomas' commentary of the raid featured in a BBC broadcast.

All except one of Letford's crew survived the war. With a total of four operational tours including a further tour on Lancasters, Ken Letford ended the war as a Flight Lieutenant with DSO and Bar and the DFC. Flight Lieutenant Ken Letford DSO* DFC served with the RAFVR and RAF for almost thirty years from 1939 to 1968, finally flying Canberras and Valiants before retiring from the RAF in 1968. Along the way, in 1949, he was once again involved in a headline-breaking exploit famously portrayed in the 1957 film, Yangtze Incident, *starring Richard Todd.*

On the afternoon of Wednesday 20 April 1949 88 Squadron's Sunderland aircraft at Kai Tak in Hong Kong were occupied as usual with the transport of mail and freight between Japan, Singapore and Borneo. Sunderlands were particularly useful where there were no adequate airfields. But when news was received that HMS *Amethyst* a modified Black Swan-class sloop of the Royal Navy commanded by Lieutenant Commander Bernard Skinner, which was on her way from Shanghai to Nanking (now Nanjing) had been fired on by Chinese Communists guns on the Yangtze River during the Chinese Civil War between the nationalist Kuomintang and the Chinese Communists, the mood changed. Air HQ Hong Kong tasked 88 Squadron to prepare to render assistance to HMS *Amethyst*. All available aircraft were made serviceable and after urgent talks between the Royal Navy and RAF it was decided to send a Sunderland flying boat to Nanking with medical supplies. These would then be sent overland to the *Amethyst,* which had been en route to replace Consort, which was standing as guard ship for the British Embassy there. At around 0831, after a burst of small arms fire, a People's Liberation Army (PLA) field gun battery on the north bank of the river fired a salvo of ten shells, which fell well short of *Amethyst* and was assumed to be part of a regular bombardment of Nationalist forces on the south bank. Speed was increased and large Union flags were unfurled on either side of the ship, after which there was no more firing.

At 0930, as the frigate approached Kiangyin (Jiangyin) further up the river, she came under sustained fire from a second PLA battery. The first shell passed over the ship, then the bridge, wheelhouse and low power room were hit in quick succession, the captain was mortally wounded and all the bridge personnel were disabled. The coxswain on the wheel was seriously injured and as a result the ship slewed to port and grounded on the bank before control of the ship was resumed. Before the ship was hit, the order to open fire had been given, but when the director layer pulled the firing trigger, nothing happened, because the gun firing circuits were disabled when the low power room was hit. The first lieutenant, Geoffrey L. Weston, assumed command of the vessel, though wounded. The order was given to fire in local control with each turret firing independently, but *Amethyst* had grounded in such a way that neither of the two gun turrets at the front of the ship could be brought to bear on the PLA batteries, leaving the single stern turret to return fire. This turret was soon hit and disabled. None of the close range weapons could be brought to bear on the PLA batteries. The shore batteries continued to fire at *Amethyst* with their artillery, causing more damage and casualties to the ship. PLA shells exploded in the sick bay, the port engine room and finally the generator, just after the injured Weston's last transmission: *Under heavy fire. Am aground... Large number of casualties.* When it was learned in Hong Kong that *Amethyst's* MO was among the dead, the plan to send a Sunderland to Nanking with medical supplies changed. The plan was now for a Sunderland to land on the river as close to the ship as possible, so that an RAF doctor could be sent on board.

On board the *Amethyst* sometime between 1000 and 1030 Weston ordered the immediate evacuation to shore of anyone who could be spared. A boat was manned to take people the short distance to shore and some men swam ashore. The batteries switched their fire to the men being evacuated and further evacuation was stopped. Fifty-nine ratings and four Chinese mess boys made it to the Kuomintang-controlled southern bank, but two men were assumed drowned while swimming ashore. Those who survived were joined by the seriously wounded from Amethyst who had been landed by sampan, with the assistance of the Chinese Nationalists on the following day. Both parties were taken to a missionary hospital in Kiangyin where they were met by a party from the British Embassy in Nanking and put on a train for Shanghai. Remaining on board were about sixty unwounded men. The shelling had stopped, but no one could move without drawing the attention of PLA snipers.

By the time the shelling stopped at about 1100, 22 men had been killed and 31 wounded in all. *Amethyst* had received over fifty hits and holes below the waterline were plugged with hammocks and bedding. During this time the destroyer HMS *Consort* which had been ordered from Nanking to go to the *Amethyst's* assistance, was sighted, flying seven White Ensigns and three Union flags, steaming down from Nanking at 29 knots. *Consort* reached the *Amethyst* at about three in the afternoon and was immediately heavily engaged. She found the fire too heavy to approach *Amethyst* and therefore passed her at speed down river. She turned two miles below and again closed *Amethyst* to take her in tow. But again she came under such heavy fire that she was obliged to abandon the attempt, although she answered the shore batteries with her full armament (including 4.5-inch guns) and signalled that she had silenced most of the opposition. Half an hour later her signals ceased, though she was making a second attempt to take the *Amethyst* in tow, having turned downstream again. This attempt also failed and she sustained further damage and casualties during which her steering was affected. She therefore had to continue downstream out of the firing area with ten men killed and 23 wounded.

Flight Lieutenant Ken Letford had taken Sunderland ML772 'D-Dog' off from Kai Tak bound for the *Amethyst* at 2225 hours.[1] Letford and his crew carried medical supplies, food and water and Group Captain John N. Jefferson, Kai Tak's station commander and ten others including an RAF doctor, Flight Lieutenant Michael Fearnley.[2]

In 1942 Kenneth Henry Francis Letford flew as a flight sergeant but he was commissioned on 10 September 1942. As a result of his wartime exploits, he was awarded three gallantry decorations. He was awarded the DFC on 7 September 1943 and his citation for his service on 207 Squadron stated: 'This officer, now on his second tour of operational duty, has attacked most of the enemy's heavily defended targets. A first rate captain of aircraft, he has consistently shown the great determination to press home his attacks regardless of difficulties or enemy opposition. He has obtained some excellent photographs.' Letford was awarded the DSO less than three months later when his citation, announced on 23 November 1943, stated:

'One night in October 1943 this officer was captain and pilot of an aircraft detailed to attack Leipzig. During the sorties, the bomber was engaged by a fighter and was hit by a hail of bullets. The mid-upper gunner was wounded and his gun turret rendered useless; the wireless operator was also wounded and some of his wireless equipment was destroyed. The inter-communication gear was put out of action and other damage was sustained. The situation became alarming when some incendiary bombs and accumulators caught fire. Nevertheless, Flight Lieutenant Letford coolly organised his crew to fight the flames and under his able directions they succeeded in quelling the fire. When base was reached, Flight Lieutenant Letford affected a perfect landing without the aid of flaps. In circumstances fraught with danger, this officer displayed inspiring leadership, great courage and determination. His final wartime gallantry award was announced on 21 September 1945 for his courage on Lancaster bombers on 156 Squadron PFF. The citation to the Bar to his DSO, announced on 21 September 1945, stated: 'Squadron Leader Letford is now on his fourth tour of operational duties. His skilled airmanship and fine fighting spirit have earned him the confidence of his crew and of the squadron. He is a fearless captain who has shown complete disregard for any opposition when pressing home his attacks. His courage and devotion to duty have been a splendid example to those who have served with him.' After the end of hostilities, Letford gained a permanent commission in the RAF and in 1949 was serving on 88 Squadron at Kai Tak, Hong Kong.

Flying at 5,000 feet 'D-Dog' had almost reached the beleaguered Amethyst when Letford was told by HMS *London* that because of intense gunfire from communist forces landing would be too dangerous and at the mouth of the river the Sunderland was ordered back to Shanghai, where it landed just after 4am on 21 April. After lunch Letford and his crew heard that the *Amethyst's* situation was even more desperate than first reported so it was decided to try again. He took off again at about 1630 hours. This time they were to take a Padre with them to bury the dead. During the flight it was realised that there might not be enough time to transfer the cases of medical supplies to the ship so the crew broke open the boxes and the doctors filled their pockets and knapsacks with plasma, anaesthetics etc. After a low run over *Amethyst* and with no sign of gunfire, the Sunderland landed and taxied towards the ship, which had been re-floated just after midnight on 21 April after lightening the ship and she had moved five miles upstream. The Sunderland's anchor was dropped and the engines were shut down. A sampan rowed across from Amethyst but just as it reached the Sunderland heavy and accurate artillery fire began.

'As we got closer to HMS *Amethyst*' recalled Gerry Moreby, the WOp/Air Gunner,[3] 'Ken Letford came down very low along a creek. Suddenly, there was the main river in front of us and as we circled we saw the ship close to the sand bank, the crew waving to us from the deck. Ken decided to land in the lee of the *Amethyst* where we would have some protection from the communist batteries. The landing was uneventful and we came to rest less than 100 yards alongside the *Amethyst*. Eric Monaghan, the *Amethyst's* Commissioned gunner [who had survived the sinking of the battle cruiser HMS *Repulse* and the aircraft carrier HMS *Hermes* during the Second World War] had left *Amethyst* in a sampan rowed by Chinese women. He persuaded them to row to the aircraft. We opened the door and Monaghan climbed in. At that moment the Communists opened fire and Michael Fearnley saw that the terrified women were rowing away rapidly so he hurriedly jumped in the sampan which proceeded to zigzag away back to the *Amethyst*, leaving Monaghan and the Naval Doctor plus most of the medical supplies behind on the aircraft. We opened the rear door and launched a rubber dinghy, attaching it by rope. Once again several bursts of shell and other gunfire forced us yet again into an immediate take-off. Goodbye dinghy. Although everything was open and the anchor down, Ken Letford shouted that he was going to take off at once. Sig. Price and I rushed down to the bows and chopped the anchor free. The rest of us shut what doors we could and we climbed away, pursued by fire from the Chinese guns.'

The RAF doctor and some medical supplies were transferred to the sampan and the Sunderland prepared for immediate take-off. Because of the gunfire the take-off run had to be performed down-wind and with the current; it was later estimated to have extended for three miles. Immediately the aircraft came under accurate gunfire and began to suffer damage as it was swept past the Amethyst on the strong current. The Sunderland eventually returned to Shanghai after being shadowed by communist aircraft and fired upon by ground forces.

'We were airborne again on the 23rd from Shanghai' continues Gerry Moreby 'to carry out reconnaissance in the area where HMS *Amethyst* was. We were hit by ground fire and the port main tank was holed causing heavy leaking into the bomb bay. Also on landing we discovered the main aileron control wire between the Signaller's position and the Captain's position running along the floor was almost severed and that two bullets were lodged in the navigator's computer which was in his navigator's bag. The bullets had entered through the portside of the wardroom, continuing upwards through the control housing in the floor of the upper deck. Luckily, the computer had stopped the bullets travelling in line for the Group Captain's bottom, which was strategically placed between the two pilots. Also, the 0.5′ round that had entered the starboard side, passed through the sleeve of Ken Dillon's uniform and did no harm, so we all reckoned that lady luck had been on our side.[4] Quite an eventful few days away from Kai Tak. Clearly, any further attempts to repeat the exercise could prove to be even less successful and the Royal Navy and RAF jointly decided to abandon any further plans for supplying by air. It retrospect, it is difficult to understand the logic of sending a warship down a river between two opposing armies in the first place.

The Assistant British Naval Attaché in Nanking, Lieutenant Commander John Kerans, joined the ship on 22 April having reached the *Amethyst* after a eventful journey overland and after he had dealt with all the wounded and unwounded men who had been sent ashore assumed command of the ship that day. During the next few days *Amethyst* moved several times, but each time she got under way the batteries opened fire at her and the ship was forced to anchor finally finishing up off Fu Te Wei. On 21 April a signal was received: HM ships *London* and *Black Swan* are moving up river to escort the *Amethyst* downstream. Be ready to move. The cruiser *London* and the frigate *Black Swan*, which had been ordered to sail from Shanghai to Kiang Yin, 40 miles downriver from the *Amethyst*, were heavily shelled as they attempted to help Amethyst and retreated with three killed and fourteen wounded.

By Monday 25 April the Chinese Nationalist resistance was collapsing and the Navy decided to move its ships out of Shanghai to the mouth of the Yangtze and the Sunderland returned to Kai Tak. It was not until the very early hours of the morning of 31 July that HMS *Amethyst* was able to break out of the Yangtze. Throughout the ship's dash down the river, the Sunderlands of 88 Squadron were fully armed and on stand-by to go to the ship's aid if she grounded in the river. Fortunately, the ship made a safe escape and sailed into Hong Kong three days later.

On 30 April the PLA demanded that Britain, the United States and France quickly withdraw their armed forces from any parts of China. During the negotiations the Communists insisted that the British ship fired first, but eventually in 1988 the PLA commander Ye Fei admitted that it was his troops that fired first. *Amethyst* remained under guard by the PLA for ten weeks, with vital supplies being withheld from the ship. Negotiations were stuck because Kerans would not accept the demand from Colonel Kang Yushao, the PLA representative, that the British state had wrongly invaded Chinese national waters and had fired upon the PLA first. Because the communists (and later the People's Republic of China) did not acknowledge any treaties between the previous Chinese government and the British, they insisted that it was illegal for *Amethyst* to cruise in the Yangtze.

On 30 July *Amethyst* slipped her chain and headed downriver in the dark, beginning a 104-mile dash for freedom running the gauntlet of Communist guns on both banks of the river. She followed the passenger ship Kiang Ling Liberation in the hope that the observers ashore would be confused and not see *Amethyst* in the dark. When the battery opened fire, the fire was directed at the Kiang Lin Liberation which was sunk by the gun fire, with heavy civilian casualties. At 0500 hours on 31 July *Amethyst* approached the PLA forts at Par Shan (Baoshan) and Woosung (Wusong) with their searchlights sweeping the river. At 0525 a pre-planned meeting with the destroyer *Concord* took place. *Concord* had been ordered to prepare to provide gun support to *Amethyst* if she came under fire from the shore batteries at Woosung. To achieve this she had moved up the Yangtze during the night, at action stations. Fortunately, *Amethyst* was not spotted by the shore batteries and the two ships then proceeded down river until at 0715 they stood down from action stations and after clearing the river mouth arrived at the Saddle Islands at 1200 hrs to anchor and transfer much needed oil and stores. After a short stay at anchor, *Concord* lent *Amethyst* sailors to fill gaps in her ship's company and the two ships set sail for Hong Kong. Next day the cruiser *Jamaica* and destroyer *Cossack* took over as escort and proceeded to Hong Kong. *Concord* was sent to Japan after being sworn to secrecy.[5]

The operation cost the lives of 46 seamen with a further 68 injured. Lieutenant Commander Kerans sent a wonderful signal: *Have rejoined the Fleet south of Woo Sung. No damage or casualties. God save the King.* Back in London and being kept updated on the situation, HM The King was quick to have a signal made to the C-in-C: *Please convey to the commanding officer and ship's company of* HMS *Amethyst my hearty congratulations on their daring exploit to rejoin the Fleet. The courage, skill and determination shown by all on board have my highest commendation. Splice the mainbrace. George R.* Fifteen of the *Amethyst's* crew were decorated or Mentioned in Despatches. Commander John Simon Kerans MP DSO RN (30 June 1915-12 September 1985) was awarded the DSO, while Michael Edward Fearnley was awarded the DSC. For his part in the Yangtze incident Ken Letford was awarded a Bar to his DFC, thereby creating a unique set of gallantry awards - only twenty-five airmen had equalled his earlier combination of a DSO and Bar and DFC in World War II. Additionally all personnel taking part in the operation were awarded the Naval General Service Medal (Yangtze 1949).[6] Letford, who retired from the RAF in 1969, died in British Columbia, Canada, in October 1985, aged sixty-three.

An historic aircraft because of its part in the Yangtze Incident,

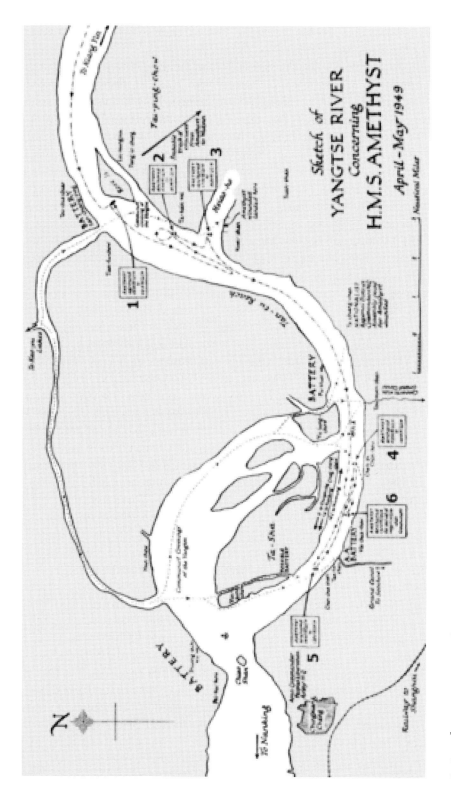

1-6 = the successive locations of HMS *Amethyst*

Sunderland ML772 'D-Dog' could have been a candidate for preservation. Sadly, this was not to be and this Sunderland was Struck Off Charge on 30 June 1955. For the 1957 film *Yangtze Incident: The Story of* HMS *Amethyst. Amethyst* was taken out of storage to play herself. As her engines were no longer operational, her sister ship, *Magpie*, was used for shots of the ship moving. *Amethyst* was scrapped at Devonport in January 1957 shortly after the filming was finished.

Endnotes Chapter 19

1   ML772 began life as a Rochester built Mark III. It had two accidents at Castle Archdale when with 201 Squadron (as S-Sugar) in 1945 and conversion to a Mark V followed.

2   Letford's crew were Pilot Officer Ken Dillon, 2nd Pilot, Flight Lieutenant Maurice Marshall, navigator, Engr.1 Lofty Doyle, Sig.1 Gerry Moreby (WOp/Air Gunner), Sig.2 Price (WOp/Air gunner and Gunner Devany, Air Gunner. Also on board were Group Captain J. M. Jefferson, Station Commander, RAF Kai Tak (who had elected to make the trip himself) Flight Lieutenant Michael Fernley RAF Medical Officer, a Royal Navy Medical Officer and two experienced Army parachute droppers as they would be able to accurately release supplies over the ship if a landing was not possible.

3   *A Mercy Mission to HMS Amethyst – April 1949* by Gerry Moreby.

4   ML772/B was replaced by NJ176/F.

5   On 1 October 1949 Mao Zedong proclaimed the establishment of the People's Republic of China. Chiang Kai-shek, 600,000 Nationalist troops and about two million Nationalist-sympathizer refugees retreated to the island of Taiwan.

6   *Heroes of the Skies: Amazing True Stories of Courage in the Air* by Michael Ashcroft (Headline 2012).

Index